UNDERSTANDING HUMAN NATURE
AN OWNER'S MANUAL

UNDERSTANDING HUMAN NATURE
AN OWNER'S MANUAL

GEORGE S. HOWARD

Academic Publications
Box 478
Notre Dame Indiana 46556

Published by Academic Publications
                    Box 478
              Notre Dame, Indiana 46556

Library of Congress Cataloging-in-Publication Data

Howard, George Stephen, 1948–
        Understanding human nature / George S. Howard
              p.   cm.
        Includes bibliographical references
        ISBN 0-937647-03-9 (alk. paper)
        1. Psychology. 2. Human behavior. I. Title
BF121.H694   1996
150—dc20   96-586
                                                    CIP

To my wife, Nancy

Contents

PREFACE

Students often have a number of goals as they begin their study of psychology. While many of these desires (e.g., to learn how psychologists think, to understand some of the causes of mental illness) are often achieved, there is one goal that is rarely reached. Many people undertake the study of psychology to come to understand themselves better. While educators often hold that satisfying Plato's command to "know thyself" ought to be a fundamental component of *all* education, many psychologists and most basic psychology texts (e.g., Introductory, Personality, Abnormal) do little to promote better self-understanding for students in basic psychology courses. This book is intended to remedy that situation somewhat.

This is an owner's manual for people who would like to understand themselves a little better. As the title suggests, the book is about human nature. It is an essay on the nature of human beings—which is, after all, a large part of what psychology is all about. But this book will be different in one fundamental way from the hundreds of other books written to introduce the field of psychology. Psychology will be explained from a first-person perspective rather than using the discipline's traditional, third-person approach.

Most scholarly pursuits in the Western intellectual tradition employ the third-person perspective (autobiography being a noteworthy exception). The sciences rely almost exclusively on the third-person approach. While it is reasonable for autobiographers to tell us their life stories from a first-person perspective, it makes no sense to think that the nonhuman objects of scientific investigation would be able to offer insightful, first-person accounts of their behavior. That is, can planets tell us what causes them to spin about the heavens as they do? Can elements such as sodium and chlorine tell us why they are attracted to one another? Can a species of cats tell us why its teeth are evolving and becoming longer over time? It turns out that these questions raise very complex issues and might best be answered by, "well, yes and no." "No" because planets, chemicals, and species neither speak nor possess insights into why they behave the way they do. Thus, a planet speaking directly to us and claiming, "Gravity is pulling me around," is ludicrous. But a "yes" answer can be justified also, as science represents a procedure wherein scientists "question" a particular subject matter via scientific theories and experimental investigations. Nature "replies" to scientists who then convey these answers to the rest of us through their scientific reports. Note, however, that this question-and-reply sequence is a completely third-person approach. At no point do the planets, chemicals, or species give their first-person impressions of why they behave the way they do.

In the last century it has become commonplace to see psychology as the scientific study of humans. We have perfected an array of third-person research approaches and theories of human behavior, and much has been learned about human nature in this way. Most of the standard introductory psychology textbooks explain quite nicely what we know about humans from the third-person perspective. This essay does *not* attempt to explain the findings from the third-person approach to psychology as thoroughly as they deserve. Hence, I trust this book will be used as a supplement to a strong, traditional textbook in the field. But why is it helpful for students to learn about human nature from both the first-person and third-person perspectives?

You'll only be able to answer that question for yourself after you've completed the exercises and personal experiments in this book. But let's suggest an answer by an analogy. Think of your right eye as the third-person approach to understanding, and your left eye as the first-person approach. As I sit in my office, I look out over Notre Dame's north quad. If I cover my left eye it seems as if my vision is unchanged. Ask me any question about the quad (e.g., How many trees are there? What are the colors of the buildings? Are the students moving or standing still?) and I'm pretty sure I could answer the queries—even without the use of one eye. But I know that I've lost something. My depth perception (i.e., the ability to gauge distances) has been severely impaired. True, I can use cognitive strategies to guess distances. For example, objects at a distance appear to be smaller, so students who appear to me as about half the size of other students are more likely to be farther away. However, I am now laboring under a severe visual liability *if the task at hand involves judging distances accurately.* This is why, years ago, when eye trouble forced me to wear a patch over one eye, my doctor strongly urged that I not drive my car—even though I could see everything on the road with my usual acuity. Without the aid of binocular vision and accurate depth perception, I would have been even more of a menace on the road than usual!

A typical basic psychology textbook helps you to understand

the psychology of "the other" (knowledge gained through third-person techniques). In addition, most basic psychology courses offer you the opportunity to serve as a subject in experiments. This experience will give you a feel for what it's like to be a "data source". Finally, competent debriefing at the end of each experiment will enable you to understand how the data that you contributed to that study will be used to answer some theoretical or practical psychological question. Thus, you will have glimpsed the psychology of "the other" (from the third-person perspective) in several ways. But this understanding of human nature often lacks "depth". Students often feel that knowledge of "the other" alone somehow loses the richness, complexity, and mystery that one experiences when one also employs first-person approaches that allow us to witness human nature binocularly.

In fact, you already know a great deal about human nature from the first-person perspective. There's a little voice inside your head that furnishes a running commentary on everything that happens in your life. My little voice sounds exactly like me—or at least I thought it did until I watched myself being interviewed on a local television show. That guy on the screen looked and sounded a lot like me, but he had a New Joisey accent.

"I don't sound like that. I don't have a New Jersey accent," I objected to no one in particular.

Greg, my six-year-old son, looked at me in disbelief and said, "Yes you do—just like Gramma Sissy and Pop-Pop." That kind of feedback is tough on us acorns, as we like to think that we've fallen very far from our family trees.

As part of your study of basic psychology, I'll try to entice you to listen more closely to what your little voice is saying to you. I'll share some of my conversations with my little voice to model how you might proceed in this sort of self-examination. I'll also suggest some exercises you might undertake that are called personal experiments. These experiences will straddle the border between first-person and third-person approaches, because you will serve as both the experimenter and the subject in these investigations. Finally, I'll present segments of interesting and unusual first-person accounts that other people have authored to suggest the range and diversity of human experiences that psychologists sometimes encounter. While one could fill volumes with rich and provocative material from published autobiographies, clinical case studies, psychobiographies, life-histories, and the like, it is not proper for me to have others write my little book for me. Thus I'll keep my use of others' writing to a minimum, but I will alert you to the existence of several wonderful first-person works and urge you to read liberally in this literature.

One final point, and then we'll begin. I think that each of us needs time for serious reflection in order to become a wise and virtuous person. Certain kinds of music, quiet places, and some activities (such as walking) can facilitate fruitful reflection on our lives. Since no one else can hear our thoughts, we can let those thoughts roam wide and free. However, I believe there is value in writing out (and rewriting) our first-person accounts. In fact, several exercises in this book will help you to write first-person life stories. My students' experience is that writing about themselves is even more difficult than writing traditional papers. Their additional reluctance involves their feeling that it is somehow prideful or egotistical to write about themselves. Traditional third-person essays feel more objective and dispassionate, and so we are not encumbered by this additional emotional reluctance in composing them. Personal essays are more difficult than third-person scholarly writing for me too. Practice reduces the reluctance a bit, but I doubt my reticence will ever completely go away. The only helpful hint I've discovered is to decide that no one else will ever see the first draft of my autobiographical material. Using this strategy may also give you a good deal of freedom to follow your heart's desire in composing your life story. Having done so, you can decide if minor modifications will make it appropriate to be read by others. If not, the essay assumes the status of most people's diaries—a personal exercise never to be read by others.

This book also helps instructors to introduce students to an important development in modern psychology—the scientific study of self-determination. Part II of the book urges students to take part in self-experiments that will show them the portion of their behavior in a domain (e.g., alcohol consumption, amount of exercise) that is self-determined, as well as the portion attributable to nonagentic causes. Complete scientific explanations of human actions will soon routinely include both the first-person (volitional) and third-person (mechanistic) causal influences on our actions. Part II presents the most basic introduction currently available to this binocular approach to understanding human nature. Part III recommends that students write a teleography—an imaginative projection of their life story into the future. This is another first-person approach that helps people to play more active roles in the creation of their own futures. We are not the hapless pawns to fate in life. Teleographies help us in the crucial task of creatively molding our own futures.

We've spent enough time talking about first-person accounts. Let's now examine a few of these accounts and begin to compose our own life stories. While this Preface is written in proper academic prose, the rest of the book consists of a collage of non-traditional writing styles. While academic prose engages the mind, it rarely touches the heart and soul. If one's study of psychology is limited to scholarly, third-person approaches, the picture of human nature that emerges could well be "flat" and lacking in depth. My hope is that by alternating between first-person and third-person investigative strategies, mixed with traditional and innovative writing styles in a basic course, a fuller, richer image of people will emerge. Being human consists of far more than what might be learned from an extraspective, third-person perspective alone. But we must also avoid the complementary pitfall of relying only on subjective, first-person insights to know ourselves. By keeping both eyes wide open and firmly fixed upon human nature, we might come to know ourselves and our fellow human beings in all the richness and complexity that we humans possess.

ACKNOWLEDGMENTS

I would like to extend thanks to the American Psychological Association for granting permission to reproduce portions of the following articles:

Albee, G. W. (1991). Presidential message: No more rock-scrubbing. *The Scientist Practitioner* . American Association of Applied and Preventive Psychology, *1*, no. 1, 26–27.

Howard, G. S. (1991). Culture tales: A narrative approach to thinking, cross cultural psychology, and psychotherapy. *American Psychologist, 46*, 187–197.

Howard, G. S. (1992). Behold our creation: What counseling psychology has become—and might yet become. *Journal of Counseling Psychology, 39* , 406–434.

Richardson, M. S., & Patton, M. J. (1992). Guest editors' reflections on a centennial series in process. *Journal of Counseling Psychology, 39* , 443–446.

Thanks is extended to Academic Publications for permission to reproduce portions of the following books:

Howard, G. S. (1986). *Dare we develop a human science?* Notre Dame, IN.: Academic Publications.

Howard, G. S. (1989). *A tale of two stories: Excursions into a narrative approach to psychology.* Notre Dame, IN.: Academic Publications.

I am grateful to Sage Publications for permission to reprint:

Birk, J. M. (1994). Country roads: Counseling psychology's rural initiative. *The Counseling Psychologist, 22,* 183–196, © Sage Publications. Reprinted by permission of Sage Publications, Inc.

My appreciation goes to Praeger Press for granting permission to reproduce parts of the chapter:

Howard, G. S. (1993). The stories we live by: Confessions of a member of the species *Homo Fabulans* (Man, the storyteller). In D. J. Lee (Ed.) *Life and story: Autobiography from a narrative perspective* (pp. 247–274). New York: Praeger.

My thanks is also extended to Andrew Deitch for permission to publish "My wife," My-Tien Ton for "Transplanted mangrove," Joy Germondson for "Dirt roads, jeeps, and slow pacing," and Brandi Coyner for "The playwright." Finally, I'm indebted to six other anonymous students who allowed me to publish parts of their life stories.

PART I
AUTOBIOGRAPHIES AND LIFE STORIES

The principle task for the first part of this book is to get you to write your autobiography. It would be ideal if you were able to begin without any help from me. If you feel you might be able to begin, please do so now.

"I was born at a very early age . . ."

"Coming to college really opened my eyes . . ."

"My kid sister has always been a pain in the neck for me . . ."

"Baseball seems to be the perfect metaphor for my life . . ."

Feel free to start anywhere in your life—and don't worry about where your story is heading. Just write it!

However, many students have a difficult time composing their autobiographies because they are unfamiliar with a first-person writing style and/or are uncomfortable writing about themselves. If you are simply unfamiliar with autobiographical writing, here are a few examples of excellent autobiographies that you might read in order to see how writers can make their life stories come alive.

Angelou, M. 1969. *I know why the caged bird sings.* Toronto: Bantam Books. Watch a black woman grow up in poverty in rural Arkansas to become a Pulitzer prize–winning novelist.

Gogh, V. V. 1937. *Dear Theo: The autobiography of Vincent Van Gogh.* Boston: Houghton-Mifflin. The incredible life of a tortured artist unfolds before your eyes.

Kingston, M. 1977. *The woman warrior: Memoirs of a girlhood among ghosts.* New York: Knopf. One sees the importance of culture in watching this Asian-American woman's journey of development.

Sometimes reading professionally written autobiographies can be a bit depressing to us nonprofessional autobiographers because they are so well written. To give you a feel for how some less-than-professionally-written autobiographies can still be of value, sections of my own autobiographical sketch and those of a few of my students are offered in the first three chapters. However, you must realize that these autobiographical sketches have been rewritten, edited, and improved many times over. Thus, you should not be discouraged if your initial attempt to write an autobiography comes out looking less polished than these examples. It is important to get something—sometimes anything—on paper so that you can then begin the important task of rewriting and improving your story.

Perhaps you are a good writer, but somewhat self-conscious when writing about yourself. I find that I must keep reminding myself that I retain control over who will ever read my autobiographical writing. I begin with the assumption that *no one* will ever read these written thoughts. Then, once they are on paper, my challenge becomes how to rewrite them so that I will feel comfortable with other people knowing these things about me. If I can't rewrite them to my satisfaction, I simply erase them—no harm done. However, simply putting one's thoughts into words can be a helpful, satisfying experience—whether or not anyone else ever reads them. So, if it helps you to do so, write as if you will be your autobiography's only reader.

Someone once asked George Bernard Shaw how one becomes a great writer. Shaw reportedly replied that one must place the seat of one's pants on the seat of one's chair, and write. This strategy is good advice not only for great writers but also for rookie autobiographers. First, just write the darn thing. Only later should one worry about what it all means, whether it is written badly or well, and how (and why) your life story might have been told differently. So begin writing your autobiography now. You can expect a few unsuccessful starts, but don't let that discourage you. After several aborted beginnings, here's how the initial section of my autobiography turned out.

CHAPTER 1
A STORY OF GEORGE

It's a tough job to spin a good story—be it a story about some fictitious character, an institution, a nation, or one's own story. Regarding my story, no beginning sounds really appropriate—let alone as dazzling as some starts like "It was the best of times, it was the worst of times . . . ." So I guess I'll just have to start somewhere, and hope the story gets better as it goes along. It doesn't seem that this start should have taken a week, and cost a pad's worth of false starts.

My memories of Bayonne are almost all good. I even savor the few bad memories, as they make the entire package more realistic. But it would be a mistake to tell tales of meaningful lessons and blindingly acute insights—for that isn't the way it was. It was all rather ordinary—really. My memories are of good pals, exciting games of stickball and basketball, caring and hardworking parents, days of school that took forever, wonderful summers that raced past like the blink of an eye, and of rainy Sunday afternoons that were so depressing that I was reduced to tears.

As my British friends would say, I grew up in a working-class family. Everyone in my family worked—and our discovery of someone between the stages of high school and retirement who did not work were always greeted with mild surprise. By the way, school didn't count as work—it was a natural thing people of a certain age just did. I mean, you don't take credit for breathing, do you? Work was what you did after you took care of the expected activities. Besides, an idle mind (or body, or anything) was the devil's workshop. So we worked hard, played hard, and generally tried to better ourselves. But to say that we were an achieving family would not be exactly correct.

My older sister Marion and my younger brother Billy were always much better in school than me. In fact, it was widely agreed (OK, universally accepted!) that, while I was a nice guy and a hard worker, I was a bit of a dunce. While it goes without saying that I was saddened by this analysis of my intellect, I had to admit that all the evidence suggested that it was correct. But I was very lucky—being a dunce had minimal impact on my spirits. After all, almost everyone in the neighborhood liked me, I had lots of good pals, I could run like the wind, jump like a kangaroo, throw a baseball like Sandy Koufax; and I was always the first or second kid chosen when we were choosing up sides for any game. Hell, I was on a fast track to the National Basketball Association. You really didn't need to be a genius to be a star.

But I sure was a good boy—even in school. While I couldn't get too thrilled about getting terrible grades, I definitely wasn't going to get myself in trouble by making like I wasn't trying, or—worse yet—acting like a wiseacre. You see, I was born after the invention of the telephone. Those nuns wouldn't hesitate for an instant in calling up my mother and then I could kiss away play for the foreseeable future (like a week).

If pressed to describe my grade school years, I would probably characterize them as being happy, safe (because I was in a very supportive environment), active, and simple. A word more needs to be said about why it was simple and uncomplicated. You see, we are talking about the mid- and late-1950s—the Eisenhower years! Did *anything* of importance happen during the Eisenhower years? When people reminisce about a simpler, less complicated time, I know *exactly* what they are talking about. The weightiest issues with which I wrestled were momentous problems like: having to do extra chores because I was late for supper, not knowing why everyone learned their multiplication tables faster than I, finding enough soda bottles to be able to replace the ball that had rolled down a sewer, and the like.

I lived in a ghetto. But really, it was more like a warm cocoon. We were all working class, Catholic, and of Western European ancestry (mostly second or third generation). In fact, my parents still live in the house where my mother was born. Families kind of grow together when they've been neighbors for sixty or seventy years. Besides, I had about a dozen close relatives (grandparents, aunts, uncles, and cousins) who lived within 150 yards of our home. As I look back on it now, I was never alone—I never had to face anything alone. Come what may, there were always relatives and friends close at hand to walk (or talk) me through any difficulty. It was many years, and many tears, before I realized exactly how influential that constant, early support was for me. I did work as a psychotherapist for four years during and immediately after graduate school. The most difficult clients for me to listen to (let alone to be of some help to) were the ones who had encountered severely traumatic experiences during childhood. I become paralyzed with an overwhelming guilt (because unlike them I was blessed with a wonderful childhood) that rendered me somewhat (OK, totally!) ineffective as a helper for them. Thus, the career choice to be an academic psychologist was easy—and I never seriously looked back. To give you an idea how idyllic my childhood now appears to me (in retrospect), consider my lone "brush with the law" as a youth.

I was driving home from a bowling outing with friends late one Saturday afternoon. I clearly had the right of way, but she pulled out of her parking space and her left front fender ripped the entire right side of my car. The only voice I could hear was my father's. A few months earlier (when I was awarded my learner's permit) he had stated *quite* emphatically, ". . . and if you ever get into an accident *call the police immediately.*" As I phoned for police assistance, I was very shaken (from the accident) but enormously relieved that I knew "the right thing to do." The potential problems associated with my being a seventeen-year-old who had gotten into an accident with the wife of a prominent physician in town, and whose learner's permit happened to be in the pocket of another pair of slacks, were still a million miles from my awareness.

I began to suspect that I was in trouble by the look in Officer Jones' eyes when I discovered that I didn't have my learner's permit with me. I knew I was in trouble when the physician's wife suggested she and the policeman have a private chat. And I was overcome with nausea when Officer Jones announced that I *would* sign a statement saying the accident was my fault—and my insurance company would pay to fix our cars—or he would throw me in jail. All I was able to choke out was that the accident was not my fault, and that I wouldn't sign anything. Fortunately, the ride to the police station was sufficiently long to enable me to gather my senses—and form a plan. As soon as I was led in tow to the desk sergeant, I shouted for everyone in the squad room to hear, "I wanna see my Uncle Bub! NOW!"

Officer Jones had no way of knowing it, but he had stumbled into the jaws of our family's only *bona fide* success story. By dint of hard work and fidelity to duty for over thirty years, Bub Mahon had risen from being an ordinary cop, pounding a beat, to the chief of police. The desk sergeant tried to pacify me by suggesting that,

"It wasn't necessary to disturb the chief with this small . . ." "Get him now, or you're in trouble too," I cried. The sergeant, who knew an explosive situation when he saw one, wisely punted, "Chief, your nephew is here to see you." You see, Bub wasn't really my uncle (but yelling something like "I wanna see my seventh cousin, twice removed!" would probably lack force). And, in fact, I never called him anything but Uncle Bub. [That's not completely true—if I caught him talking to someone "important" (like a mayor, or a Monsignor), I'd breeze by and nonchalantly chirp, "Hi ya, Bubbles!"] And, in fact, he never called me anything but "Nephew George" (unless, of course, I had just called him "Bubbles"). I was proud to think of him as my uncle—and so I adopted him.

But getting back to the story, no sooner did Bub appear, than Officer Jones and I began to blurt out parallel—but very different—versions of "the story." Eventually, I became so upset that I began to cry. I summarized with a sobbing, ". . . and, Uncle Bub, you know I'd never tell you a lie." And in that moment of silence, one could almost hear the great court judge in the sky announce, "Advantage, young mister Howard." I silently thanked my lucky stars for all those times I had been compulsively honest with Bub. By the look in Bub's eyes—even if Officer Jones had been a cat (with nine lives)—he still would have been dead as a doornail. "Murphy! Get a squad car and take my nephew home. Jones! My office!"

About the fifteenth time I thanked Bub for "getting me out of trouble," and apologized for "causing him all that trouble," he said that it was probably for the best that it happened. People can be very cruel sometimes—and he was just happy that this time I was around friends when I needed help. As always, Bub was right—as I'd later find out. But more importantly, Officer Jones was young and would have to determine right from wrong as the representative of the law for many years to come. Bub was convinced that the experience was one Officer Jones would not soon forget—and that he would be a far better cop for it. I hope Bub was right.

If all this sounds like so much "truth, wisdom and beauty," or piles and piles of "happy horseshit," then I'm sorry. But that's the way I remember it. I had more than my share of fights as a child. I also broke more than my share of bones while playing sports. But life seemed so good, so fair, so understandable, and so predictable—in the good sense. If you take chances, you can sometimes come up with the short end of the stick. But, in general, life wasn't cruel, or threatening, or unfair, or uninteresting. I charged into adolescence and young adulthood with enthusiasm, confidence, and more than a little naïveté.

I've pretty much avoided what was an important part of my life at that time—my religion. Being a Catholic, for me, was a lot like being a male. I didn't know how I had become a Catholic. There was never any question about it—I would no more have thought, "Maybe I'll become a Protestant," than I would have imagined, "Maybe I'll become a female." And I certainly did nothing to earn the faith I had. [The Baltimore catechism answer, "Faith is a gift from God," fit my experience perfectly.] But in Bayonne in the 1950s, being a Catholic was like being a human—everybody was one! I completely accepted the world-view of Catholicism, and thus benefited from the warm, safe certainty that it offered. I knew right from wrong; I understood what was expected of me in life; and, through religion, I began to work out "my view of the world." I began to tell myself an increasingly more coherent story regarding why things were the way they were in my life, my community, and the world. As provincial, unrealistic, and idealistic as it was, it was at least a start, and that was important.

But with 20-20 hindsight, I can now see that the seeds of change were sown even then. It would just take a few years for those seeds to germinate. The religion I learned was liberally sprinkled with sin and damnation, stories of the fires of hell, and a deep suspicion of sinful human nature. I had more than my share of childhood nightmares of the devil and hell-fires. Finally, mysteries of faith were always my Achilles heel. Perhaps it was the first stirrings of the scientist in me, but even back then mysteries were puzzles, challenges, and mind-teasers which were to be dissected, analyzed, and solved. "Just accept it on faith" was the standard advice I received. And even if it was good advice, I was constitutionally incapable of heeding it. I simply had to think everything through—even though the thinking was painfully slow and frequently faulty.

I need to talk a bit about my parents before we leave the topic of religion. My father is a Protestant—although to this day, I don't know exactly to which denomination he belongs. He certainly never actively practiced. When he and my mother married, he was forced to sign an agreement that the children would be raised as Catholics. While there were times that he chafed under the terms of that agreement, to his credit he never seriously subverted it (to deliver an occasional joke or snide remark is only human—and, in fact, highly desirable if the jokes are funny). But I know that I learned at least two important lessons from his example in the religion domain: 1) a deal's a deal (you agree on something and you don't renege on it); and 2) you don't need to be religious to be a good person and lead a good life . . .

Chapter 2
What Can Be Learned from an Autobiography?

Writing my autobiography proved to be a very rewarding experience. I came away with a fresh appreciation for some wonderful people who were important influences on my early life. I'm at a point in my life where I want to feel good about my childhood—and writing my autobiography helped me to better appreciate the benefits I received from my family and childhood friends. But who knows what the future holds? Maybe at some point in the future I'll need to tell an autobiographical tale that makes my childhood seem less the prelude to a happy, productive life. Let's be serious. Just because I haven't murdered anyone or had problems with substance abuse is no guarantee that I won't experience either of those tragedies. And if some such tragedy does occur in my life, I'll have to find a way to make my life story accommodate that reality. In short, events in our lives force us to write (and often rewrite) our life story to maintain its *narrative truth* (Spence, 1982). That is, given the direction and tone of my life at this point in time, "A story of George" is as honest and (narratively) truthful a life story as I am capable of telling. I genuinely hope I will never have to alter the narrative tone of my life story, but unfortunately, there are no guarantees in life.

However, there is another kind of truth to a life story which will not change—the *historical truth*. An early line of my autobiography, "My memories of Bayonne are almost all good," conveys a good deal about the narrative tone that my life story now possesses. But that line makes little claim to historical facts. Things would have been quite different had I begun, "I was born to John Howard and Margaret Jordan Howard on June 8, 1948 in Bayonne hospital." While that start covers a number of claims of historical truths, it would give little clue as to the narrative tone that my life story would adopt.

While I vouch for the historical truth of everything claimed in "A story of George," I believe it is more important to consider the narrative tone of any person's autobiography. For it is the narrative truth of our life stories that reveals that which is most precious, unique, and interesting in our human natures. What occurs to you and me in life is only important insofar as it plays a role in helping us to become the sort of persons that we have become.

You don't need to be a psychologist to know that people react to events in their lives in a variety of ways. A failure that will crush one person can serve as the galvanizing experience that projects another person to greater achievement and happiness. What accounts for such discrepancies in reactions to similar life-events? The only honest answer is that psychology is just beginning to understand why some people are resilient in the face of adversity, while others are inclined to crumble. But from a narrative (or story-telling) perspective, how a person interprets an event in her or his larger life story greatly determines what effect that event will produce in that life. How each of us interprets what happens to us is crucial.

Surely you've heard the apocryphal story of the identical twins who were led by their parents into a room that was filled from ceiling to floor with horseshit. One of the twins slumped to the floor, began crying, wailed that he wasn't responsible for this mess, and vowed that he would not help to clean it up. The other twin immediately threw himself headlong into the manure, yelling excitedly, "Look at all this horseshit! There's gotta be a pony in here somewhere!"

Since the time of the Greek philosopher Epictitus, we've known that one's interpretation of the meaning of any event is crucial to an event's impact on the person—"Nothing is either bad or good, but thinking makes it so." In reading someone's autobiography, we can gain a sense of the narrative tone of that person's life—how the writer tends to anticipate and interpret the things that happen in her or his life. Narrative tone is important because it causes us to anticipate some events and helps to prevent other events from occurring in our lives.

Listen as a few students, through their autobiographical reflections, describe how their lives appear to them. But remember, the most important task before you now is to write your own autobiography. So stop reading the following accounts the moment one enables you to begin composing your own life story.

"Losses and reactions" was part of a young woman's autobiography that was written after her class of sophomores read Oliver Sacks' (1987) magnificent collection of essays dealing with cases of neurological abnormalities entitled *The man who mistook his wife for a hat.*

Losses and Reactions

In my life there is one prayer that I have consistently said, every time I've knelt, every time I've so much as thought of prayer. I'm not sure if there is even any thought or feeling behind it anymore. It's more an instinct to say, "Thank You for letting me hear in one ear if not both. Please help me to hear in the other ear as I grow older." Kind of funny actually, for as I approach my twentieth birthday, there is little chance that complete hearing will be restored "as I grow older" (if there ever could have been such a chance). The prayer was in fact developed in second grade as the result of my mother's comment: "Wouldn't it be great if as you grew up, you somehow regained your hearing? But you ought to thank God every day that you can hear in at least the one ear." So I did; in second grade, there's not much more to it.

I'll never forget the day that the doctor told my parents and me that I was completely deaf in one ear. As a kindergartner, I had not often seen my parents cry, particularly my "strong" father. But both of my parents cried as they received the news; I suppose out of some sense that their little girl was no longer "perfect." I certainly did not know what the tears were about, and, as only a young child can, I asked them why they were crying. Life to me was no different; my hearing had not changed one bit with the doctor's news.

They now tell me that I did make one request, and it was a rather strange request for a six-year-old to make, but bear with me. I apparently insisted that no one besides my immediate family be told: not grandparents, not aunts, not uncles, not cousins, nor friends. I guess I thought that my grandmother would be too upset, and that no one else need know. A rather private and secretive child, I suppose. To this day, only two of the aforementioned people have ever so much as commented on my hearing to me: my cousin's husband and my mother's best friend's husband. That's it. (Okay, Mom and Dad couldn't keep the secret as well as me, I was seventeen when I first told anyone!) And so I went through all of grammar school and high school. I think I thought it would make me "different" in grammar school if others knew of my "loss"—every child's worst fear.

Humor enters the picture as I trot off to high school on the noisy bus with all of my best friends from grammar school. For all of my supposed intelligence, I believe I was thought of as the biggest airhead in the world in high school. I can't tell you how many times my friends literally asked me if I was deaf—nor can I tell you how many times I wanted to answer "Yes!!" at the top of my lungs. But I never did. As a doctor who deals with humans' reactions to losses, Dr. Oliver Sacks makes the point perfectly as he writes, "What had been funny, or farcical, in relation to the movie, was tragic in real life" (p. 13). What my friends had thought a good laugh would have been the greatest of tragedies, for why else would I have kept such a secret for all these years? I was in a quandary. How could I suddenly tell all of these old friends my secret without making it seem a tragedy—or worse—the best-kept secret?! So I remained the clueless airhead.

"It must be said from the outset that a disease is never a mere loss or excess—that there is always a reaction, on the part of the affected organism or individual, to restore, to replace, to compensate for and to preserve its identity" (p. 6). Dr. Sacks begins his account of the patients and the diseases he has dealt with by setting forth his belief in *reaction*. And, indeed, as one reads his writings, one finds that he seldom forgets the organism or the individual for the sake of the disease. *The man who mistook his wife for a hat* includes several tales of neurological losses, excesses, transports, and worlds of the simple, and in each excerpt, Dr. Sacks does his utmost to include the reactions of the persons within the disease and the illness. It is perhaps this element of Dr. Sacks' character and writing that strikes me the most, for *human beings* are the ones who have the disease; they are the ones who must cope with the changes in their lives brought about by the diseases. All too often the doctors and scientists attempting to cure the disease can lose a sense of their purpose: to restore and to replace "life" for a human being. Dr. Sacks is one of the rare individuals who instead attempts both to cure the disease and to measure the life within the disease. For him, there will always be a soul, no matter what the condition of the physical body.

Dr. Sacks begins his accounts with the story of a man who is visually impaired, a man who sees parts but fails to recognize the whole. Mistaking his wife for a hat, the patient, Dr. P., seems relatively unaware of his impairment and indeed even less bothered by it. Life for him continues without complete visual awareness.

And, although Sacks finds that, "he saw nothing as familiar. Visually, he was lost in a world of lifeless abstractions. Indeed, he did not have a real visual world, as he did not have a real visual self" (p. 15). Nevertheless, Dr. P. carried on—teaching, eating, and living with his wife. He was every bit the accomplished artist that he was with full vision, just different.

I wish I knew if I laughed or cried harder as I read Sacks' account. I had visions of Dr. P. greeting the fire hydrant as a person, just as clearly as I have memories of all the times I have tried to answer questions and to carry on conversations without really knowing what was said. For every time Dr. P. greeted the wrong person, I can guarantee I answered the wrong question. I feel as if I have an insight not only to Dr. P.'s reaction to such blunders, but also to all the strange looks Dr. P. himself must have missed from onlookers. Of course, strange looks would be lost on someone with Dr. P's "loss."

But I believe that Sacks had the right idea in deciding to leave Dr. P. to his peace of mind, rather than attempting to conduct further study of his case. People deal with such losses in the best way that they can. Dr. P. and his wife denied the change in his artwork; I kept my secret and to a certain extent denied my loss to the rest of the world. I admire Dr. Sacks' consideration for the life that Dr. P. led in the midst of his loss. For someone who cannot share the experience of such a loss, it must be difficult to understand the ability to adapt, much less to appreciate fully the quality of that adapted lifestyle. I admire Dr. Sacks' belief in the human spirit, a belief which demands recognition of the life and the reaction beyond the disease. As he exercises this belief in his daily practice, Dr. Sacks gives me greater faith in doctors.

This reflection of mine is in no way meant to completely parallel my "case" to the cases studied by Sacks. But the accounts have caused me to think about the ability of humans to react to events in their lives, their losses, their diseases and to somehow self-determine the lives they will lead in the face of such realities. My friends at college all know of my hearing loss, and I am content with my decision to tell them. Oh! Life is so much easier than I ever imagined! No longer do I have to pretend to hear the secrets whispered in the wrong ear; no longer do I spend meals in my own world for the sake of not hearing the conversation!

But I am also happy with the choice I made back in kindergarten. Growing up without the "excuse" of my hearing, I have been forced to pay special attention when people speak. Because of this reaction, I think that my hearing is not as much of an issue for me now as it might have been. Such observations and thoughts stem from a fellow "deafy" who I have met since coming to Notre Dame. Unlike me, he grew up with everyone fully aware of his impairment. I honestly believe that is why he seems so much more hindered by it now. Whether his hearing is just worse than mine, or whether I just learned to compensate better, I will never fully know. But I really believe that there is "never a mere loss or excess—that there is always a reaction" (p. 6). It seems to me that the reaction, not the loss, is the more significant of the two components of life.

What do you think of the narrative tone of our young autobiographer's life? Does an autobiography like hers mean that everything is always rosy in her life? Hardly! In fact, while her attitude toward her "loss" and her "reactions" is marvelous, her auto-biographical reflections on other aspects of her life—such as career, marriage, religion, etc.—could have quite a different narrative tone. She might profitably explore each of these domains in turn. The narrative tone of her entire life story would represent the sum of all these true stories of her life. Any life represents a complex collection of interconnecting story-lines. Did you notice that my autobiography in Chapter 1 was called "A story of George"? Many, many more true stories might have been told of my childhood— but this one was quite enough for me.

Our partially deaf sophomore received the inspiration for "Losses and reactions" from a very odd source—a collection of essays on clinical neurology. This is an example of liberal education at its best. In coming to know our world and other people better, we succeed in better understanding ourselves. Have you read any books, seen any plays or movies, or heard any stories lately that grabbed your interest? Perhaps in reflecting upon this experience you can discover a narrative voice that will lead to an expression of your life story. Each of us must first discover the narrative tone of his or her life story before we can attempt the next task—improving the narrative tone of our lives. Good luck in locating a muse and finding your "voice."

Some students have experienced great pain in their lives before they enter college. In "Death comes, and life goes on" an African-American senior recounts her experiences with deaths and defeats. However, despite her numerous trials, we see how character can sometimes be forged from the fires of life's tragedies.

DEATH COMES, AND LIFE GOES ON . . .

. . . It was my first day of kindergarten. I had a warm, loving class, so I adapted very well. Surprisingly, I didn't have any problems with the other kids or the teacher. It was similar to my Head Start class; so my transition was a breeze. I was ecstatic when it came to school. I could play, learn, and have fun doing it. I never really wanted to go home, except to have more fun with the neighborhood kids. They too were from Belize [her ancestral home in Central America]. As with all good things, kindergarten also came to an end. The real transition was yet to come; it arrived in first grade. I was the youngest in the class, and on the first day I sure acted like it. We were released for a recess break, which all the kids believed to be the highlight of the day. Well, for Sandra it was a prime opportunity to cry my head off. I threw one of the most incredible temper tantrums, as I stood at the gate in exactly the place my mother dropped me off. I grabbed the fence and cried and cried, hoping my mother would return. But no such luck! The other students began to stare, and when the bell sounded to return to class, someone told the teacher. She came to console me. She explained how my mother had to work and that she would be back soon. Well, for some strange reason I believed her and let go of the fence and returned back to class.

At this time, my grandmother was battling cancer. To me it seemed as if she just loved to smoke and to visit the hospital. After months of therapy my grandmother was released and sent home. She then began to live with us. It was fun having her around, until the good Lord decided it was her time to go. I was six years old. I really had no experience with death before—especially death so close. My grandmother was the only grandmother I ever knew because my father's mother lived in Belize. So, she was the only grandmother I had. The whole idea of her death left me awe-struck. One minute she was asleep; the next moment she was asleep forever, never to be woken. As they wheeled her body out of the bedroom on the stretcher, all I could remember was the man with the blue jumper with a name tag that read CORONER—just as bold as it is on this paper. This was really my first encounter with death, and that coroner label always remained in my head whenever I thought about her passing. But that was not the end of death experiences for me.

It must have been about eight months later when I was awakened at 1:00 a.m. by gunshots and a car skidding. A drive-by shooting had just occurred. A young boy (about the age of sixteen) from my neighborhood was shot. All I could hear was him yelling to his friends, "Man, I'm not letting go." The two guys with him dragged his body directly under my window. Why did they do that? The boy stared up as if he was looking at me. He clenched a red bandanna that he swore not to let go of. I was calm, just looking on as the paramedics tried to save his life. But even with all the electroshocks, it was just too late. The boy was lifeless and still his eyes were staring upward until the paramedic closed them. They removed his body, but left behind was a large puddle of blood as a result of the gunshot wound. As if school was not enough for a six-year-old to get used to, the streets were crazy too. But violence in my life was just beginning . . .

The years progressed, and I was tired of the whole "valley school" thing. I was fed up with the minority students always being at fault for whatever went wrong. There were many incidents that were just so crazy. I remember one time in our math class, the class was about 60 percent white and the rest were black. Well, this particular day there was one white kid who was real smart—he knew everything. He was very intelligent, but he still didn't know that drugs will kill your brain cells. Anyway, as the teacher was lecturing, this boy pulled out a bag of cocaine. This was the first time I'd ever seen the stuff. I was shocked that he brought it to school. He later asked this black guy sitting next to him, "Hey, you want to taste it? It's real." The guy replied "No, you got to be joking man. That's got to be flour." The white boy tasted it, insisting that the black boy next to him try it. He refused, but before the class was over, the white boy began to carve his arm; he explained he was giving himself a tattoo. It looked so painful. I could not believe that he sat there taking drugs in class, then offered it to someone else, and on top of it all began to give himself a tattoo. Then the administration claimed that the black students were the ones that disrupted the learning environment. Our school days would always have a lot of tension. Many of the students got along, both black and white, but more times than not they were planning to have white vs black fights after school. Throughout the day in class, if someone was disrupting the class, and the teacher had no worldly idea who did it, a black student would somehow get chosen to go to the principal's office. It was strange how that always occurred, even after reports from parents contradicted the administrator's beliefs. The only way out was to leave, and after three years that's just what I did. I had some great memories of Junior High School, like being part of the city champion cheerleader squad. Yeah, me, six-foot-one-inch, a cheerleader. But back then I was not that tall. I enjoyed it all, but the time had finally come for me to move on once again.

It was a coincidence that just as I was changing schools, I was also moving homes. We seemed to move about every six months for some crazy reason or another; whether the landlord just did not like us, or maybe the rent would increase. By this time I was tired and felt as if I was a professional mover—just call me U HAUL. I was now about fourteen years old and ready to start senior high. But I had a decision to make. Should I go to the high school in my district or attend my brother's and sister's alma mater? Well, the decision wasn't that easily made. My mother had to get permission from the school in my district, which happened to be Crenshaw, the chief rival of Dorsey, my brother's and sister's alma mater. As the paperwork was completed, I was so excited to return back to the black community and attend the school where my brother and sister had graduated.

I enrolled in summer school. It was the summer of 1987, my best friend and I were approached by these two big girls who asked if we played basketball. Well, our response was "No!" and I really did not care to play either. I was about 5'11" and had acrylic nails; I was too busy trying to check out the cute fellows at the school. "Sorry," I said, "but my mind was not on basketball." I had never really played, and it just didn't compete with being a cheerleader. Although, I loved competition, I just was not interested. But these two girls were very persistent—they wouldn't take "no" for an answer. With some coercing from the assistant coach, my best friend and I tried out and were selected for the varsity team. Can you believe it? Two individuals with no experience whatsoever were selected to the varsity team. It was definitely a case of a "height advantage." This was the beginning of something special for me.

Special it was! After the first year I grabbed the Most Improved Player Award. I was overwhelmed that I had picked up on the sport so well. I really never thought that basketball was for me. During the eleventh grade everything about basketball started to jell for me. After school I would rush home to finish whatever homework I had to do so I could watch the Los Angeles Lakers. I was developing a real feel for the game. We had a well-rounded, very athletic team with lots of heart. But this turned out to be the year that I thought basketball might disappear from my life forever.

In the last game of the season we were playing the best team in our district—Washington High School. If we defeated them our conference record would place us in the number two spot; a loss would leave us in third. So the adrenaline was pumping—especially for me. I was eager to start the game. On the first play of the game, I stole the ball and was on my way down the court. I thought I would do a nice Tim Hardaway, crossover, stutter-step. But at the end of the move there was a loud snap, and I collapsed on the floor. I was in tremendous pain. As the referee stopped the game, my coach raced out to see if it was serious. It was serious! "My knee just gave out," I tried to explain. The trainers then escorted me off the court. I was still in pain, but I tried to convince myself that it was just a little sprain. So I asked the trainers to tape my knee to give me some support, so that I could re-enter the game. I went back into the game, but I was only good for two rebounds and four points. My knee continued to give out, as if I had no control over it. As a result we lost.

But we still had a playoff spot to compete for the city championship. The next day I was anxious to find out what the situation was concerning my knee—and exactly how long I would need before I could play again. The news I received was not pleasant. I was told I had an ACL-deficient left knee. What it meant was that I had torn my anterior cruciate ligament, and also destroyed some cartilage. This particular ligament is responsible for the stability of the knee. That was only the beginning. I was later told that I would never be able to play the caliber of basketball I once played. I was given the opportunity to have surgery, but with my financial situation, who would pay for it? The doctor suggested that I select another sport, like cycling or swimming, but neither tickled my fancy. I sat up many nights wondering how I would function without basketball—weighing the long-term consequences. I also had to deal with not being able to help my team in the playoffs.

As the playoffs began, I was on the sideline and in more pain than my face displayed. I was happy that our team was there, but sad I couldn't help. Cheering was all I could do. The team advanced to the semifinals which were held in the Sports Arena, the gymnasium of the Los Angeles Clippers. Well, as with all good things, our team's dream was shattered. We were so close, yet so far, but we were proud anyway.

I believed we could win it all the next year, and I vowed I would be ready then regardless of what some doctor said. I believed that if I worked out every day, and built up my strength and endurance, I could definitely improve and be in better shape than I was to start. That is exactly what I did, and in October I was ready for the season.

I averaged about 19.9 points a game. "Sandra the Ballin Girl" was definitely back. I couldn't believe that without surgery I could perform so well. Of course there was pain every now and then, but it wasn't anything I couldn't tolerate. I thanked God every day for giving me such talent, and allowing me to use it. And I surely did use it! It was now my senior year and I had something to prove. I was on a mission to get back to the Sports Arena. I wanted to play there more than anything in the world. But luck may have placed a dark cloud in our path. We were held back by a loss in the quarter-final game against Van Nuys High. I was so upset because the referee took away any chance we had to win the game. Of course, you're probably saying, "Yeah, how did the referee take away the game?" It was the most poorly refereed game in which I had ever had participated—or even seen as a spectator—to be honest with you. I was so hurt that my chances to play in the Sports Arena were shattered. But I was granted an even more prestigious honor.

I was selected to the City-Wide, All-Star team. I had the great honor to play in the world-renowned Forum—the home of the Los Angeles Lakers. It was an exciting feeling playing among great athletes like Charisse Sampson, Detra Lockhart, and Lisa Leslie. I really felt that I had accomplished a great deal by representing my school and district—even though we didn't win the game. I felt as if it was my fate to win a championship of some sort, but I guess my time just hadn't yet come.

I really began to believe that basketball would be the only way, so I used it to my advantage. The next level was college and I had plenty of offers to attend different universities. But they didn't offer what I was looking for in a school. Schools would constantly call the house and my mother would take messages. Finally she said, "Honey, the decision is up to you, and you must select where you want to go." I received letters from the University of Portland, Idaho, Iowa, but they had goals for me that differed from my goals. I wanted to attend a school that was small, and I could get my studies done as well as play basketball. Basketball was an excellent means to finance my college education. I did know one thing—all the offers I received from California schools were definitely out of the question. Just think, if I stayed in Los Angeles or nearby. I probably would scream to go home every day, and so never get any work accomplished. Nevertheless, time was ticking and I had to make a choice. A school, that I really had no knowledge about, began to send me information on how prestigious it was; how the student-teacher ratio was low; and how they produce about 80 percent of the African-Americans that continue on to medical school. This was just what I was looking for in a school. A place that offered a great opportunity to go to medical school, as I had always dreamed of being "Dr. Sandra!"

The literature that I received led me to research the school further, and I found more information on basketball as well. Surprisingly, the school only had one sport, and that was basketball. This was right up my alley. I later sent a letter to the coach and asked how he went about recruiting athletes. He asked me to send a tape of one of my games, and I did. He was impressed with the tape, and he even expressed some interest in a teammate who happened to be best friend. He offered both of us a scholarship on the spot. I was still not sure where I wanted to go just yet, but it surely was near the top of the list. Then, about a week later I read that Xavier's team had just recently won the district championship. I was sure this was the school for me. It was a historically black university with a highly prestigious academic reputation; it was away from Los Angeles; not to mention they had a championship season.

But it seems the rough seas wouldn't take a break, for another dilemma arose—we had to move again. Another move, but this time my mother wasn't up to it. She was suffering with an ulcerated vein in her left leg which threatened surgery—something she really feared. Moving really stressed her out, and on her last visit to the doctor he gave her an ultimatum; if she didn't get any rest, she would have to be admitted immediately. The search for our new residence was on once again; for an apartment, a house, just anywhere to lay our heads. Our search lasted about three weeks and my mother's condition kept getting worse. At last, just before the doctors admitted her, we found a nice three-bedroom apartment. Our prayers had been answered. The only thing that spoiled the occasion was that our mother was in the hospital for a skin graft surgery.

I was so sad because in less than a month I would have to go to college, but my mother wouldn't be able to escort me. I would have to go alone. Well, my mother would not have any of that. She told me that since she couldn't go, that my eldest sister would have the honor of escorting me to school. My mother's surgery was successful; she was recovering and she would soon be home. I was jumping for joy that my mother would soon be home—I just couldn't wait. I decorated her room and mine too. I couldn't wait for her to see the apartment.

Finally, it was time for my mother to come home. She was so excited, too. She was assigned a nurse who came by to visit and check her vital signs and to make sure she was doing well. During one check, the nurse detected a slight irregularity in her heart beat, so she insisted that my mother relax. While this was occurring, I was off to get booster shots for school; which can really be a pain in the butt. Anyway, as I was out getting shots, my brother and sisters were at work, so my mother was left in the care of her best friend. She sat there with my mother and made sure she was comfortable. So, as I returned home, I was so thrilled to see the whole family together. It was really a moment to remember for the rest of our lives. I had to get some papers for my college financial aid, and as I ran upstairs to get them I heard a loud cry. My sister had yelled, "Dial 911!"

I was scared. I didn't know what was going on, although I remained calm. I dialed the number but my sister grabbed the phone and began to babble things to the operator. The operator was trying desperately to calm her down, but she was too erratic. The operator was also receiving another call about the same emergency from the back house where our cousins were trying to help. I was so scared as we stood watching our mother have some sort of attack, and we knew of nothing we could do to correct the situation. The operator talked to me until the paramedics arrived, which was about ten minutes later. Once help arrived they began to question us as to who was going to pay for the service—they needed to find out if she had insurance. It was weird. I couldn't believe they would ask such questions, as my mother sat there without a clue as to what was going on. She really was incoherent, and unable to reply to anything the medics asked. I wished they would hurry and take her to the hospital, which was about fifteen minutes away, even if they were speeding.

We went to the hospital where there was a dire feeling in the air. The day that every child dreads had arrived for the five of us. My mother had passed away. I was so hurt I could not describe the pain. My sister was so devastated that she attempted to break through a wall with her bare hands. I really couldn't believe she had died. They allowed us to go back to view the body. As she lay there I just thought she was sleeping. She looked so peaceful without a care in the world. I really couldn't believe that she was gone. As I left the room, my best friend told me she had spoken with my mother earlier that day, while I was at the doctor's office. She said she asked my mother how she was doing and if she felt better, and my mother replied, "Honey, I feel fine, I just need some rest. And tonight I'm going to rest like I've never rested." After hearing that, and listening to my mother in the past, I believe she knew she was going to pass away. That was her way of warning us. She was more than a provider and a caretaker, she was a friend and I think that she really knew she was leaving. I looked back on the whole scenario before her death and realized that she had warned us in various ways. Telling me she wouldn't be able to escort me to school and that my sister would go was one way.

I truly believe if my mother was still here on earth with us she would have suffered with ulcerated veins for years to come, and that is not the way she would have wanted it. So, through all her preparation, she knew all her children were ready to take care of themselves. Her work was done. I, the youngest child, had finally graduated and received a full scholarship to college. My sister was engaged to be married. What more could my mother ask for? I really wish she could still be here, but I know that in spirit she is everywhere. . . .

I've worked with Sandra for two years. She is a wonderful person! People like Sandra never cease to impress upon me the resilience of the human spirit. In "Transplanted mangrove" an Asian-American student relives the trauma of being uprooted from her homeland.

TRANSPLANTED MANGROVE
My-Tien Ton

To understand a mangrove tree, one needs to examine the roots and seed out of which it grew.

When my father turned nearly half a century old, he questioned assumptions about life. The answers to the questions were rooted in his origin. He dug up old archives and commenced the family tree of the Nguyen Phuc Ton That ancestry. Our first generation, Nguyen Phuc Ton That Tu, was the eighteenth son of king Hien Ton Mieu Minh. My father is the ninth generation, and the first generation yanked out of Vietnam's soil, into the soil of the United States. Though the soil of the United States nurtures my father, it is the nutrients of Vietnam that best suit him. I think that is why when my father chose to examine the present and look into the future, he first reached back into his past in Vietnam. My father did not simply put names and arrows down on paper while making the family tree, instead he found himself. The family tree has not been completed. A letter was enclosed with my copy of the family tree. In the letter my father wrote the following:

> In late April 1975 when your father was working for the National Oil Exploitation Agency in Saigon, the war was so close to the city that the people were in panic and didn't know what to do, everyone was prepared to run but didn't know where to! Your mother made for each of you a small linen bag to be put around the neck and inside each bag was a note with your name, names of your parents, relatives and addresses . . . just in case we may need to run and you may get lost or we may get shot! Hung was then 6.5 years old, Quynh was 5, My-Tien was almost 4, Huong almost 3 and Quy only 18 months. On April 21, 1995, your Uncle Bang informed your father that the Tan Son Nhut airport entrance could be closed the next day and that might be the last day we could enter the airport for any hope of evacuation by airplane!
>
> We did not think that we can run by boats or on roads with five small kids . . . Hue had been taken over by the communists. Uncle Lu came along just to help carry My-Tien. Your mother and your father, each one carries a kid in one hand and a small bag on the other hand; Hung and Quynh were big enough to walk by themselves. In the airport we had to wait for three long days, we did not have any priority to embark any airplane, thousands of people were ahead of us. No one would know what might happen to us in the last twenty years should we have returned home that day; our life might turn out differently.

Though this is supposed to be an autobiography about myself, I included the words of my father, because it shows my own origin. I grew up knowing so little about my heritage, that I knew scant about my family, culture, and ultimately myself.

The following is a mixture of facts and fiction about the day my family left Vietnam. The main points are true, the particulars are dreamed, just the way I think of that day.

Leaving Saigon

In my Saigon, the sunset is a bloody red. The redness accentuates the pale yellow concrete houses, as a fever does to a sick man's face. Saigon's a living hell because of the Communist soldiers and the exploding bombs that tear apart the yellow concrete houses and the frail human bodies. Hue has been toppled by the Communists. Soon the American embassy will fall, and this once simple town of fishermen and dignity will turn into a place of soldiers and violence. It is busy, for many wish to escape the Communist oppression, including my family.

"Hurry, hurry the plane will come soon," Ba yells to the family. Mama quietly, always quietly whispers, "Do not yell so, it will hurt the children's ears." Though Ba is sorry, for he loves his children, he is unrelenting and demands that we finish packing our two suitcases. Ba's hand trembles in his fear of leaving Vietnam, his only home. However with the rise of the Communist party four days ago, home has become a stranger's abode. My family quickly finishes packing our white shirts, black pants and mangos for us children. Photographs and letters are inessential at this time. Only memories take no space in our suitcases.

"Mama, can I take Anh?" I ask, for she is my favorite stuffed doll. "Yes, my little one you may," Mama replies. I look for Anh under my thin bed and behind the warped wooden chairs. I stand upon my toes to peer over the bamboo cupboard; alas I am too tiny and cannot see. "Ba, will you please, please, please, please, pleeeaaase help me find Anh?" I plead. Ba is very busy from worrying and packing, but he sees the tears in my eyes and stands on his tip-toes to look above the cupboards. He cannot find her. I already miss my friend Anh's black yarn hair, brown button nose and companionship. Since I can no longer control my tears, they explode down my face of their own free will.

Before my family leaves our house, I want to peek outside the window. Looking outside, I see streams of tiny black-haired people marching like army ants to the savior queen (the plane). Soon my family joins the marchers and becomes a part of the swarming horde of ants.

I am finally in the boarding area of the plane. It is a jungle here. There are American soldiers with their rifles in hands, for the time has come to escape. They are prey, Vietnamese people and American soldiers, running away from the predators, the Communists. Peoples' shouts are like lion's roars, loud but incomprehensible. The aircraft's mechanical sound pierces the air. We are all animals who claw our ways to the plane. We fight to survive, nothing else matters because there is nothing but survival.

We wait for the plane. "Mama!" I cry impatiently for she is tightly pulling me towards her so much that I can barely breathe. Mama does not notice my voice or my pain for she is lost in her thoughts of a new life away from squalor and toward freedom. Her face contorts into a strange expression, as if she is afraid but does not want to show it. Mama's eyebrows arch high up while her mouth makes a crooked frown. Her face makes me sad, and I cry a single tear of blood in my heart.

I am not afraid, but everyone else around me is. I am only three, no, nearer to four years old, and I know only of the far-off three-toed monsters under my bed. This crowd of thousands has but one face, a fearful mask thinned from hunger. The adults talk in such angry tones that it is shrill in my ear. It seems as though only the adults are afraid. To the young this is merely an adventure, rather than a beginning of a new life in a new land.

I look around and spy Hoa, a girl from my village. Hoa looks pretty in her light teal kimono and white ribboned hair. Her eyes spy mine and for two minutes we stare at each other; though we do not smile, our eyes laugh. I yell, "Hello" at the top of my youthful lungs and try to walk towards her. Mama's strong arms hold me back. I am sad, for Hoa is the first person I see who is not afraid. I yell at Mama to let me see Hoa, squirming my frail body from her steel grasp, but Mama holds me still.

Mama is becoming so impatient that she can no longer control her emotions. She is crying now. Only Ba comes to comfort her. No one else comes or even notices, for in their animal-like states people are deprived of all tenderness. Just like animals gripped by fear, these deprived people could only feel fear. Mama still holds me. I look up to see her face's redness blending into the bloody-red horizon. I am sorry for making her cry. "Mama, what is wrong?" I ask. Mama sees me and becomes stronger. "Ti, nothing is wrong," Mama replies. Mama has five children and cannot afford to break down yet . . . not yet.

The plane's door opens and the humans claw towards it. No one cares if they run over others as long as they are not run over themselves. I feel elbows and knees shoving my back. The people roar. I see men battling with their claws at the gate to see who will get in first. Some have no ticket so they cannot get on the plane. They are so desperate as to try to fake their way in. The American soldiers, however, are not easily fooled. They send away the bluffers, young and old alike. I see families with no tickets. I see a ticketless woman, whose husband has already made it to the U.S., she cries and collapses. People continue to run past.

I am waiting to get on the plane. I see soldiers (who are supposed to keep the crowds in order) pass by. They are ineffective at their jobs for they are afraid of this strange land and its people. The elders are afraid of American soldiers, many of whom have bombed their village. I am not afraid. I stare quizzically at their uniforms and faces, for their pale faces and light hair seems strange. A blond soldier passes close by and sees me. I study his youth, he is not a pretty boy, but his eyes are a beautiful sea green. He slowly picks me up and pats my silky head. It seems as if he is as intrigued by me as I by him. Then he gently lowers me to the ground. Off his neck, he takes away a dull piece of metal and gives it to me. It is a dog tag. Believing that American soldiers only destroy and never give, the elders look on suspiciously. I do not care, for I am excited over this gift. The sunset's red rays shine on the dog-tag, making it glow a warm orange. I show off my dog-tag to Ba, who just smiles and puts me on line for the plane.

I walk up the stairs to the plane holding on to Mama's hand. I look down to see the masses of crying people and imagine each teardrop as crystals shattering on the ground. As I start to see the reality of leaving the only place I have ever lived, sung, and breathed the air in, I grow afraid. Soon I will be breathing the air of another land. I hope that it will be the air of freedom, for my people have been oppressed by many successions of government. We are sick of being mangy animals and demand to be treated as we really are, as human beings. My family is going to the United States for democratic freedom and for hope. We must leave Vietnam, but we cannot help being sad. Vietnam, which holds our land and our people, will always be our home.

Ba gives the soldier my family's plane ticket as we pass through the plane's door. We follow a soldier's lead and sit down where he points. We squat on the plane's hard floor. It is warm. The plane engines suddenly increase in power and the plane is airborne. I look around and see air and clouds. I see the plane's wing and it becomes the wing of an eagle. The plane flies like an eagle, soaring and passing through time and space. The eagle is free and strong as it carries us towards freedom.

"Mama, what is under this gray ship?" I ask. Like an eagle in flight, mama puts her arms around my waist and lifts me up towards the window. As she holds me by the window, she clutches me closer to her heaving chest. Fair heartbeats pulsate to the curve of my back. I wipe away some of the dirt which hides the window. I peer through the smudged window. There are thin strands of clouds underneath, like a silky shroud over the ocean. The clouds magnify and contrast the brilliant blue water. As the plane speeds off, clouds are transformed into wriggling water snakes weaving in and out of the water. Each snaky strand of cloud slides past another snaky strand over and under. Gradually the snaky clouds give birth. Peering through the window, I see a pure blanket of milky clouds.

As more thousands of clouds pass, I feel the tension in the air. Sandaled feet tap to the flow. Most in a slow . . . tap . . . tap . . . tap, others in a fast tappity, tappity, tap rhythm. Eventually, we stop worrying about the synchronization of our feet and pay more attention to the rumble of our stomachs. There will only be one meal during our arduous flight. Ding! A bell signals the beginning of our meal.

I am a black mangrove tree
rooted into a tiny island
floating in the Pacific ocean.
Life starts in chaos.
I precariously lie
on the edge of Vietnam's ocean shore.
Incoming waves wash away sandy soil,
exposing me to salty water.
During an enormous night storm of the Vietnam war,
pelting rain and lightning cracks the earth
surrounding the mangrove.
Rain cried down the bark of the mangrove.
Mother Vietnam screams
as she gives birth to the dividing ground.
Pelting rain cuts the placenta,
till the mangrove island is on its own.
A mangrove island floats through life
into the unknown of another land.
Though my soil and soul combines with the earth of the US
I will remember always the child mangrove.

MEMOIRS FROM THE MELTING POT
A Senior

I come from a biracial family. My mother is Caucasian and my father is African-American. They had a horrible courtship and their wedding was even worse. Everything had to be done in secret, my mother constantly feared that her parents knew. My parents had to make a decision very quickly. Did they love each other enough to get married and face all the consequences? Obviously the decision was "yes," and my parents have been happy ever since—but there was hell to pay. My grandparents were so unreasonable that my mom gave them an ultimatum. Either accept this marriage or never again see their daughter and her future children. My grandparents chose not to accept the marriage, and the relationship was not reconciled until after I was born. I grew up hearing this story and wondering how my grandparents could ever have not liked my dad. Sure he had darker skin than them, but he is such a great guy. My biracial background never allowed me to consider that anyone could be judged on the basis of color.

My parents decided to raise their kids as African-Americans. They wanted us to think of ourselves as members of the minority race because they knew that as we grew up that we would face discrimination. Never would people in this country consider us as half White. Rather, people would see us as Black, with all the stereotypes that went with that classification. My parents figured that if we thought of ourselves as Black, we would have an easier time dealing with racism and identifying with others who were discriminated against.

The hard lessons in life came early for this little girl. We moved all the time. My dad was in the military and that was what military families did. We ended up in Europe right after my first year in school. Life was good until the question of school came up. We lived an hour from the nearest American school, and my mom just did not want us to be bused that far. So, we went to a German school. My mother thought that being immersed in German culture would be the ultimate in an educational experience.

I will never forget the first day of school. The only German phrases I knew were "Yes," "No," and "Where is the bathroom?" My mother took me to school with our next door neighbor who also had a child in my class. I was terrified that my mother was going to leave me there alone. Suddenly, as she was leaving, I wanted to run but I was frozen—unable to move. Breathing became a chore, I felt like a truck had parked on my chest. Then came the tears—hot, stinging, and salty. The teacher showed me to my seat and introduced me to the class. She spoke some English, so at least I could understand enough to kind of blend in.

Recess was supposed to be the happiest time of the school day, but I wanted to throw up. How could I play with these kids? Out of nowhere Petra came over, I will never forget her. She grabbed my hand and dragged me out to play. After we came back to the classroom, I knew it was sink or swim. So, I swam beautifully. I learned German fluently in six months, became best friends with Petra, and managed to raise hell around our little town.

Just when I had gotten comfortable, the news came—another move. We packed and headed out. Karlsruhe was so different from Schalodenbach. We had to live on base. My mother decided that I would still go to the German school. Every morning I got up and rode my bike about two miles to school.

My new teacher was excellent. In fact, my teacher reminded me of my grandmother. The students had been learning how to play the recorder since kindergarten, so my teacher offered to help me catch up by giving me extra lessons in the morning before school. Pretty soon, in music class, I could play with the best of them. Some of the kids were not happy with me. The boys started teasing me. I did not mind being teased, but I did not understand why they teased me about the color of my skin and the other language I spoke.

The teasing got worse. I did not know how to handle the situation. My parents just could not understand the depth to which this harassment had gone. I refused to have my dad take me anywhere. I thought that if my mother took me places that people would think I was White by association. If they saw my dad then they would know my shame.

I was distraught. Eventually, I decided to stop going to school. I would ride my bike around town until my mom and dad had left for work, and then I went home to enjoy my day in peace. Then I rode around again until it was time to come home. This was my routine on the days when I felt like getting out of bed. On other days, I played sick and moped around all day in my night gown.

Two months later, my parents became aware of the situation and the things started happening. My parents and I had a meeting with my teacher and the principal of the school. Everyone was very concerned, but no one truly understood. I went back to school and the teasing got better. I still had to beat up one kid, he just did not know when to stop. I knew the other people were on my side. After that no one bothered me. I excelled in my classes and all was forgotten.

Deep in my heart, though, the teasing and the hurt will never be forgotten. I still cringe when I think of not letting my father take me any place and the shame I felt when he showed up at school events. I can never forget that split second when an innocent child realizes that her skin color separates her from other kids.

As I got older the memories and feelings faded into the background as I tried to conquer acne and boys. Then after my awkward period, eventually things became very comfortable again. I was a cheerleader, the only woman of color on the squad, and I was the best. My academic career was pretty successful and I received several awards for academics as well as sports. I dated anyone, crossing racial boundaries without a problem. I began to look at the world as if most people were not prejudiced. If they were prejudiced, I thought, when they got to know me they would change. This feeling lasted until I graduated from high school and came to college at "good old Notre Dame."

I expected to have a Beverly Hills 90210–type college experience. Why not? I was an attractive girl who enjoyed a good party. I expected lots of dates, and if not dates at least a group of good friends. At first I thought things were going well. I had a great group of friends, we went out all the time. Academically I was doing well. Then the questions started. Questions about my family: if my parents were educated, if I had any sisters or brothers in jail, and so forth. Stuff that was really outrageous. My father has a Ph.D., my mother has a masters degree, and I have never even met anyone who has been in prison. The questions did not bother me at first. Then people asked how it felt to be African-American, and how it felt to be biracial. The kicker was when people told me they just could not consider me Black because I did not act Black.

My question is "How do people act Black?" In my family, being Black is not about actions, it's about being part of a legacy, a heritage. When I take advantage of opportunities given to me by my ancestors I complete a circle. Being Black is about being proud of a history and striving to make the future brighter. Nowhere is talking a certain way, or wearing certain clothes, mentioned in what being Black is all about.

College continued. I did not date at all. Most of the men I knew were white and they could be my friend but not my boyfriend. One guy actually told me that to my face. Parties came and parties went—all with me being alone. I suppose this seems like a trivial problem, but watching all my friends go out and have a great time was hard. I decided that something was wrong with me. People made derogatory comments about African-Americans. I was told that affirmative action was the reason that I was accepted to Note Dame. I cried myself to sleep. I was depressed. I was confused about my identity.

Daily calls to my mother were not unusual at this time. My grades started to slide. The social side of my life was over. I refused to go anywhere. I didn't have any real friends—at least no one that truly felt I was as good as them. I talked to my dorm rector, to my resident hall assistant, and to a counselor. But no one was telling me anything that was helpful. When I talked to my dad it helped a little, at least he understood somewhat. He knows what coming into a room is like when at least one person in that room is making assumptions based on the color of his skin.

Eventually I found a support group for women of color, and I made some African-American friends. I thought my troubles were over. Wrong! I was too White to be Black. My new friends found my past dating of White boys unacceptable. I talked too White, and the music I chose was definitely not hip: Not White enough to be White and not Black enough to be Black.

I suppose being rejected by the Black community hurt more. These were supposed to be my brothers and sisters. Where was my piece of Black unity? This experience was the last straw. I tried to find refuge among my own people, only to find that they were part of my problem. I had no idea where I might turn. My identity was shaken. I thought of myself as Black, but I was being told that I was not.

After a horrible year I found other people like me. These new friends were all different shades of brown. They were as mixed up as I was. We started talking and I discovered I was not alone. Together we figured out who we wanted to be. The next year we roomed together and our room was nicknamed the U.N. Tina was half Native American and half Spanish. Mary was African-American but she acted too White for that community, so they ostracized her. Theresa was half Indian and half Caucasian. We used to joke that between Theresa and me, we made a whole White person. Color became a very important topic of discussion, we were always aware that we were not really any race.

Through the year we gave each other the support and affirmation that we needed. During that year I came to the realization that no one had to be comfortable with me but me. I know who I am, and what I stand for. As long as I am true to myself the rest of the world can go away. No, I am not totally Black and I am not totally White, but I am totally human. That's what counts.

After having this realization, I began to attract new kinds of friends. They were people who wanted to enrich their lives by knowing all sorts of people. I have become comfortable with myself and I love being biracial. Why? Because I am the melting pot that this country hoped to become. I was born out of the love of two people who judged other people based on the "content of their character, not the color of their skin." I represent the hope that eventually this country will be able to treat all its citizens equally.

After reading hundreds of students' autobiographies, I've come to realize that everyone has some issue with which he or she is struggling. Life is anything but problem-free. In good autobiographies we come to grips with the issues that are forging our characters—we face seriously our challenges of living. It is a liberating and healing experience to commit one's demons to paper—and to see them for exactly what they are. One's problems don't completely go away, but somehow the writer is able to become less caught up in the problems' snares.

Because these last few stories were so gripping, I'll bet you've forgotten that we cut short my life story during my adolescent years. Well, the next chapter is another installment in my tale that begins in adolescence and ends when I'm in my mid-thirties—about a decade ago. If the theme of "A story of George" centered around what I learned during a happy childhood, this next segment entertains the theme that my life wasn't one big, happy game. Everyone's life has some darker moments. Although compared with the tragedies that some others encounter in life, I've been quite lucky indeed.

CHAPTER 3
SOMETIMES LIFE CAN BE TOUGH

I really don't remember his name, so we might as well refer to him as Tony. I'll never be able to forget her name, so I guess we should just call her Marcia. I began falling in love with Marcia around the time we were graduating from grammar school, and by the end of my freshman year of high school—I could think of little else but her. You wouldn't believe the elaborate daydreams I fantasized about Marcia and me. It was clear to me—and probably to everyone else also—that ours was a most special relationship. The darkest cloud on my horizon was the prospect of having to wait eight years (until we graduated from college) before we could get married. Now fourteen-year-olds are not real strong on checking the fine print—even in relationships. So I can't certify that Marcia felt as strongly and deeply about me as I did about her. She certainly seemed to like me; she wanted to spend a lot of time with me; and all my friends said she really liked me a lot. It was ludicrous to even imagine that I could be so smitten by Marcia and she not feel exactly the same way about me. Wasn't it?

Well, to make a (potentially) long story really short, there was a high school dance and I was talking with my friends and somebody said, "Hey George, look at Marcia. She's dancing with some ape." Well, she was. It was this Tony guy. He was huge! Somebody said they thought he was a hood from Jersey City—but nobody knew for sure. He looked to be about three years older than me, so he was probably a senior—or more likely—a freshman who had been "left-back" three times. Well, he and Marcia danced the whole night—and I did nothing about it. "Hey Howard, shouldn't you go over there and do something about that?" I knew the right answer—but I couldn't make myself do anything. I was rooted; paralyzed like a wooden statue. As I left the dance I felt depressed, betrayed, humiliated, brokenhearted, and a dozen other terrible emotions. I didn't want to see, be with, or talk to anyone—friend or foe. I was a beaten young man—beaten in love, in self-respect, and in spirit.

But guess who was waiting outside for me—Tony and three piranhas he'd brought with him. It was clear Tony was dying to fight—and I never wanted to avoid a fight more in my life. You see, there was nothing to fight for. Marcia had a grand old time for herself. If she had given the slightest signal that she wanted to get away from that ape, I would have gone over and tried to help her out. But it was clear that things were proceeding exactly as she wanted. So there I was—feeling more hollow and vulnerable than I ever had in my life—and I was supposed to fight this cretin. He hurled every derisive, provocative insult that an IQ of 64 can generate. But frankly, anger and fighting were millions of miles away from me. If he wanted to hit the human equivalent of a sack of wheat—fine, go ahead.

Well, Tony never got a chance to have his fight. Jimmy and Micky Hart were neighbors of mine. I played ball with their younger brother Gerry. When they went on vacation I delivered their *Bayonne Times* route. If we visited my grandmother on weekends, Gerry would deliver my *Newark Sunday News* route. If Tony and his boys were piranhas, the Harts were sharks. Jimmy mentioned something about them slithering back to Jersey City—and they did. You see, even piranhas know they have to watch their dorsal fins when swimming in shark-infested waters. I probably mumbled something like "Thanks, guys" to the Harts, and I must have gotten home somehow, but I honestly don't remember another thing about that night.

Even though I never saw Tony again, I somehow felt less safe knowing he—and others like him—were around. I realized how vulnerable I was because I had been "in love" with Marcia. While love is heaven when you're in it, I was devastated by the realization of its potential drawbacks. I was frightened by the lability of my own emotions. One moment I was reveling in fantasies of undying love, and the next moment I never wanted to see that hussy again in my life. Finally, I hated having the entire misadventure occur in public. While the epsiode probably lasted less than a week in everyone else's mind—I stewed over it for about another three years. Strike that—I'm writing about it twenty-five years later—this stew is seriously overdone.

Family and religion were two important parts of my life through my college years. As I was finishing high school, I wondered if I might not have a religious vocation. Recently, I saw the movie "MacArthur" and, apparently, MacArthur was fixated on the phrase "duty, honor, and country." So he went to West Point. Makes sense.

For me it was "duty, God, and education." So I entered the novitiate of an order of teaching religious—the Marist brothers. My parents didn't want me to enter the novitiate—they wanted me to complete college first, and then try religious life. But as with all my life-decisions, they told me their opinions and then urged me to decide what to do for myself. They supported my choice as enthusiastically as their disappointment would allow. They did their best. You can't ask for more than that.

Religious life was a very interesting experience. I stayed in the Order for six years. Overall, it was a wonderful experience for me—and a good time of my life. But you'll probably miss that reality, because I intend to focus upon the reasons why I chose to leave. I guess I ought to tell you the bottom line up front—I left the Marist Brothers because I lost my faith. My belief in God had always been a natural, strong, and sustaining part of my life. One day at Mass it hit me that I could no longer imagine God any more. I'll try to suggest some reasons why this shift in perspective might have occurred, but the truth is that I really don't know. Faith left as mysteriously as it had come.

Why? Well, I can list some things that I know didn't help my faith at all. I took a psychology course in which we read Sigmund Freud's *The future of an illusion* and a philosophy course in which we read William James' *The varieties of religious experience*. I found both books (and subsequent discussions about them) very unsettling. I knew it was coming with *The future of an illusion* but I was a newly declared psychology major, and I couldn't start off by refusing to consider certain parts of psychology, just because they might threaten my faith. Besides, it never really seriously occurred to me that I might possibly lose it. Ah, the invincibility of youth. The impact of the *Varieties* experience came as a bit of a surprise. I took the course because the teacher (nicknamed "The Dragon") said James' ideas would be "an uplifting experience" for me. While James' ideas might indeed be uplifting, the Dragon was a bummer. Too bad I couldn't see the uplifting forest because of one downer tree. I realized that nicknames are not randomly assigned to people—all too often they are hard-earned and richly deserved.

Speaking of people making it tougher to maintain one's belief in God, while in the novitiate our pastoral needs were met by the Redemptorist monastery just up the road. Thus we were treated to a strange parade of representatives of God. We either had old priests who'd been put out to pasture or rookie priests who were in the process of making (and, hopefully, learning from) their mistakes. I can't tell you the number of times I counted the fingers on my hand over-and-over-again, just to keep my mind off the content of the homily. One time I failed and wondered (aloud) whether the sermon was the proper place for "thinly veiled political biases." Interrupting a homily is rarely a good idea—for a monk-in-training it is always a not-very-good idea. I had to be punished—but the punishment was really no problem. I could tell my superiors' hearts weren't in it. You see, those were the troubling days of the late sixties, when almost everyone doubted whether he or she would ever again be able to tell right from wrong. I think my Marist friends rightly saw my actions as manifestations of a wrenching soul-searching process that included far more than issues of religion.

Vietnam was a black cloud that hung over my college years. I was a senior when the Kent State tragedy occurred. But through it all I had a curious feeling of guilt. You see, in the draft lottery my birthday, June 8th, came up 366th. I knew I would never have to go—but I felt very guilty that many of my friends were so much less lucky than I. Upon hearing that I was number 366, I was so relieved that I blurted out "Three hundred and sixty-six! That's the special women-and-children-first category." It seemed like a harmless joke, but no sooner had I said it, than I realized that my single- and double-digit lottery number friends would fail to appreciate the humor—because for them the issue had a life or death seriousness. That's the thing about whether or not a joke is funny—it often comes down to whose ox is being gored.

But there were other tensions as well. These were the years immediately after Vatican Council II. All religious orders were in chaos and we Marists were no exception. I was trying to develop an identity as a Marist brother at a time when the identity of the Marist brothers was undergoing wrenching changes. Of my class of forty, I think there are only two monks left.

Finally, death touched my life closely for the first time. My mother's brother—Uncle Bocky—died in an automobile accident. He was driving along a two-lane highway and an oncoming, drunk driver crossed into his lane. Bocky swerved off the road and on to the right shoulder to avoid him, but the crash was head on. If Bocky had simply stayed in his lane, the car might have whizzed past on his right. But hindsight is always perfect. Bocky never married, and he had enormous physical problems (shrapnel in the eyes in World War II, four-fifths of his stomach was removed due to ulcers), and so his attitude was often bad—to others. But he never showed that side to me—we were always best buddies. Bocky played favorites— no doubt about it—and I was perhaps his most favorite.

We probably became a team when I was having enormous

difficulties in grammar school. He took summers off and tutored me. Bocky taught high school, so he had long summer vacations. But wait a minute—that makes him sound too good. He helped me study in the early morning. By 10 a.m. we were on the Stamford, N.Y. golf course. Bocky spent more time on a golf course—with less success—than any human being who ever lived. Simply put, he was terrible. But for two kids raised in Bayonne (Bocky and me) a golf course was as close to heaven as we'd ever get. And since no one gets rich being a high school teacher, golf was an expensive habit for Bocky. Membership, green fees, a drink in the 19th, and *six to eight* lost balls per round—we're talking big bucks. Oh, did I mention that I never golfed with Bocky? I was his "caddy." But I rarely carried his clubs. You see, I was a professional ball-retriever. I was a ten-ball swing in Bocky's game. Instead of losing six to eight balls per round, we'd come home two to four balls to the good. Ponds and streams were as close to a swim as I was going to get and woods and thickets weren't hazards; they were challenges. The Stamford club pro never referred to me as anything but "the Bayonne Bloodhound." And he took a dim view of anyone who slowly waded through water hazards rather than walking around them. One time the pro gave me a hard time and pointed out that most caddies are employed to carry clubs, not to contract poison ivy. Well, Bocky heard him, and he just wasted him. I'd love to tell you exactly what he said, but that would completely blow any chances of getting a *nihil obstat* for this book. You see, Bocky's bite could be worse than almost anyone else's bark.

But, getting back to my story, in my senior year of college, things were very tough. I was graduating a year early, so I had to take 24 credit hours (15 is normal) that spring semester and it was killing me. A Friday morning in late April, I was just trying to drag my ass to classes one more day to make the weekend, when a dorm-mate said, "George, a guy downstairs says he's Arnie Palmer and he definitely is not. He wants you to come downstairs—and bring your golf clubs." Sure enough! "Bocky, what are you doing here? Why aren't you working?" "Teachers' convention! Where are your sticks? Come on it's almost 10 a.m. and I want to get 27 holes in today." After three and a half years of religious life, finally a command I was thrilled to obey. Well, to make a very enjoyable story very short, Bocky left after four days—and over 100 holes later—to "see if that convention is still in session." About a week later, at Bocky's funeral, I was telling my mother how incredibly lucky I was that Bocky had had that convention. There was no convention (she confessed); she had spoken with me a week earlier and she was very concerned that I was pushing myself too hard. So she called her brother for reassurance—as she always did. And as always, she got it: "Don't worry, Sis, he'll be just fine." One strong belief in my family has always been if you want something to happen, make it happen! But I digress.

A few months later, I realized for the first time that I no longer believed in God. Beliefs that were so natural and self-evident all my life were no longer possible. As mysteriously as religion had come, it went. I continued the life of a religious for almost two more years. Of course, I spent thousands of hours praying and discussing my inability to believe with friends and religious superiors, but nothing changed. Religious life makes no sense at all without a strong belief in God—so I had to leave. I was truly sad to leave the Marists, and they hated losing me. You probably have a hunch as to why I lost my faith—and if you're right, then you're a better analyst than I, because to this day I still don't know what happened. I left the East Coast for the first time in my life and began graduate studies in psychology at Southern Illinois University. For the first time in my life, I was truly "on my own" in many, many ways.

The theme of this chapter deals with some "bad times" in my life. You've probably guessed by now that the good times weren't as uniformly good as I depicted in Chapter 1, and my young adult years weren't as consistently troublesome as this chapter implies. But a theme's a theme—so I'm going to speed by my graduate school years in Carbondale, my predoctoral internship at Duke University, and my postdoctoral year at Wichita State University. Why? Because they were wonderful times! I worked hard, learned a lot, began to form my professional identity, made many wonderful friendships, and best of all, I met (and married) my wife Nancy.

But then I took my first tenure-line job at the University of Houston—"It was the best of times, it was the worst of times . . ." The people who hired me genuinely wanted to do something to improve the poor quality of undergraduate instruction at UH. In addition to being a good teacher (if one can believe teaching excellence awards), I had an extensive background in teaching evaluation and improvement—so I was a natural for their job. And the job seemed good for me also, as I was much more interested in teaching than research. While I was a member of the clinical psychology faculty, I was to devote most of my efforts toward improving teaching in Houston's enormous undergraduate program. Of course, the usual promises were made that "if I was successful in these endeavors, I would receive tenure for them." These weren't lies *per se*. If the people who hired me had been in power when I came up for tenure, I would have received tenure in an instant. But other friends on the faculty quickly pointed out that: 1) the current department chair would not be department chair when I came up for tenure; 2) the faculty as a whole were not interested in quality undergraduate education; and 3) the upper administration was hell-bent on going from "Cougar High" to "Harvard on the Bayou." Research, not teaching, was what would get one tenured. Their points were well taken, so I fired-up my research program. Since no one had purposely tried to mislead or deceive me, the voiding of my initial job agreement did not bother me terribly. Besides, I had good research instincts, skills, and some interest in doing research—so off I went in my investigations. By the way, I kept up my teaching improvement efforts also—I simply worked 70 hours every week. Since Nancy also worked 70-hour weeks, it wasn't a hardship on our relationship. The non-work time we had together was good—so we were both free to be happy workaholics.

Well, to make a long, sad story short, my research program flourished beyond anyone's expectation. By tenure time, my research credentials were very good—every faculty committee, departmental, college, and university, voted positively on my candidacy. But by that time the administration of the department had fallen into the hands of people with whom I disagreed on issues of intellectual, professional, and ethical values. They had to get rid of me because I would always be opposed to their vision of psychology, the university, and perhaps life itself. Besides, I occupied a position that could be filled by one of their loyal true-believers. It was just politics—really. But as I said earlier, how it feels is often a question of whose ox is being gored. In this case it was my ox. Besides, in a divorce if one is told, "I'm sorry, we just grew apart," one almost has to take it personally. That's just part of the way people are constructed. So things got ugly. One of the reasons it got bad is because the departmental chair had to be supported by the dean and the dean by the provost. But it would be very difficult for the upper levels of administrators to reject a set of credentials that said excellent teacher, researcher, and university citizen, and then deny tenure because they just don't like where he stands on theoretical and value issues. So, politics being what it is, the administrators had to construct a plausible scenario of "how it was that George didn't quite measure up to their high standards." It was doubly tough taking that abuse from a departmental chairman whose total scholarly output in quality journals for his entire career does not equal my output for any single year of the past fifteen years. But I had to live with this nonsense for several months.

Nancy was wonderful during this time. She was the only family I had in Houston. Bub, Bocky, and Vince Harren (whom you'll meet later) were my protectors from earlier episodes—but by this time they were all dead. And so no protector arose—I was on my own, and I felt as lonely and vulnerable as I had in my entire life. I didn't want to bring my parents into it (I didn't want to upset them—and besides what could they do?), I had no God to whom I could turn (that would be hypocritical), and aside from Nancy I had no life outside of work. As work goes (for a workaholic) so goes your life. And life was going none too well at this point in time.

As Nancy always says, "When the going gets tough—the tough go shopping!" So I went shopping for a job. I was plenty marketable, but the real rub was Nancy. She had a wonderful private practice in Houston and she didn't want to leave it. You don't just pack up a practice and take it across the country. And that is what hurt me the most—if I didn't get tenure, Nancy would suffer most. But perhaps her greatest strength is her flexibility. She said that she would like to get closer to home. So if I were able to get a job within a hundred-mile radius of Chicago, she might be willing to leave her practice in Houston for it. I grabbed the *APA Monitor* and the *Rand-McNally Road Atlas*. There was only one job possible: Department of Psychology; University of Notre Dame; Notre Dame, Indiana—95 miles from that Windy City.

"Hello! George Howard, please."

"Speaking."

"George, I'm the head of the search committee for the counseling position at Notre Dame. We just received your credentials, and they come real close to what we're looking for. What would it take to bring you to Notre Dame?"

"Well, an invitation would be nice."

The decision wasn't hard. Our interview went well, they offered Nancy a job also, and we were on our way to South Bend.

"Hello, mom. It's George."

"Hi! Where have you guys been? We've been calling but getting no answer."

"We've been traveling. Mom, I didn't want to bring this up until we had something definite. We're leaving Houston. Nancy and I have just accepted jobs at Notre Dame."

"Oh my God! Has Catholic education deteriorated that badly?"

"Mom!???!!?"

"Oh honey, I'm only making a joke. Of course, I'm delighted for both of you. Boy, your sense of humor has just gone to hell-in-a-handbasket lately."

"Well, things here have been rough recently. I haven't had a whole lot to laugh about lately."

"Well, I'm glad for you that that's over now."

CHAPTER 4
MODELS OF HUMAN NATURE

I hope that you now agree that reading autobiographies can be both enlightening and fun. Writing one's life story can also be an educational and enjoyable experience. I trust you've begun to imbibe those pleasures, as you write your autobiography. If you haven't begun yet, please give it the "old college try" now, because the remainder of this chapter is unlikely to be of any help in getting you started. Here are a few more opening lines that might get you "over the hump."

"I always wondered what life would have been like if my parents hadn't divorced . . ."

"I never thought about what makes people tick until that day in seventh grade when my best friend . . ."

"My family is one-of-a-kind . . ."

"All my life, I wanted to be a doctor . . ."

This book isn't only about experiencing first-person approaches to psychology—it's also an essay on human nature. However, since philosophical treatises can be awfully dry, I'll try to help your motivation by presenting my ideas in as interesting an array of writing styles as I am capable of producing.

Today in class I heard myself saying some things that were shocking. I usually know what I will say in class, but in my own defense, today I was under a lot of pressure. The final assignment for my honors social science course was to write an essay on "What is distinctive about a social science?" As their instructor, I was to be a resource in helping them to puzzle through this thorny problem. And as humans are wont to do, the students were sorely testing the limits of this old resource. They were relentless—as bright, motivated students (under the gun of a writing assignment) often are. You see, their problem was to pull together what appeared to be only tangentially related approaches to understanding social action, such as psychology, political science, economics, anthropology, and sociology.

It quickly became clear that the students' difficulty lay in integrating what they had learned throughout the semester in a manner that made sense. I decided that a quick exercise in how one might integrate what appear to be disparate lines of thought in a science might be helpful. Being a psychologist, I chose as an example that which I know best—psychology. I'm telling you this story because it traces a formal model of human action from a story-telling, active agent perspective. Here's how the class went.

"Let me give you a lesson in the art of integrating seemingly incompatible lines of thought which might help you with your writing assignment. You see, psychology is no different from any other science. In order to understand something, you first try to simplify it. Strip away distracting elements, the irrelevant, the peripheral, and get to the heart of the issue. Then you work with the central mechanism, the core entities, the driving parts of the thing you are studying until you really know them well. For example, we read a little bit of Freud about a month ago. What were the core elements or constructs in his view of humans? Mary, what do you think?"

"Well, he thought there are biologically based psychological forces in a person's id that are in conflict with a person's conscience or superego. And this third entity in people, the ego, kind of negotiates or referees the battles between the id and superego. But some of these conflicts go on unconsciously, and so we try to understand behavior we can see (like the neurotic behaviors that Freud's patients were exhibiting) as caused by these unconscious conflicts."

"Exactly! Now many of Freud's followers couldn't buy a view of humans that was that simple. People such as Carl Jung, Otto Rank, and Karen Horney, who basically agreed with Freud's core position about the unconscious determination of behavior, pressed for a more sophisticated view of human action. They argued for the importance of a particular event in a person's life (such as Rank's 'birth trauma'), factors beyond the individual (such as Jung's 'collective unconscious') and so forth. To the end, Freud tried to keep his theory simple, pure, and uncluttered by these additional factors. But contemporary psychologists, who see themselves as intellectually directly descended from Freud (usually referred to as psychodynamic psychologists), try to consider a broad array of factors in explaining human action. However, the thread that ties all psychodynamic-types together is their view of the importance of intrapsychic factors in human behavior. Mike, you have a question?"

"Is B. F. Skinner a psychodynamic psychologist?"

"Bite your tongue, fellow! Nothing could be farther from the truth. Skinner sees human behavior in terms of the rewards and punishments that follow our actions. Behaviors that tend to be followed by a reinforcing set of circumstances (usually a rewarding, pleasant, or satisfying state of affairs) will increase in frequency over time. So if you wish to understand a person's actions, look at his or her current set of circumstances, and the individual's prior learning history in similar situations, and you will be able to understand his or her behavior. For example, if you hoot, whistle, and scream in this class, or in Sacred Heart Cathedral, you are probably going to get in trouble. But at a Grateful Dead concert or at a football game—hoot-on—such behavior is appropriate and even reinforced. So, according to Skinner, present reinforcement and punishment circumstances (or contingencies) control our behavior. But everyone doesn't act exactly alike in the same circumstances. This is because we each have different learning histories. Some of you were often punished for giving answers in class in the past, while others were generally reinforced. Patricia?"

"Does knowing the right answer have anything to do with who puts her hand up?"

"Considering this class, I have my doubts. Come on! Stop the yelling! Settle down! I'll get serious again. As happened to Freud, over time other behaviorists forced Skinner to expand the scope of his central theory. With regard to your question Pat, Michael Mahoney, Carl Thoresen, Albert Ellis, and other theorists forced Skinner to consider closely what the person is thinking about as an important element in explaining the person's behavior. For example, if one of you were to do something that annoyed me and I berated you in class, most of you would find my abuse punishing and would be less likely to do whatever you did again. But consider the unlikely event (I hope!) that one of you—Mr. X—hates my guts. Mr. X does something really out of line, and I berate him for it. Mr. X thinks, 'Great, I really got that joker's goat!' For him my abuse was reinforcing and might serve to increase his acting out in class in the future. We call this phenomenon 'obtaining secondary gain.' Even more interestingly, consider this scenario. Mr. X also has his eye on Ms. Y and he knows that she likes me even less than he does. If he disrupts class not only does he get secondary gain from it, but he also believes his action will win him points with Ms. Y—and he is *highly* motivated to win points with Ms. Y."

"Excuse me, Dr. Howard. Is the point you are making that a

good teacher should do *everything* in his or her power to stay in his or her students' good graces in order to avoid a situation where they might obtain secondary gain from inappropriate actions? I was thinking about the term paper assignment and wondered if you might see important educational benefits in reducing the scope of that, perhaps overly ambitious, assignment."

"Tim, I'm thrilled that you profited so thoroughly from our discussions of Karl Marx and his treatment of 'class interests'. But getting back to behaviorism, the thread that ties behaviorists together is that it is the consequences of our actions that determine what we will do in the future. Yes, Betty, you have something to say?"

"In the *Notre Dame Magazine* a while back they had an article that suggested that advances in the scientific understanding of the biochemistry of behavior would eventually lead to pharmacological methods of curing all psychological disorders, enhancing memory, curing criminals, and an incredible number of other human problems. What do you think of those claims?"

"I saw that article too, Betty. I thought it was an interesting, but rather misleading, article. But to understand my reaction, we must analyze the article from several perspectives. Remember when you read Freud's *Psychopathology of everyday life*? Your reaction was 'Ridiculous! He tries to explain everything with a few simple constructs.' Or remember your reaction to Milton Friedman's monetarist view of inflation in the economy? 'Probably too simple,' you concluded when you also considered John Maynard Keynes' fiscalist position and Arthur Laffer's supply side approach. Rarely (if ever) can social scientists furnish a complete and satisfactory explanation of complex human behavior with one, or only a few, basic principles. Later I'll flesh out why, in my opinion, this must always be the case. For now, suffice it to say that some very interesting work is being done in psychopharmacology which will hopefully contribute to human welfare in the future. But in my opinion, the important human problems that psychology faces will *not* be improved appreciably by fine-tuning people's biochemical balance. Drugs undoubtedly influence our moods, our thinking, and our actions. This is so because of our material natures, the way our bodies have evolved over hundreds of thousands of years. However, I believe that the potential benefits of biopsychology are currently being oversold. But, as suggested earlier, the outlandishly optimistic claims of the author of that article probably represent something of a rhetorical device that scientists have long used to reenergize themselves to tackle the enormously difficult and tiring work involved in converting a research idea into a scientifically demonstrated reality. Question, Paul?"

"But if they could come up with a pill that could totally cure psychological disorders, wouldn't that prove Freud wrong?"

"Well, if that were to happen, it would certainly cause all psychologists, who hold models of humans that emphasize psychological phenomena more than biological phenomena, to scurry back to the drawing board and rethink the model of humans that is presupposed in their approach to understanding human behavior. But let's slow down a bit here. I introduced a number of new ideas in that last sentence very quickly, and I must explain them clearly or risk having some of you not understanding my position. I think it is enormously unlikely that anything like the pill you suggested will ever be found. At this point what we have found are some chemical agents that are rather helpful in combating some of the symptoms of emotional difficulties. But this is a far cry from using drugs to effect a cure of the fundamental causes of psychological problems.

"The more interesting issue at stake here involves the relationship between a scientist's model of humans and how that scientist will interpret the results of his or her studies. Let me demonstrate this by some simple diagrams. Assume in these diagrams that the area inside the square represents a person's behavior, and the circles represent how much a particular class of potential causal factors (such as psychodynamic forces, biological influences, environmental contingencies, societal influences, astrological influences, and so forth) actually influence that person's action. Now in Figure 4.1 we'll crudely try to diagram Freud's view of the causes of human behavior.

FIGURE 4.1
Rough schematic drawing of Freud's view of causation in human behavior

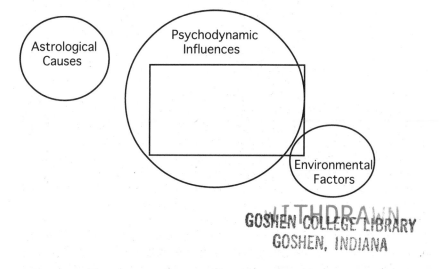

"You can see in Figure 4.1 that psychodynamic factors are overwhelmingly responsible for a person's actions (diagrammatically, they cover the greatest area of the box). Environmental influences have a slight role in behavior, as Freud recognized their role as triggering mechanisms for the expression of repressed intrapsychic conflicts—thus, environmental factors overlap slightly with the box. To my knowledge, Freud did not believe that astrological forces played any role in human behavior—thus, no overlap with the box. In Figure 4.2 we will depict a fictitious psychologist who is a bit more balanced than was Freud in his or her view of human nature.

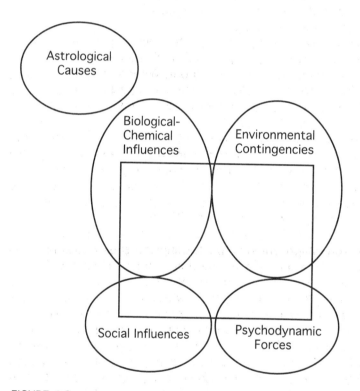

FIGURE 4.2
An atheoretical, eclectic view of causality in human behavior

"This psychologist might be described as a thorough eclectic who takes no strong position (except an aversion to astrological influences) on the question of what makes people tick. This individual sees reason to believe that psychodynamics, environmental contingencies, societal influences (such as social class, societal institutions, and so forth), and biological-chemical factors each play a role in the genesis of behavior. You can see that each of us has an implicit set of beliefs regarding the wellsprings of human behavior. But beware, I have employed a number of simplifying strategies in constructing this picture of the real situation. I have implied that one can easily assign a potential cause of human behavior to one and only one domain of influence, which is not really true. For example, remember from your reading that Freud considered his drives to be biologically based. So which are they—biological or psychodynamic in nature? Do you want to say something Tom?"

"What about psychic forces like E.S.P., psychokinesis, and that stuff? Do they influence our behavior?"

"I haven't a clue. Mary?"

"What about religion? What effect does that have on us?"

"I'm not a theologian. I haven't a clue there either."

"Wait a minute!! That's a cop-out. We didn't come to Notre Dame for the football team. Part of being at a Catholic university is that we will get at least an honest effort at integrating what we learn with our religious beliefs."

"You're right, Mary. I'm sorry. I try to confine my comments in class to areas where I feel my training gives me some special expertise. I certainly don't want to waste anyone's time or patience with ill-formed or stupid ideas. Please excuse me if my grasp of theological issues is naïve or unenlightening. But I will give your question my best shot. Please bear with me.

"One of the things I learned from my study of calculus is that it is often enlightening to push things to their extremes. You know, what is the value of a function as X approaches zero? What is the function's value as X approaches infinity? Analogously, how would we characterize the situation where our circle for spiritual causes completely dominates a person's box to the complete exclusion of environmental, psychodynamic, biological, and all other potential influences? That would be something like the case of predestination, wouldn't it? God set up everything, and so anything that happens is simply God's will. Conversely, if the spiritual domain does not overlap with the box at all, then religion is like astrology in our previous examples. What would that mean? Well, it could mean that there is no spiritual domain, and hence it couldn't possibly influence human action. Or perhaps the spiritual domain really exists, but God chooses to leave human affairs totally alone. That also would show up in our diagram as no overlap between the spiritual circle and the square. Fred?"

"What do most psychologists think? How much overlap is

there between the spiritual circle and the box?"

"I have two answers to that question. First, I honestly believe that question is more appropriately answered by theologians than by psychologists. As I structured the problem, I believe that questions about the amount of overlap are simply outside of the area of psychologists' competence. We have no special insight to offer. Second, history tells us that psychology and religion have been, at best, uneasy bedfellows. For example, Freud's thoughts on religion are in a book entitled *The future of an illusion*. As you might have guessed, in that book, religion was the illusion. But it's my impression that all of the social sciences have historically had a rather uneasy relationship with religious thought. Remember, for example, in your readings, Marx called religion the 'opiate of the masses.' Hardly a view that will win you friends in religious circles."

"Well, professor, what do *you* think is the amount of overlap between the spiritual circle and the box in your model?"

"I'd like to answer that question, but I don't think you would understand my answer yet."

"Try us; after all, we are honor students. Witness the outrageously difficult writing assignments you have been giving us!"

"*Touché!* But I wasn't questioning your intellectual capabilities. I simply meant that I couldn't present my view yet because I haven't specified what, in my view, is the most critical causal element in human behavior. Would anyone like to take a wild guess at what that element might be? Nancy?"

"Free will?"

"My god, that's right! How did you know that?"

"A woman's intuition? Maybe my guardian angel whispered it to me? Just a lucky guess? Who knows? Maybe it's a mystery?"

"Maybe. Who knows? Anyway, free will isn't a totally correct label for my central explanatory construct in human behavior, but it is remarkably close. Let me say that a large number of psychological theorists have speculated about a number of human powers such as volition, self-determination, self-actualization, personal constructs, autonomy, active agency, self-control, free will, and many more. I associate names of psychologists such as Carl Rogers, Abraham Maslow, Gordon Allport, Paul Secord, Bill Tageson, and George Kelly, as well as philosophers like Rom Harré, Charles Taylor, Larry Wright, and Stephen Toulmin as speaking to the human powers that I feel are central to what it means to be a human. Terms such as *humanistic, teleological, person-centered, growth-oriented*, and *action theorist* are at times given to subsets of these thinkers, but I would be surprised if any one of them would agree that all of the labels I just mentioned are descriptive of their thinking. In its most blatant form, my position might be characterized as follows: If you want to know why a person behaved in a particular manner, ask him or her! The answer may sometimes be incomplete, or uninformed, or even purposely misleading. But in leaving out an individual's account of why he or she behaved as he or she did, we lose access to what, in my opinion, is the central human capacity in the formation of human action. A first-person account asks for the role of personal agency in our actions. But science has relied upon third-person accounts which usually leave agency out. Schematically, my view of the wellsprings of human action is depicted in Figure 4.3.

FIGURE 4.3: My view of the causal factors in human action

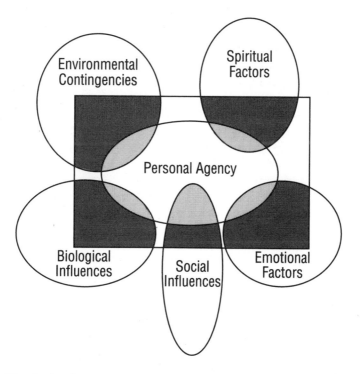

"For lack of a better term, let us refer to the core construct of human action, which was loosely described above, as personal agency. Figure 4.3 locates personal agency at the center of human behavior. As can be seen from the diagram, biological, social, environmental, and psychodynamic influences can exert their influences independently of personal agency (the shaded areas).

But from this perspective, other potential influences (such as environ-ment, biology, etc.) of human behavior sometimes (perhaps often!) achieve their effects in the formation of human action through their interaction with personal agency (the striped areas). This conceptual move stands the conventional wisdom in psychology on its head. For example, let me assure you that there is a very close relationship between the amount of coffee I drink at the office and how much writing I get done. Any biologically oriented psychologist would im-mediately begin to talk about the effects that the stimulant caffeine has on my activity level, and how this facilitates my writing. Now that analysis is not totally incorrect. It simply misses the most in-teresting aspect of the phenomenon. Let me assure you that when I decide to write, I choose to drink a good bit of coffee in order to facilitate my desired action. How about an example involving en-vironmental contingencies? I also get a lot more writing done when I leave my office door closed than when it is open. Environmental psychologists would jump at this relationship and maintain that I am under the control of this environmental condition. But that's not the most important thing going on here. I'm altering the environ-ment (by closing the door, or turning off the stereo, or whatever) in order to help myself meet my goals. Or as Albert Ellis maintains regarding the genesis of our emotions: our emotions are primarily the result of the things that we keep choosing to tell ourselves. Yes, Ed, you have a question?"

"Not a question really; I think I understand what you are saying, and I'd like to take a shot at how you will handle the relationship between spiritual factors and the self."

"Go for it, Ed!"

"Insofar as one believes in a spiritual dimension to his or her life, the person actually brings a spiritual reality into existence in his or her life. And in so doing, the spiritual dimension becomes a causally efficacious entity in the formation of that person's action. Something like that?"

"Something like that. But remember that there is a far stronger claim that can be made (and actually is quite frequently made) about the real existence of a spiritual reality that is inde-pendent of whether or not people choose to believe in its existence. But here I can't see where psychologists have anything special to say. We each simply have our own opinion on this topic. Bob, you look puzzled."

"What is this personal agency entity, anyway?"

"You, Bob! It's *you* who is acting upon the world for your own purposes, plans, and so forth. I could have called it "the self", but that's a slippery, nebulous term. I could have called it 'mind,' or 'ego' or 'consciousness,' or 'personhood,' or any other term. But, in my opinion, 'personal agency' or 'self-determination' comes the closest to the human power (or capacity) I am trying to describe. It's that little voice inside your head that furnishes a running commentary on what is happening in your life.

"Now one might wonder exactly how the ability to self-determine is achieved by a person. I wrote a rather speculative book entitled *A tale of two stories* that suggests that at its core, human thought is story telling. Some stories allow people to have greater control over their lives, whereas other stories picture people as pawns to other powerful forces in their lives. In believing one cannot self-determine, a person actually brings about (or creates) the reality that he or she cannot self-determine. As Heraclitus pointed out over two millennia ago, one must hope, for one will not find the unhoped for. That is, it is one's hope that leads one to the discovery of something. *Some stories are simply more 'hopeful' than others.* And certain people, like therapists, ministers, and so forth, are trained to discriminate "Winner" from "Loser" stories, and to help a person to retell (or reconceptualize) their story in a way that is more hopeful. Of course, these retold stories must be realistic—but a good story will have someone striving for goals that represent both desirable and possible goods, but which are as yet unrealized. Claire, is your hand raised?"

"Well, psychology is a science, isn't it? What does research have to say about self-determination in human action?"

"Almost nothing, Claire!"

"Come on, Doctor Howard. There must be thousands, maybe hundreds of thousands, of studies in psychology. None of them test whether personal agency is an integral part of the formation of behavior?"

"I am so glad you all had Professor McMullin for your philosophy of science course. Anyone without a good grasp of the essence of science will find it tough sledding from here on out. Also, because of time constraints, I'll need to simplify complex arguments and summarize large bodies of literature. I have published some articles on these topics recently, and I'd be happy to let you read them if you need the complete arguments to be satisfied that you fully understand the moves I make. So let's jump right in.

"Kenneth Gergen claims, 'Observers of the sciences frequently comment on what they take to be a deep and pervasive discontent with the outcomes of traditional research pursuits. With increasing outspokenness, investigators of high visibility and lengthy research experience have begun to raise sobering questions concerning the promise of traditional science' (Gergen, 1982, p. 190). Gergen then documents his point by citing eighty-five recent books and professional articles dealing with this discontent. I know of at least a dozen additional critiques that Gergen failed to cite. But why am I engaging in an extensive airing of my discipline's dirty linen? Simply because psychologists, when threatened, are often tempted to employ defensive strategies such as denial ('The problem isn't really that serious!) or obfuscation (as Koch suggests, usually couched in scientistic terminology with a thick coating of statistical jargon). Don't be misled. With precious few exceptions, research in most content domains of psychology is in some degree of trouble. But after all, psychologists are human beings also, so why shouldn't they defend their professional domains? Why shouldn't they have access to the same protective strategies also employed by other humans? The problem is that defensive attitudes do not get the deficiencies in our current research practices remedied. So what do I have to offer toward a solution? Mike, you have a question?"

"Hurry! We're running out of time! First, unless I miss my guess, you're going to suggest that research in psychology that includes first-person perspectives, such as your self-determination construct will furnish a superior explanation of human action than research as it is currently practiced. Are you suggesting that psychological research currently only deals with the influence of non-agentic (e.g., environmental, biological, psychodynamic, and social) influences on human behavior? Second, are you saying that nobody does research on the role of personal agency in human action? I can't for an instant believe that is true!"

"You're a sharp cookie, Mike. You've guessed correctly where I am heading. But with regard to your second point, I'm not nearly as negative on psychologists' research efforts to date as you think. More on that later. However, I do think psychological research, as currently practiced, often strives to furnish a completely mechanistic account of human action. Joseph Rychlak makes the point this way: 'Most of us can describe in general terms how our stomach or heart works, but we haven't the foggiest notion of how to describe the workings of our free will. If we turn to scientific texts we are sure to be disappointed because the going assumption in science is that we are *not* really free but mechanistically determined. Even though there is growing scientific evidence in support of a free will conception of human behavior, the public never gets this message because such findings are put through a mechanistic wringer before they are presented to us as "facts"' (Rychlak, 1979, p. vii). Remember, Skinner has a particular view of what represents the *proper form* of any scientific explanation, and seemingly indeterminate constructs like 'free will' simply don't fit that view. Thus, in his opinion they're out! Plus, I bet his personal belief is that human behavior *is* totally determined by personal historical factors interacting with current environmental contingencies. Unless I miss my guess, all of the world looks pretty coherent through Skinner's eyes. Question, Fred?"

"You bet! How can someone who doesn't believe in freedom, autonomy, and human dignity be a Catholic? How do you behaviorists reconcile your professional views with your religious convictions?"

"Fred, I hope you haven't been asleep for most of this class. I am a psychologist! I am anything but a behaviorist! However, you do raise a good point. First, Skinner does not speak for all behaviorists. He is an extremist. Second, there are some good behaviorists who are also good Catholics. But none of them has ever explained to me exactly how they integrate their religious and scientific belief systems. So I guess we'll just have to ask them how they manage it, won't we? Third, many professionals make no effort to integrate their professional views with their personal lives. They simply see them as separate domains. Speaking for myself, it never occurred to me that my personal agency model wouldn't be completely compatible with Catholic beliefs. Mike, you are nervously eyeing the clock again."

"I am! I'd hate to miss the punch line to this story because the bell rang. Your suggestion that Skinner has a narrow view of the types of explanations that are appropriate for science really got me thinking about what sort of explanation your attribution of causal force to this personal agency construct would represent. Unless I misunderstand my philosophy classes, it's a teleological explanation of sorts, isn't it?"

"You've read my mind. And here's the bottom line: teleological explanations have a bad reputation in science, in general, *and research in psychology has traditionally been designed so as to systematically exclude them altogether!* I believe that fact has had an enormous amount to do with the dissatisfaction many feel with what psychological research has accomplished thus far. But let me flesh out that point in a bit more detail. Remember Jacob Cohen's (1977) point, that even under the best of circumstances, psychological research seems to have an effective upper limit of prediction of about 25 to 33 percent of the variance in human behavior? Well, if I'm right, and much of human action is volitional in nature (that is, a reflection of this capacity of humans for personal agency), then variance due to volition inappropriately gets thrown into the pool of unexplained variance, along with other sources of variance that rightfully belong in this pool of unexplained variance (such as error in measurement, etc.). If personal agency accounts for a huge portion of human action, then our studies are doomed to account for a minor portion of the variance in human behavior, *even if we understood all the nonvolitional causes of the particular behavior* under study, and were able to measure all constructs perfectly! And those are really big 'ifs.' I see Madalene has a question."

"I'm afraid you lost me. What are teleological explanations? And why don't scientists like them?"

"I'm sorry. I'll try to be clearer. Simply stated, a teleological explanation is generally one that appeals to a purpose, an intention, or a reason. Sometimes an appeal to a plan or a strategy can also represent a teleological explanation. With regard to your second question, it requires a bit of an interpretation of some of the history of science in order to understand it. In my opinion, psychology adopted its conception of what constituted appropriate types of scientific explanations from the natural sciences. During the seventeenth century, the natural sciences began systematically to exclude teleological accounts as explanations. Up until that time, it was not uncommon for scientists to anthropomorphize their subject matters and explain their behavior via teleological accounts. But given the enormous success of the mechanistic, deterministic Newtonian paradigm in physics and the other natural sciences, some scientists and philosophers of science overgeneralized the importance of all scientific explanations being nontelic in nature. Claire, you have a question?"

"So why don't psychologists run some studies to test whether self-determination is an important cause of human behavior?"

"Good idea! But it's not quite that simple. Scientists know that good theories are those that can predict the outcomes of experiments the best and . . ."

"Oh no! You're wrong there, professor! Professor McMullin says that the task of choosing among various theoretical accounts in science is an enormously complex enterprise. Appeals to criteria, other than predictive accuracy, such as internal consistency, coherence, fertility, unity, and simplicity are often . . ."

"UNCLE!! UNCLE!! You and Professor McMullin are undoubtedly correct, and I am wrong. I am glad to see you are staying awake in his class. As I should have said, for the working scientist, perhaps the single most important criterion in choosing among competing explanations of a particular phenomenon is predictive accuracy. Is that better now? But here is the rub: For every other science on the face of earth, the prediction and control that served as the warrant for enhanced understanding *was prediction and/or control of the phenomenon by the scientist, not by the object of investigation.* Scientists predicted the behavior of planets, or chemicals, or falling bodies in their studies. The planets, chemicals, or falling bodies didn't predict their own behaviors. But personal agency, of its very nature, implies prediction and/or control by the behaving agent, not by the scientist. To make a long story real short, all the existent models of experimentation were inadequate to the task of assessing the portion of variance in human behavior that could logically be attributed to personal agency. Important technical modifications, in the manner in which studies are conducted, needed to be devised and refined. I've got a paper totally devoted to those problems and solutions, if anyone is interested in considering those issues closely. Tim?"

"Thank God, you are *finally* ready to run some studies! Quick, tell me. Do people really have volitional control of their behavior?"

"*Touché!* Turnabout is fair play, Tim. You're using sarcasm on me. Of course humans can behave volitionally! If our studies had suggested that they couldn't act volitionally, we would have suspected the inadequacy of the technical modifications we had made. I keep forgetting that because of your philosophy of science background, you people have a sophisticated understanding of the role of evidence in science. Well, as it turns out, the evidence shows that people *do* in fact behave volitionally. What was shocking was how perfectly the evidence fit with what one would logically predict. For example, shy people in fact demonstrated little ability to control volitionally their dating behavior. Similarly, obese individuals had only a modest capacity for volitionally controlling their eating and exercise behaviors. Conversely, using a broad sample of Notre Dame students, we found they had an enormous amount of volitional control over how much they eat. We compared the magnitude of this volitional control with a few environmental factors that previous research suggested were important, and found that on the average volitional control was *much, much more effective in controlling eating behavior than were the environmental factors!! In fact, in a recent set of studies (Howard et al., 1988) we found that about 90 percent of the variance in a human action (drinking) can be unequivocally attributed to self-determination . . .*"

"Is that a lot?"

"Is that a lot??? Oh! I see. Sarcasm again. I guess I do get wrapped up in this stuff a bit. You know, I keep thinking of what physicists found when they investigated the nature of light to find out if light is basically a wave or a particle. It seems these investigations led to a rather unsatisfying but important conclusion: *If you ask it a wave question, it will give you a wave answer; ask it a particle question, and it will give you a particle answer.* It seems to me that in psychology we have been asking only nonagentic, mechanistic questions. We did so because those were the only types of questions we knew how to ask scientifically. But now we are also able to consider human action from the volitional/self-determining perspective. That's progress, and that's all you can ask from a discipline—that it try to improve.

"Let me add that this research with personal agency (or first-person approaches) is but one of hundreds of ways that psychology is improving as a scientific discipline. For example, since you know that theory development is the most important task of any science, you will be interested to know that a second generation of multivariate statistics (structural equation modeling techniques) have recently been developed that make the direct test of theory more likely to occur than had formerly been the case in psychological research. The field of psychoneuroimmunology is yet another area of promise. Recent developments demonstrate the important relationships among psychological states, subsequent levels of immune surveillance, and an individual's susceptibility to physical illness. Similarly, the insights of General Systems Theory have been brought to bear on a variety of human problems such as child abuse, alcoholism, and so forth. I have focused upon the recent developments that I know best, while a different psychologist might have attended to any of a number of equally promising scientific breakthroughs. But we don't have time to consider any others, do we?"

"No way!"

"You're right, people. This is an Honors Social Science course. You ought to take a good Introduction to Psychology course to learn about all the exciting developments in first-person and third-person approaches to understanding human nature. Tom, you have a question?"

"Yes, Professor Howard, getting back to that term paper that's due next week . . ."

"This time you're right, Tom. Let me try to put what we've covered in a slightly different perspective by noting the following possibility. Almost five years ago, at graduation, I learned that Mahatma Ghandi felt there were seven sins in the world: wealth without work, pleasure without conscience, knowledge without character, commerce without morality, science without humanity, worship without sacrifice, and politics without principle. What did

Ghandi mean by science without humanity? It appears the meaning might be very different for every science. For example, the possibility of the nuclear destruction of the human race represents a legacy that most physicists sorely regret. But psychology's ill-conceived bequest might be of a quite different sort. Our legacy could be an impoverished vision of humanity. By viewing humans from an unduly narrow perspective, we may perpetuate a paralyzing myopia that serves to diminish rather than expand humans' potential as individuals and as a species. Our challenge, then, would be to construct a science of humans built upon an image of humanity that reflects and reveres human nature in all its diversity, complexity, and subtlety. That is, an intellectual enterprise that truly deserves the designation of *A Human Science.* Well, there's the bell. Bet you thought it would never come."

"Professor, how much of this should be in our paper?"

"None of it! This was just an example of how to integrate some disparate ideas within psychology. This was easy. You people have got your work cut out for you. You've got to integrate all of the social sciences."

"Don't you think that assignment is a bit outrageous? After all, we're only sophomores."

"You're honors students, aren't you? Sit down and start playing with your ideas. You can sometimes amaze yourself when you work hard to polish up your thoughts. And then you will find out what you really do think. Or to paraphrase Shakespeare, 'What a piece of work is mind!'"

CHAPTER 5
CULTURE TALES

One typically begins a fairy tale with the phrase, "Once upon a time . . ." This introduction serves to tip-off the reader as to the genre of the story being offered. Thus, when the author speaks of fairies, dragons, leprechauns, and the like, the listener is not unduly troubled—for imaginary creatures routinely roam the world of fantasy. Lots of strange, fanciful possibilities can be comfortably entertained in a fictitious story. But there are other story-forms where talk of fictitious creatures is forbidden. For example, even at Notre Dame, one could not get away with a research proposal that purported to study the role of incentives in learning by leprechauns.

But the acute ear should be troubled because I just made an important claim in the context of the quip about research on leprechauns. I implied that science was another form of story telling, and thus of the same genus as fairy tales, although undoubtedly of a very different species. That is precisely the claim being made. If it can be shown that science represents a case of meaning-construction via story telling, then the more general hypothesis that most forms of thought reflect instances of story elaboration becomes quite plausible. Finally, by demonstrating the storied nature of all thought, I believe that an important goal—namely, proposing that cultural differences might be rooted in the preferred stories habitually entertained by ethnic, class, racial, and cultural groups—might gain a degree of credibility.

DOES THE NOTION OF "STORY TELLING" DEGRADE HUMAN THOUGHT?

The claim here is that when we think, we do so by fitting story themes to the experience we wish to understand. Have we demeaned human thought by suggesting that it is nothing but story telling? To answer, consider what might be a competing explanation of human mentation. One of the oldest views of mental processes (dating back at least to the very beginnings of Western civilization) is that humans are rational and logical beings. Are humans rational and logical? Indeed sometimes they are. However, psychological research continually turns up ways in which humans are imperfectly logical (e.g., Nisbett & Ross, 1980) or logical thinkers with limited capacities (e.g., Simon & Newell, 1964). But one might wonder: Are humans innately rational and logical? While that question might never be answered definitively, any student of human thinking knows that there are numerous instances of irrationality in human thought and action. That rationality and irrationality persist in spite of our culture's diligent efforts to teach rational modes of thinking suggests that rational thought represents a singular achievement for individuals, even if we might be naturally disposed to think rationally.

But narrative psychologists (e.g., Bruner, 1986; Howard, 1989; Mair, 1989; McAdams, 1985, 1993; Polkinghorne, 1988; Sarbin, 1986; Spence, 1982) would want to make a slightly different claim. Logic or rationality represents *a type* of story (or kind of analysis) that one might choose to apply to a particular problem (or situation) in order to understand the issues at stake and discover plans of action that one might entertain. So, through education and practical experience, we might learn to solve problems logically and rationally. But obviously there are many instances where one is instructed to entertain story-lines other than logic and rationality. [Seeing aspects of one's life through the eyes of religious belief is but one, obvious example.] So the narrative psychologist believes that scientific theories represent refined stories (or rich metaphors) meant to depict complex causal processes in the world. And when human thought turns to issues of "what caused something to occur," many would argue compellingly that scientific stories represent the best analysis available. But when our thinking is drawn to a consideration of issues of meaning in our lives (e.g., What do I wish to achieve in my life? What would be the moral or ethical action in a particular circumstance? What is the good life?), scientific stories might lack the rich resources of other nonscientific perspectives like philosophy, literature, clinical wisdom, religion, and the like. The moral is: different types of stories best serve different functions. Some important scholars now take quite radical positions on this point. For example, Kenneth Gergen claims, "It is my view at this point that the separation between fact and fiction is only one *of style*, and that the scientific style is the inferior in many ways because of the enormous number of limitations by which it is encumbered. (How many experiments do you know, about which anybody cares?)" (Gergen, 1989, personal communication).

One should realize that even mathematical thinking is story telling. Mathematical stories involve the workings of abstract symbol systems where the demand for internal consistency (that there be no logical inconsistencies within the system) is paramount. This reality was brought home to me a few years ago as my children watched a "Smurfs" cartoon where the Smurfs were trying to free a captured princess by solving the following riddle:

$$4X + 3Y = 23$$
$$2X - 2Y = 8$$

I took a piece of paper and began solving the simultaneous equations, in the hope that my three- and four-year-old boys would: (1) be impressed with their dad's knowledge of riddles; and (2) recognize that the benefits of education sometimes pop up in the strangest places (like Smurf cartoons). I first took the second equation and solved it for X—as I had learned in high school—to yield:

$$X = Y + 4$$

By then substituting Y + 4 for X in the first equation, or so the story goes, one will obtain a value for Y:

$$4(Y + 4) + 3Y = 23$$
$$4Y + 16 + 3Y = 23$$
$$7Y = 7; Y = 1$$

Now replacing 1 for Y in either equation will yield a value for X. Replacing Y with 1 in the first equation yields

$$4X + 3 = 23$$
$$X = 5$$

One is able to check the accuracy of these results by substituting the obtained values of X and Y (namely, 5 and 1 respectively) into the second equation, and noting whether or not it is a balanced equation:

$$2(5) - 2(1) = 8$$

Thus, our solution is correct. Armed with the key that would unlock the Smurf-princess from her unjust imprisonment, I awaited the perfect moment to dazzle my sons with my bit of mathematical magic. A statistician-friend was staying as our houseguest at that time. He walked into the room just as I finished my calculations, and asked what I was doing. When I showed him the equations and explained that the princess' safety hung upon the Smurfs accurately solving this algebraic riddle, my friend paused for about fifteen seconds and then stated matter-of-factly "X = 5, Y = 1." While my friend is smart, there is no way he could have solved the problem that quickly by using my method. He must have known a different story (or method, or algorithm) for solving simultaneous equations, so I asked how he did it. He traced the outline of an approximation technique whereby he guessed at initial values of X and Y and revised those guesses in light of the direction in which his computed values missed the original equations' values (namely, 23 and 8). I had never before been told that story for solving simultaneous equations with multiple unknowns. But that story works also. By the way, the Smurfs rescued the princess—without needing to solve the algebraic riddle. My kids still think math is boring and their dad is a nerd.

But this "mathematics is a process of following story lines" position can be demonstrated in the most simple cases also. Consider the following problem:

Problem	Step 1	Step 2	Step 3
23	23	23	23
x 46	x 46	x 46	x 46
	138	138	138
		92	92
			1058

The multiplication sign (x) tells us we are not telling an addition story, nor a subtraction tale, nor a division fable. Multiplication stories proceed in the following manner: first multiply the top number by the right hand part of the bottom number, and put that result under the line (Step 1); then multiply the top number by the left hand part of the bottom number and put this value under the first value (but you must move this second value one place to the left of the first value under the line) (Step 2).

Why do you move this second product one place to the left? I haven't a clue—that's just the way the multiplication story goes. But you have to tell this multiplication story in exactly this manner in order for it to work (i.e., to yield the correct answer). Put the second product directly under the first (or two places over to the left) and you get the wrong answer every time. The climax to the multiplication story comes when you add these two intermediate products (Step 3).

Follow the story line perfectly, and you'll usually get the right answers (unfortunately, computation errors do sometimes occur). Are there other ways of multiplying? Yes, there are. The abacus, for example, tells a different tale of how to achieve the correct outcome.

Why have I spent this much time suggesting that mathematics can be seen as learning how to tell mathematical stories? Similarly, why did I (Howard, 1985, 1991) argue that scientific theorizing involves telling stories that maximize the values inherent in the epistemic criteria (i.e., predictive accuracy, internal consistency, external coherence, fertility, and unifying power) for theory choice? If we can reasonably understand scientific and mathematical reasoning as instances of story telling, it should not be difficult to imagine other forms of human thinking (e.g., practical reasoning, intuition, pathological thinking) as instances of story telling also. This is not to demean human thinking—it simply sees several forms of thinking as important variations on a central theme, namely, story telling. And so, might not our cultural differences be due, at least in part, to the differing stories that we learn as part of our socialization into different cultures? Think back to my auto-biographical stories (Chapters 1 & 3) and the stories of the rest of my life (Chapters 12 & 13). Were they not dripping with stories of Jesus, Science, Irish wisdom, and Family? Aren't they the substance that makes up my "self"—that makes George Howard who he is? Now for the critical question: What are the great stories of our race and place that have formed you as a person? Please strive to compose an autobiography that honors the central values and great stories that define your uniqueness as a person.

CULTURE: SOME OF THE STORIES WE LIVE BY

LeVine (1984) defines culture as "a shared organization of ideas that includes the intellectual, moral, and aesthetic standards prevalent in a community and the meanings of communicative actions" (p. 67). He further emphasizes that a recurrent experience of ethnographic anthropologists "is that they [anthropologists] are dealing with shared, supraindividual phenomena, that culture represents a consensus on a wide variety of meanings among members of an interacting community approximating that of the consensus on language among members of a speech-community" (LaVine, 1984, p. 68). Thus, a culture can be thought of as a community who "see" their world in a particular manner—who share particular interpretations as central to the meaning of their lives and actions. From this perspective, education can be understood as the initiation of the young into the dominant meaning-systems of that culture. In a more negative construal, one might see indoctrination rather than initiation. Translated into the terms of this book, the young learn to believe and tell the dominant stories of their cultural group—be those stories scientific, civic, moral, mathematical, religious, historical, racial, or political in nature. As individuals tell increasingly more deviant stories (and act upon those antisocial beliefs) they are labeled as criminals (if the deviant story and subsequent actions have an antisocial theme), or mentally disturbed (if the story is not so much illegal as it is different from accepted notions of "reality"). Thus, institutionalization of criminal deviants can be seen as: (1) protecting society from further infection by illegal beliefs and acts; (2) punishing individuals to reduce the likelihood they will act illegally in the future; or (3) concentrating the criminal element so that members can become even more conversant with the criminal point of view and more closely enmeshed within the criminal subculture—as many critics of our judicial and penal systems fear. A similar analysis could easily be offered for the practice of institutionalizing psychologically disturbed members of our society.

Then what kinds of stories does our culture suggest we entertain as fundamental? As already noted, rational, logical, mathematical, and scientific story-lines are highly regarded. But the preponderance of Americans also report strong religious beliefs, belief in our democratic political institutions, belief in the importance of the family, and a plethora of other value commitments. So one might assert that we are urged to entertain a pluralistic stance toward thinking about life. Depending upon the nature of the issue, the circumstances involved, and one's objectives at the time, any of a number of disparate story-lines might be called upon to make sense of a particular issue. Being able to consider issues from a number of different perspectives (a skill demonstrating cognitive flexibility) is generally praised as the mark of an educated, perceptive citizen. While we might in our professional roles (e.g., scientist, politician, religious leader, mathematician) specialize in particular types of story-lines (e.g., scientific, political, religious, mathematical), one mark of a liberally educated individual is his or her ability to consider problems or issues from all the perspectives deemed legitimate by our American culture. But, of course, some types of stories (e.g., astrology, witchcraft, sorcery) are deemed illegitimate at this time in our culture, and thus are generally not taken seriously.

Modern anthropology thoroughly demonstrates the collective and organized nature of each culture. One does not need large numbers of informants to learn the dominant stories of any culture. Virtually all competent, adult members of a culture can repeat the consensus view on a variety of storied meanings in their culture. And unlike earlier anthropological findings, modern ethnography consistently finds cultures to evidence organized, coherent belief systems.

> No ethnographer who has followed Malinowski's (now standard) program for intensive fieldwork has failed to find increasing connectedness and coherence in customs—particularly in their ideational dimension—as he or she becomes better acquainted with their meanings in vernacular discourse and practice. There is controversy about the degree and kind of coherence—claims that cultures are deductive systems, pervasive configurations, seamless webs, have been repeatedly made and just as often disputed—but even those most skeptical of cultural coherence would not return to the earlier view of customs as discrete traits. The "shreds and patches" concept of culture has simply not survived the test of intensive field investigation, because the ethnographer, in learning to communicate with people of another culture, discovers the orderliness not only in their communicative conventions but in their version of "common sense," the framework of ideas from which they view, and act upon, the world. The framework may not be as orderly as a syllogism or a formal taxonomy, but it is far from a random assemblage of discrete elements. Most important, it is an organized set of contexts from which customary beliefs and practices derive their meaning. (LeVine, 1984, p. 72)

Of course, the history of anthropology amply demonstrates that the dominant stories of other cultures have not always been accorded legitimacy by Western cultures. Cultures organized around the wisdom of a set of stories that are quite different from our (i.e., Western) dominant cultural tales were labeled as "backward" or "primitive" cultures—even by anthropologists. Shweder (1984) shows a long history of what he calls "Enlightenment thought" (e.g., Frazer, 1890; Turiel, 1979; Tyler, 1871) in anthropological thinking. Enlightenment thought "holds that the mind of man (*sic*) is intendedly rational and scientific, that the dictates of reason are equally binding for all regardless of time, place, culture, race, personal desire, or individual endowment, and that in reason can be found a universally applicable standard for judging validity and worth" (Shweder, 1984, p. 27). To an anthropologist of an Enlightenment temper, Western culture was the paradigmatic example of a rational, scientific belief system. Therefore, any culture's distance from this Western ideal became the measure of its backwardness or primitiveness. Other cultures weren't merely different from ours—they were seen as inferior to our culture. This Enlightenment myopia not only gave certain Western anthropologists grounds for their brand of cultural elitism, but it also served as a set of lenses through which they could view their professional tasks and goals.

> From that Enlightenment view flows a desire to discover universals: the idea of natural law, the concept of deep structure, the notion of progress or development, and the image of the history of ideas as a struggle between reason and unreason, science and superstition. (Shweder, 1984, p. 28)

But there has always been a countertheme to this Enlightenment approach in anthropology. The Romanticist view (e.g., Geertz, 1973; Levy-Bruhl, 1910; Whorf, 1956) holds "that ideas and practices have their foundation in neither logic nor empirical science, that ideas and practices fall beyond the scope of deductive and inductive reason, that ideas and practices are neither rational nor irrational but rather *non*rational" (Shweder, 1984, p. 28). The Romanticist view is implicit in "symbolic" anthropology (e.g., Geertz, 1973; Sahlins, 1976; Schnieder, 1968; Turner, 1967) wherein nonrational ideas (presuppositions, cultural definitions, declarations, arbitrary classifications) are of paramount concern. Or as Shweder (1984) says it, "Indeed the main idea of a symbolic anthropology is that much of our action 'says something' about what we stand for, and stands for our nonrational constructions of reality" (p. 45). Nonrational constructions of reality are what one gets from stories. Stories slice the world up (or urge us to view the world) from a variety of different perspectives, points of view, and value positions, and thus construct noncomparable frames of reference through which reality might be grasped. One can view reality from a political perspective, as an ethical exercise, scientifically and empirically, rationally and logically, superstitiously, aesthetically, or from any of a number of other frames of reference.

> The whole thrust of Romantic thinking is to defend the coequality of different "frames" of understanding. The concept of nonrationality, the idea of the "arbitrary" frees some portion of man's mind from the universal dictates of logic and science, permitting diversity while leaving man free to choose among irreconcilable presuppositions, schemes of classification, and ideas of worth. (Shweder, 1984, p. 48)

Returning to the theme of "thinking as instances of story telling" that was developed at the beginning of this chapter, we can see that anthropologists in the Romanticist tradition have no trouble seeing different stories as embodying differing themes, perspectives, or frames of reference. Further, the Romanticist would want to argue for the fundamental noncomparability of different perspectives, such as racial tales, religious narratives, political themes, scientific perspectives, family narratives, and so forth. Different frames present differing views of reality. But no one frame is superior to another. The anthropologist in the Enlightenment tradition, on the other hand, argues that scientific and rational visions of culture and history are not only *different*, but also *better* perspectives from which to view cultural differences. So while all anthropologists might see the stories a culture habitually invokes in understanding its reality as being important in the formation of its unique cultural identity, there would be great disagreement as to whether all stories are created equal. Science and rationality would be the obvious candidates for deification by Enlightenment anthropologists.

It might well be impossible to draw a line of demarcation that demonstrates where microanthropology ends and cross-cultural psychology begins. A crude distinction would see anthropologists as being more interested in differences between cultures, and how cultural distinctiveness manifests itself in various practices. Cross-cultural psychology also dwells upon cultural distinctiveness, but here the emphasis is often placed upon how an individual's distinctiveness is partially informed by cultural factors. Crudely put, anthropology tends to focus upon large cultural differences, and considers the origin, purpose, and unintended consequences of these gross cultural patterns. Cross-cultural psychology, on the other hand, tends to consider how culture effects the individual, and vice versa. Perhaps a recent, formal definition of cross-cultural psychology would help.

> Cross-cultural psychology is the study of similarities and differences in individual psychological functioning in various cultures and ethnic groups. It attempts to discover systematic relationships between (a) psychological variables at the individual level, and (b) cultural, social, economic, ecological, and biological variables at the population level. Researchers in the field examine the individual's actual experience of these population variables as they change. (Kagitcibasi & Berry, 1989, p. 494)

One can see in this definition of cross-cultural psychology a strong concern for how large differences between cultures actually find their way into the psychological world and actions of individuals. This tendency to study cultural influences as they act on the individual took an important turn with Triandis' (1972) work on subjective culture. It is not as if each of us has been dropped into some monolithic culture, which then exerts its inexorable effects upon us. Rather, we are raised in a plurality of cultural subgroups, each exerting a multiplicity of influences upon us. For example, each of us belongs to a racial group, a socioeconomic group, a sex group, a religious preference, a political constituency, and so forth. The subjective culture of each of us is strongly influenced by the degree of contact we have with people and institutions that focus upon (or see the world in terms of) their own subcultural perspectives. This fact can be seen as the basis for the old saying "Show me your friends, and I'll tell you the kind of person you are." We are molded by the subjective culture of our reference subgroup.

Initially, a child is greatly influenced by the cultural milieu of his or her family. With maturation the influence of the family generally declines, relative to the potency of other subcultural groups such as the neighborhood, the schools, and society in general. Many of the classic struggles between parents and their children in adolescence and early adulthood come about as children espouse the values and beliefs of their subjective culture subgroup which conflict with the beliefs and values of their parents' subjective culture.

Stated in the terms of this chapter, struggles for independence by adolescents and young adults represent cross-cultural struggles as much as do misunderstandings and conflicts among members of different religions, races, nationalities, and the like. The stories advocated by the subjective cultures of adolescents often clash with the storied perspectives held near-and-dear by their parents.

How Stories Constitute Subjective Culture

The claims of narrative (or story-telling) psychologists have become more strident of late. For example, Sarbin (1986) in referring to human psychology (and after explicitly exempting the part of psychology that deals with sensory physiology) makes the following remarkable claim "So psychology is narrative" (p. 8). What part of psychology, then, is narrative in nature according to Sarbin? Almost everything of interest! Or consider Mair's position:

> Stories are habitations. We live in and through stories. They conjure worlds. We do not know the world other than as story world. Stories inform life. They hold us together and keep us apart. We inhabit the great stories of our culture. We live through stories. We are *lived* by the stories of our race and place. It is this enveloping and constituting function of stories that is especially important to sense more fully. We are, each of us, locations where the stories of our place and time become partially tellable. (Mair, 1988, p. 127)

Polkinghorne (1988) makes a similar point, "We make our existence into a whole by understanding it as an expression of a single and developing story" (p. 150). While McAdams focuses upon the role of story telling in the development of identity.

> My central proposition is that identity is a life story which individuals begin constructing, consciously or unconsciously, in late adolescence. As such, identities may be understood in terms directly relevant to stories. Like stories, identities may assume a "good" form—a narrative coherence and consistency—or they may be ill-formed. . . . The life-story model of identity suggests how the personologist, or anyone else seeking to understand the whole

person, may apprehend identity in narrative terms. Furthermore, the model suggests hypotheses about identity which can be tested in research, and less rigorously, in personal experience. (McAdams, 1985, pp. 57–58)

According to all such theorists, the essence of human thought can be found in the stories we employ to inform and indoctrinate ourselves as to the nature of reality. But how do human beings grow into their role as *homo fabulans* (man the storyteller)?

While human infants might not have the sort of hard-wired instincts often seen in many infrahuman species, children certainly do have some strong tendencies or predispositions. The two related tendencies that I wish to focus upon are language use and a struggle toward finding meaning in one's experiences. At a very early age, children pepper their parents with a seemingly endless barrage of questions. Questions generally fit the following generic form: How can I understand (or make sense of) these puzzling aspects of my experience? Careful parents not only try to provide concrete answers to their children's' questions, but they also strive to point them toward the general frames of reference (such as science, social customs, religion, cultural history, etc.) that make claims regarding meaning in our lives. For example, a child's simple question of "How did the world start?" could be answered either by summarizing Genesis or by offering a thumbnail sketch of Big Bang Theory. One answer offers a frame of meaning that sees the Bible as the Good Book; the other response suggests that Stephen Hawking's (1988) *A brief history of time* might be a good book. Both stories might be true (i.e., might actually have occurred), and the relative validity of the two stories depends upon the perceived plausibility of the two frames (science and religion) to each listener.

Lee Cronbach (1982) reminds us that, "Validity is subjective rather than objective: The plausibility of the conclusion is what counts. And plausibility, to twist a cliché, lies in the ear of the beholder" (p. 108). And while I suspect that you, Cronbach, the Pope, and I all have rather strong preferences for one of those frames (the scientific or the religious) over the other, I doubt that we'll ever all agree on the proper interpretive lens. But since a dissertation on epistemology is usually lost on a three-year-old, most parents usually answer the question with, "God made the world," or "A long time ago there was a big explosion." But most three-year-olds (or at least my three-year-olds) would find either answer less than complete, coherent, and comprehensive. And so question #2 would be a novice storyteller's attempt to get me to tell the whole story (either of science or of religion) within which my first answer makes some degree of sense. Nine hundred ninety-eight questions-and-answers later, our neophyte narrativist might have some rudimentary grasp of either the culture of science or the culture of religion.

But parents aren't the sole source of stories—even for very young children. Beginning at a very early age, most American children watch many hours of cartoons each week. Cartoons tell stories ranging in length from eleven minutes (one must leave eight minutes per half hour for commercials) to several hours (feature-length cartoons). Even at two or three years of age, children are entranced by cartoon stories, and they often try to explain the meaning or themes of the cartoon plots to their parents. Because children's thinking is more fluid than adult thought, the "impossibility" of cartoon plots does not often bother children. Adults are generally more constrained by proper notions of time, space, and causality, and thus prefer that the stories they seriously entertain be more "rational," "realistic," or "believable" than are cartoons. But children are far less discriminating in their fascination with stories. Tell, read, or show them a children's story, and you have their attention—often for longer than you had thought their attention-span could endure. Only later (at four, five, and six years of age) do children typically concern themselves with weighty discriminations, like which stories (and characters) are "real" and which are "pretend."

Finally, one should not think of cartoons as portraying only silly or superficial story-lines to children. On three successive Saturdays "Alf Tales" presented *The legend of Sleepy Hollow*, *Peter Pan*, and *Romeo and Juliet* to the author's children. Similarly, my children's favorite Walt Disney videocassettes are *Cinderella*, *Sleeping Beauty*, and *Pinocchio*. Such classics play out the eternal conflicts of good versus evil, issues of life and death, as well as the role of love and hate in human interactions (Bettleheim, 1976). This is psychologically heavy material packaged in a medium that is attractive to very young children. The Jungian, Hillman (1975) says that we are motivated, not by reason or by reinforcement, but by *fantasy*—the images and myths with which we have grown up. Jungians feel that many of the story elements that we live by are buried in our unconscious and are linked to the great myths that have captured the experience of the whole human race over eons of time.

But even if all members of a society told themselves exactly the same stories, the meaning and implications of these stories for different members of the society would not be the same. This is because there are many roles described in any story, and each of us must choose which role we will play in a story. Take *Romeo and Juliet* for example. Our sex could immediately eliminate half the roles offered as viable options. Further, one's age might suggest whether a "star-crossed lover" or one of their parents represents the most relevant role for us to fill. But here the literature in cross-cultural psychology might shed some light on this process.

Kagitcibasi and Berry (1989), in a recent review of cross-cultural psychology, claim that, "Cross-cultural psychology, like many other branches (of psychology), still lacks, and badly needs, a conceptual framework" (p. 495). But Brislin (1988) indicates how it is that people know what are the relevant roles for themselves in stories. He suggests that, "the four concepts of class, ethnicity, culture and race are social categories (Gardner, 1985) that *people use to think about themselves and others and to make decisions about their behavior*" (pp. 174–175, emphasis added). All stories offer a multiplicity of roles. Cross-cultural concepts direct us to the roles that are especially important to us in stories. For example, the recent film, *Cry freedom,* had two protagonists: a white newspaper reporter and a black anti-apartheid advocate who both lived in South Africa. The story was about friendship, oppression, and the sacrifices one makes to live out his or her values. But Brislin (1988) suggests that race might serve to direct some of us to identify more closely with the black activist, whereas others of us would be more inclined to identify with the white reporter. And whereas the movie clearly exhalts friendship and resistance to oppression, it is instructive to inquire about what happens to people when they speak out against oppression (at least in this particular morality tale). Imagine you identified with the black activist—he was brutally tortured and murdered by the police. The white reporter's efforts met with a rather different ending—he wrote a book about his friend which won a Pulitzer Prize that was later made into a movie, *Cry freedom.* So after seeing that movie, will people be more likely to speak out against oppression? It depends.

LIFE—THE STORIES WE LIVE BY

PSYCHOPATHOLOGY—STORIES GONE MAD

PSYCHOTHERAPY—EXERCISES IN STORY REPAIR

If we have learned anything from the cognitive revolution in psychology, it is that the things that occur between one's ears are critically important in the genesis of human actions. There is a fair amount of disagreement as to how the hardware of the brain interacts with the software of the mind. And there is a great deal of disagreement as to which analogy is most appropriate to describe the various processes of cognition. Is thought best understood as scripts (Schank & Abelson, 1977), possible imagined future selves (Markus & Nurius, 1986), stories (Mair, 1988), or any of a handful of other possible models? But beyond these disagreements, one thing is clear—psychology once again appreciates the importance of mind and thought.

If one considers thinking as story telling; and if one sees cross-cultural differences as rooted in certain groups entertaining differing stories and roles within stories; then one might see some examples of psychotherapy as interesting cross-cultural experiences in story-repair.

Have you noticed that therapy usually begins with an invitation to the client to tell his or her story? Therapists have favored ways of phrasing their readiness to hear the client's tale, such as "Can you tell me what brings you here?" or "How can I be of help to you?" or "What seems to be the problem?" Clients generally know that these invitations do not request the telling of one's complete life-story. Thus, we rarely hear replies like, "I was born on June 8, 1948 in Bayonne, New Jersey to John and Margaret Howard." Rather, clients understand that their task is to tell the part of their life-story that appears most relevant to their presenting problem. Thus, one hears appropriate beginnings like, "While I've always been a bit shy and withdrawn, since the break-up of my engagement last year I have been completely unable to . . ." or "I never worried too much about my weight, but since coming to college I've been afraid of gaining . . ." or "Drinking and socializing were always a large part of my job in sales. While I always drank a lot, I could always handle it. But lately . . ."

In the course of telling the story of his or her problem, the client provides the therapist with a rough idea of his or her orientation toward life, his or her plans, goals, ambitions, and some idea of the events and pressures surrounding the particular presenting problem. Over time, the therapist must decide whether or not this problem represents a minor deviation from an otherwise healthy life-story. Is this a normal, developmentally appropriate adjustment issue? Or does the therapist detect signs of more thoroughgoing problems in the client's life-story? Will therapy play a minor, supportive role to an individual experiencing a low point in his or her life-course? If so, the orientation and major themes of the life will be largely unchanged in the therapy experience. But if the trajectory of the life-story is problematic in some fundamental way, then more serious, long-term story-repair (or rebiographing) might be indicated. So, from this perspective, part of the work between client and therapist can be seen as life-story elaboration, adjustment, and/or repair. But, unfortunately, our therapeutic efforts are not uniformly successful.

An extensive literature has developed that demonstrates the importance of the therapist-client match upon therapy outcome. But the search for "the important matching variable" has proven frustrating. Research has at times shown the importance of client-therapist match on the dimensions of: race (Sue, 1988); social class (Carkhuff & Pierce, 1967); sex (Tanney & Birk, 1976); cognitive style (Fry & Charron, 1980); personal constructs (Landfield, 1971); conceptual level (Stein & Stone, 1978); personality variables (Dougherty, 1976); complementarity of therapist-client needs (Berzins, 1977); and personal epistemologies (Lyddon, 1989). One thing is clear, however, getting a good client-therapist match is an important problem in therapy.

Many therapists conduct telephone interviews with clients prior to an initial therapy session, and intake interviews are standard operating procedure in many agencies. Therapists are attuned to issues that suggest whether or not they represent the optimal therapeutic resource for a particular client. Thus, referrals early in treatment (or even before it begins) often represent shifts to pairings that represent better client-therapist matches on critical dimensions. For example, if a client's story involves fundamental religious beliefs or problems due to childhood sexual abuse, I know therapists who are uniquely well equipped to help people with such problems—while I am ill prepared to help (and uncomfortable with) such life-stories.

Recall Mair's (1988) point that "Stories are habitations." It is a fact that many people currently live in fundamental religious construals of their lives. That the stories of fundamentalists represent quite different habitations than the story in which I dwell is also a fact. The salient professional issue for me is whether I can wholeheartedly enter into a fundamentalist worldview. Can I be effective in helping a client to effectively rewrite his or her story while still remaining within the fundamentalist story-line, if that is what the client so desires. Since others are more skilled than I in moving through the fundamentalist religious life-world, I feel that I am ethically bound to let the client know that such specialists exist, and that his or her best interests might be served by engaging such a specialist. Finally, I would no more engage a fundamentalist in therapy in order to move him or her out of a fundamentalist worldview, than I would applaud a nonfeminist's efforts to undermine a feminist's belief system in therapy. After all, who died and left me God? Or, stating this last point more properly, only an Enlightenment thinker would have the hubris to see a fundamentalist, or feminist, or any other cultural frame, as inferior to their own story of reality. All such instances of cultural elitism are distasteful to thinkers of a Romanticist temper.

We might also reconsider Mair's (1988) point about the influence of culture on our stories and lives, "We inhabit the great stories of our culture. We live through stories. We are *lived* by the stories of our race and place. . . . We are, each of us, locations where the stories of our place and time become partially tellable" (p. 127). I am a creation of middle class, American culture of the latter half of the twentieth century. I am also strongly influenced by the cultures of psychology and higher education (see Howard, 1989). If I can see and understand the world at all, it is through spectacles colored by the worldviews of the cultural times and institutions in which I have dwelled. This is my world—the world I understand and operate within best. But other worlds are not completely opaque to me. I spent a brief moment in black South Africa in *Cry freedom*; I visited Ireland at the turn of the twentieth century as I listened to stories at the knee of my Irish grandmother; Dostoevski showed me a snapshot of nineteenth-century Russia in *Crime and punishment*; my wife has helped me to understand what it is like to be a woman in a male-dominated society; and a newscast gave me the briefest glimpse of what life in war-torn Bosnia is like in 1994. Empathic experiencing is perhaps the psychotherapist's greatest aid in escaping our inevitable limitations in understanding people from different cultures, races, belief systems, sexes, places, and times.

Beutler and his colleagues (Beutler, 1981; Beutler et al., 1990) speak of a "convergence of values phenomenon" that occurs in therapy. Treatment is experienced as effective when the participants begin with somewhat different perspectives, but close the gap between them as therapy progresses. Therapy might be seen as a cross-cultural experience where two life-stories come together with each life-trajectory being altered somewhat by the meeting. We are in the process of creating value in our lives—of finding the meaning of our lives. A life becomes meaningful when one sees himself or herself as an actor within the context of a story—be it a cultural tale, a religious narrative, a family saga, the march of science, a political movement, and so forth. To some extent, early in life we are free to choose what life-story we will inhabit—and later we find we are lived by that story. The eternal conflict of freedom versus destiny is revealed in the old Spanish proverb:

Habits at first are silken threads—
Then they become cables.

The same could be said of stories. Thus, a paraphrase of one of Shakespeare's more dire warnings becomes appropriate,

Beware of the stories you tell yourself
—for you will surely be lived by them.

PART II
SELF-EXPERIMENTS

Virtually all basic psychology textbooks devote a good deal of attention to issues of research methodology; to what distinguishes science from nonscientific disciplines (e.g., philosophy, theology, history); and to why science is different from pseudoscience (e.g., astrology). Your background understanding of methodological issues (such as control over extraneous variables, rival interpretations to the experimental hypotheses, random assignment, statistical inference, etc.) will enhance your understanding of (and appreciation for) the self-experiments that follow. However, because the research backgrounds of readers will vary from little experience to extensive knowledge and sophistication, my examples will range from the very simple (and therefore scientifically less compelling) "Bourbon and me" to the more sophisticated and scientifically compelling (but unfortunately more difficult to understand) "A pound here, a pound there" and "How depressing."

Even though psychology has learned a great deal from the natural sciences, and employs many of the same research techniques and forms of explanation as these physical sciences, psychology must be a somewhat different enterprise from the natural sciences *if human beings are active agents* (with some degree of ability to self-determine their actions). Chapter 6 ("Dare we develop a human science?") is a thought experiment (i.e., a fictional story that can highlight important scientific points) that shows why an adequate science of human beings must transcend the types of explanations that were sufficient for the natural sciences. Self-experiments test our ability: 1) to directly control our behavior in important domains (e.g., alcohol consumption, exercise, depressive affect), and 2) to indirectly control our behavior by modifying the conditions related to that behavior (e.g., regular physical exercise helps to reduce depression somewhat, spending less time with one's "drinking buddies" can lower alcohol consumption).

Returning to the theoretical model depicted in Figure 4.3, self-experiments can probe the direct power of self-determination in a domain (as symbolized by the blank parts of the oval labeled "Personal Agency") and they can also assess the striped areas (indirect volitional control by altering the nonagentic factors related to the action). Finally, the shaded areas of Figure 4.3 can be probed via traditional, third-person, psychological experiments. But before we can consider concrete studies of self-determination, the next chapter will present a fantasy that highlights the profound differences between studying inanimate objects and studying humans.

Chapter 6
Dare We Develop a Human Science?

> It does not 'hurt' the moon that I look at it.
> ('Hurt' meaning 'alter the behavior of')
> — Albert Einstein

You're not going to believe this story—and in fact you shouldn't believe it, because it is pure science fiction. It is a story that couldn't possibly happen—but it is important to remember that the impossible can often illuminate what is commonplace. This story is a bit special because you have a role in it. You are telling the story. I'm thrilled that you've made it this far in the book, so I'm going to give you a dynamite part to play. Brace yourself! You are the current holder of the Galileo Galilei Chair of Astronomy at a prestigious Eastern university. Yes, you are Professor Ivy League! Your career was solid and satisfactory until late one evening as you were taking measurements of a meteor shower, you became the first human to observe what later became known as the League Comet. Discovering a comet would be wonderful in-and-of-itself, but you were doubly blessed because your comet happened to pass within one thousand miles of an unmanned space probe. Since it was "your comet" you were on the ground floor of the group of astronomers and astrophysicists who got immediate access to the data transmitted back to earth by the space probe. But it was your mind—out of those two dozen scientists—that recognized that in those data lay the key to a theory that would (three years later) supercede the Big Bang Theory of the origin of the universe. While you never downplayed the importance of your findings, you maintained the proper level of scientific caution and understatement. Your style caught the eye of an ambitious provost, who suggested to a donor who wished to remain anonymous, that a Galileo Chair of Astronomy might entice you to the East Coast.

Well, the hubbub about your discoveries has now pretty much subsided, and you are looking forward to a pleasant American Astronomical Association Convention. In fact, you are now walking to the auditorium where you will hear your beloved old dissertation advisor, Professor Big Ten, deliver his Presidential Address to the Association. Suddenly you hear the voice of a classmate, Professor Cal Tech, calling out to you.

"Ivy! Ivy, slow down. I bet you're all excited about hearing The Big One give his Presidential Address. By the way, Ivy, did I ever tell you that you look great in tweed?"

"Oh, Cal! Thank you. It's good to see you. I hope you got a lot done on your sabbatical. Yes, I am looking forward to this talk, but I'm also a bit apprehensive. I called about a week ago to get a sneak preview and our old mentor said the Presidential Address would either be the high or low point of his career—but he couldn't tell which. It's not like him to be uncertain about his work. I hope there isn't any problem. Here's the auditorium. It's mobbed. I hope we can find two seats."

Cal saw two empty seats first. "Here are two. Ivy, what a crowd! Every top astronomer in the world must be here. It's quite a tribute to Professor Ten. Look, he's going to begin."

"This talk is supposed to be the crowning achievement of my career. But I'm afraid that I'm more frightened than a graduate student about to give his or her first public lecture. It should have been a sheer joy to review for you the achievements of my career— to summarize what I've learned over the course of a lifetime devoted to science. But I'm afraid I can't do it. You see, I've been shaken to the very core of my existence these past three weeks. Either I'm on to the greatest astronomical discovery of this or any other century—or I'm crazy as a coot! I'm afraid the odds are long that it's the latter. But please bear with me as I try to say what I have to say as clearly as I can."

Cal grabs your arm and whispers, "Ivy, I don't like this. I hope our friend doesn't do something stupid."

Professor Ten clears his throat and begins nervously, "Well, let me say it and be done with it. Over the past three weeks, I have come to believe that the moon is alive. All along, humans have considered the moon to be an inanimate hunk of rock traveling mindlessly through space. Well, I now believe that that view of the moon is incorrect. You see, the moon has communicated with me telepathically. The moon has told me that it is orbiting in the manner that it does for good reasons, but that it could move in another manner, if it so desired. You see . . ."

Bedlam! Pandemonium breaks out in the auditorium. Some people are yelling, "He's crazy! Get him off the stage!" Others are shaking their heads and saying things like "I can't believe someone would say such things" and "It's simply outrageous that something like this could have happened." Your head is spinning and you seem to be thinking ten different thoughts at once: What is *your mentor* up to? This must be some sort of a joke! The entire place is in an uproar. Could an entire career of dedication and accomplishment be ruined in one minute? What a completely preposterous set of claims for anyone—let alone your intellectual idol—to make. Events are moving in a sort of surrealistic slow-motion. You look toward the podium and your heart crumbles completely. Your beloved mentor and friend is leaning heavily against the podium, sobbing softly—a completely broken person. How could everything have gone to pieces so completely, so quickly? You are suddenly gripped with a rage that seems to come from nowhere. You hear yourself shout at the top of your lungs, "Shut up! Everybody, shut up! Be quiet! Shut up! Everybody shut the hell up!!"

Your last command is unnecessary, as it is issued to a completely silent auditorium. The silence suddenly terrifies you because as you look around, all eyes are on you—it's your move—and you haven't the faintest idea of what to do. You look toward the podium and even your mentor is staring at you—startled by your fury.

"Oh Ivy. I'm sorry, my friend. This must be so embarrassing for you. I'm terribly sorry that you have to . . ."

"'Sorry' just won't do it!" you explode. As if by magic, the fury is back and you bark a command to the one person to whom you had never had the temerity to raise your voice. "Those things you said were completely ridiculous. Now, take them back while you still have a chance. You couldn't possibly believe any of the things that you've just said!"

All eyes shift back to the podium. To your utter astonishment, Professor Ten is obviously thinking—weighing what he will say next. What could there possibly be to think about? What is going on here? This has to be absolute insanity—some fool's terrible, twisted idea of a joke!

"I'm sorry, Ivy. I'm afraid I do believe it. The moon is a person— I mean, a being—who can freely choose to continue to do what it is doing—or act differently if it so desires. I know that sounds preposterous to you, but I believe it."

Suddenly the rage is back. Almost without thinking you snarl, "Your beliefs don't mean a damn thing! This is science. We don't care what ridiculous beliefs you hold. You must furnish evidence—*hard evidence*—of your beliefs before you as a scientist can make any claim. Where is your evidence? You don't have a shred of evidence to support these outrageous statements. *You*—who has made dozens of graduate students and countless thousands of undergraduates *prove* their assertions—how could *you* say anything so stupid?"

Suddenly the old fire flashed again in Professor Ten's eyes. Maybe it was the sight of a former student presuming to lecture him on what science is—or is not—but instantly, you are once again facing that challenging, taunting adversary with whom you've done wonderful battle over the past two decades. "Ivy, might you do me the kindness of considering for a moment that there is not one shred of evidence that is clearly inconsistent with my claim that the moon is simply doing whatever it damn well pleases."

"Wait a minute!" you bark, "Don't give me any of that *Intro to Natural Science* crap about the rules of evidence in science. Professor Ten, so help me, if this is some dumb classroom demonstration technique you're pulling on us, then I'll . . ."

"Relax, my friend." It was clear that the old master was now back in control. "I wouldn't be so stupid as to pull an adolescent stunt like that in a Presidential Address. What do you think? That I'm nuts? Hold it! Don't answer that question just yet. But Ivy, my friend, I'm afraid that I will stick by all of the claims I've made thus far, and ask you as a fellow astronomer to put them to a fair test."

"A fair test? How would one go about testing such a preposterous thesis? I don't even know how to begin to set up a test of that theory." Much to your surprise, a colleague a few rows in front of you raises his hand, which you quickly acknowledge.

"Excuse me, I'm not sure what is going on here, but I'll say this anyhow. We're in Fort Lauderdale, Florida, right? The Atlantic Ocean lies to the east, right? It's early evening and so, as every astronomer knows, the moon rises in the east in the early evening. Now Professor Ten, since you stated that the moon communicated with you telepathically, I presume that means that you could make statements or requests to the moon." Your mentor nods his assent, and the stranger continues. "OK, here's my proposal. Tell the moon to instead rise in the west tonight, and while I can't speak for everyone here, that would certainly get my attention. I'm not sure I would say that I would be convinced that the moon is a self-determining active agent—but I guarantee that I would be at least nine-tenths of the way toward being convinced."

"No doubt a dazzling demonstration like that would compel everyone to consider seriously the possible validity of my thesis," Professor Ten offered. "But I'm afraid the moon can only alter its own behavior—it cannot perform miracles such as you ask. But I thank you for what I consider to be a friendly suggestion—you are at least trying to put my claim to a fair empirical test."

Suddenly you are intrigued by the stranger's suggestion, and so you inquire further, "Professor Ten, short of a miracle, what would your self-determining moon be willing to show us as evidence that it can influence its own behavior? We'll try to be fair in our requests for evidence that your moon is self-determining, but as scientists we cannot simply accept your claim that the moon is behaving volitionally because we like you, or because we respect your earlier work. Finally, you have us at a disadvantage, Professor Ten, since you are the only one who can communicate with the moon."

"Fair enough, Ivy. We've agreed that we will not ask the moon to perform miracles on the one hand, but if on the other hand I tell you that the moon chooses to continue to behave exactly as it has in the past, you have no reason to believe me. So what intermediate action can we agree upon that will be compelling?"

For the first time in the session, Cal Tech spoke, "Old friend, despite your protests to the contrary, I still believe you are simply leading us upon an intriguing thought experiment. There is simply no way that the moon is an active agent. But since I have always learned quite a lot from your excursions into science fiction fantasy, I'll happily go along on this mind-trip. Here's my proposal: Since we have extraordinarily precise measurements and knowledge of the moon's behavior, if the moon would but alter its orbit by one degree, we would detect it and find the demonstration compelling. And surely asking the moon to alter its trajectory by one degree would not be an overly ambitious request of an agent."

The stranger from several rows ahead, who had spoken earlier, objected, "I'm afraid you've given away too much with that offer. I can think of at least three problems with your proposal. First, no matter how accurate measurements have become in any science, there is still room for error in measurement. I suspect that there will be some controversy regarding whether or not a change of only one degree did or did not occur. Further, a change of that magnitude would not be obvious to the naked eye. I'd like some more dramatic proof—if that isn't asking too much of our active agent moon. Second, imagine that Professor Ten, who is after all a noted astronomer, discovered a force out in space that is traveling toward us. Suppose he calculated that it would engage the moon first, and deflect it from its orbit by one or two degrees. Now with Professor Tech's test of agency, the moon would move a degree or more and suggest (incorrectly) that we were dealing with a lunar agent. Third, as a general rule of thumb, I would want to see some action that reeks of intelligence before I would feel comfortable that the demonstration undeniably was the work of an intelligent agent. For example, if the moon could turn on and off whether or not it reflected the sun's light to us, I would love to see the moon flash on and off a message in Morse code—how about 'Moon Person on Board.' That would sure knock my socks off! Or if the moon's agency only enables it to alter its direction of flight, then I'd like to see it dance across the sky in a pattern that writes out in script something like 'Moonperson'."

Professor Big Ten is obviously tickled with the points being made because he roars with laughter at the thought of the moon writing a letter across the sky to astronomers everywhere, "That would certainly turn quite a few heads in our discipline," he observes, "but I'm afraid that would be asking too much of the moon. However, the moon likes the thrust of the stranger's challenge. Set an unusual course for the moon to follow over the next four hours and the moon will follow it. Now, who should we ask to lay out the moon's atypical course? Three people from the audience have spoken up thus far. Since Cal and Ivy are former students of mine, we ought to rule them out to avoid the appearance of collusion. The young man closer to the front who spoke earlier is an astronomer whom I've never met. He might be a good candidate to set the moon's course for the next several hours. Are you game for it, young man?"

With obvious apprehension, the stranger rises and speaks, "The reason that we haven't ever met is because I'm not an astronomer, but rather I'm a psychologist who is interested in the sociology of science. I'm now doing research comparing the topics covered and participants' behaviors at professional meetings for various disciplines. I'm supposed to be an unobtrusive observer at your meeting—not a central player in it. My name is Doctor Santa Barbara. By the way, this session is completely bizarre—not anything like I expected. If you have Presidential Addresses like this every year, I might permanently skip the American Psychological Association convention and come listen to your wild speculations."

As everyone waits for the laughter to subside, you review your feelings. You are a bit embarrassed that this psychologist thought all of your Association's Addresses would be as crazy as this one—that certainly wouldn't be good PR for the field of astronomy. But you are a bit relieved to hear that the stranger was a psychologist, and not an astronomer. You are more than a bit suspicious that he so quickly came up with three perfectly reasonable objections to Cal Tech's seemingly reasonable suggestion that the moon alter its course by one degree. Your suspicion was based upon the assumption that he was just another astronomer. He should have found all this talk of the moon as an active agent quite unsettling and the issues of testing for agent self-determination quite novel and perplexing. This Santa Barbara's comments were too lucid and came too quickly to be from someone who was an astronomer and who would have been as shocked at the turn of events as were you. But being a scientific psychologist, you think, he probably deals with issues of self-determination and active agency daily. That knowledge makes his response more believable. Finally, you look toward the podium and catch your mentor's eye. He manages a weak smile that conveys his enormous relief that your colleagues are taking his preposterous claims seriously for the moment. You see in the old man a tremendous vulnerability that you have never seen before. You realize his entire career is on the line—bet on what has to be one of the most improbable longshots in the history of science. Frankly, you think that the hypothesis that the moon is made of green cheese has a much greater likelihood of being true. But because of the personal and intellectual debt you owe to this warm and wonderful human being, you smile and gave a "thumbs up" signal of encouragement to him—in this, his hour of greatest need.

The stranger begins to slowly outline how he would have the moon behave to prove to the audience that it is a self-determining active agent. "You would probably like me to issue the instructions in some kind of space-coordinates—but unfortunately I don't know any. So instead I'll tell you how I want the path of the moon to appear to us here on earth and, Professor Ten, it's then up to you to communicate to the moon what it is to do. OK! Here we go. The moon normally moves across the night sky from east to west. Let's consider that path to be something like a straight line. Now, what I'd like to see the moon do is to immediately move perpendicular to that line. That would make it look as if it made a right-angle turn and is now moving straight up into the night, relative to the path it would normally take. How does that sound? Oh, I almost forgot. I want the moon to triple its speed immediately."

Cal leans forward and comments rather sardonically, "Shall we then kiss the moon bye-bye forever? Following your commands, our lunar friend is gone forever. At least give me something good to hope for. If the moon continues its current path—my mentor looks foolish. If it makes your right angle veer—our solar system is forever altered. I lose either way."

Santa Barbara takes the comment good-naturedly, "Good point! Every potential lover for eons to come would blame *me* for any failed romantic relationship. I don't want that on my head. Moon! One more instruction, please! Maintain the new course for two hours only. Then proceed at your new accelerated speed to the closest possible rendezvous point on your original orbit path. Then proceed at your normal speed and orbit path, until Professor Ten again requests that you change the path of your heavenly flight. Have I undone any possible harm? Are those instructions hopelessly obtuse, Professor Ten?"

The old academician smiles and says, "The instructions are received, understood, and, hopefully, being executed. I guess all that's left to us now is to go outside and see what our lunar friend does. Thank you all for being open-minded enough to entertain these incredibly improbable proposals of mine. I'll see most of you outside, I guess."

You and Cal are swept out of the auditorium by the crowd. Once outside everyone immediately orients themselves, locates the moon, and traces with his or her arm the path the moon will take—if Professor Ten has not been talking nonsense. There is complete agreement as to the moon's normal trajectory at this time of the year. From behind you hear Professor Santa Barbara's voice as he questions Professor Big Ten, "So under normal circumstances the moon would move toward that large building over there? Is that right? OK! So has the moon changed direction and speeded up its movement? What do you think?"

Professor Ten seems rather surprised to have to break the bad news to the visiting psychologist, "I'm afraid you can't detect the types of changes we're considering with the naked eye until an hour or two has passed. Had we set up the proper instrumentation in advance, we would have known almost instantly whether or not something had changed. But certainly in two hours we will know whether or not the moon's path had been altered. Might I suggest that you, Cal, Ivy, and I go get a cup of coffee while we wait for the results of our experiment."

Once comfortably ensconced in a nearby cafe, you are able to follow up a few thoughts you had earlier with Santa Barbara, "I suppose that in your research on human self-determination you have people change their normal behavior patterns in order to demonstrate their ability to self-determine their actions."

"Oddly enough, we don't. I guess we should have been

conducting studies of that sort all along, but for years we simply didn't try it. I suspect the reason was because no other science ever offered 'self-determination' as a scientific answer to why their object of investigation behaves as it does. I mean, before today, did astronomers ever offer an answer like 'the moon is following its orbit in order to check out the other side of the earth'? Would any physicist claim that an object fell at a certain speed because it was in a hurry to get to the ground? Or would a chemist claim that sodium combined with chlorine at a low combination temperature because the sodium was anxious to get together with the chlorine? And would any biologist today suggest that the gradual lengthening of the teeth of a species of cats was the result of the cats' desire to have longer teeth? Final causality, agent causality, self-determination, or whatever you want to call such an explanation, seemed to be unscientific in form, and often represented pre-scientific and amateurish theorizing that was eventually replaced by better, mechanistic, scientific explanations. Remember, a little more than 100 years ago there were no experimental psychologists. We attempted to free ourselves from the 'dead hand of philosophy', and to become a science like the other natural sciences. Thus, we developed research methods designed to find the mechanistic, nonagenic causes behind human behavior. We did so because that was exactly what the other sciences did. We studied the effects of various environments upon our behavior, levels of chemicals in our body and how they related to behavior, how early childhood experiences led to later emotional states like depression, how various patterns of family interaction produced stunted relationships, and other mechanistic influences upon humans too numerous to mention. It seems we looked at the forms of explanations in the other sciences and said to ourselves 'if we can also find explanations of this same type in human action, then we will have performed our function responsibly—we would have developed a properly scientific analysis of human behavior.' That ambition would have been quite appropriate, of course, if human self-determination actually accounted for little or nothing in the genesis of human action. But it is pretty clear to many psychologists now that self-determination is a very important element in human action. Or to answer an ancient philosophical question, 'Yes, reasons can be causes.' But now we are confronted with a huge problem—how does one study such a human capacity scientifically? Obviously, the other sciences are no help to us in this endeavor—for you folks simply assume that your objects of investigation are *not* self-determining. That is, until today that was a standard assumption."

Since Professor Barbara has gotten close to a question that is burning in your heart, you decide to shift gears in the conversation. Addressing your mentor you ask, "Dear friend, why did you do it? Do you really think the moon is communicating with you? Do you really think that when we go outside that the moon will have taken a right angle turn and be speeding along on a new path? Did you need to jeopardize your entire career just to test this incredibly improbable thesis? Oh friend, I'm afraid you've exposed yourself to some terribly harsh criticism."

Your mentor is obviously touched by your concern. But even in this, his most desperate hour, the class and humor that was the hallmark of his entire career does not desert him. "Ivy, I want to be sure that no one will ever forget my Presidential Address—we've had too many of those boring, nondescript talks of late! And I suppose I could have asked our lunar companion for a sneak preview before I went public with the possibility that the moon could self-determine. But I hope you remember that all my life I have attested that science should be conducted in the public domain. Why should I change my tune now? And think of it—what colossal hubris on my part to say to the moon, 'Perform a trick for my personal edification, and only then will I go public with the message you have entrusted to me.' Do I really think we will find that the moon will have drastically changed its orbit when we return outside? Frankly, it's quite unlikely. But if the moon hasn't changed its orbit, then I guess I have been hearing voices that really aren't there. If that's the case, I think we'd all better face up to that fact—and do whatever we can about it. I'm not terribly frightened, Ivy. With a loving family, and dear friends like you and Cal, I'll be properly taken care of. In fact, things have turned out far better today than I'd expected. When everyone started shouting early on—I thought it was all over. But thanks to you, Ivy, things got settled down again. You never told me that you had background in crowd control. And since the moon has indicated to me that the proposed test of its agency seems fair, who am I to complain? But tell me friends, what do you think the odds are that the moon has altered its heavenly course?"

You and Cal stare at one another, neither wanting to deliver your pessimistic message, when Santa voiced his reservations. "I'm sorry, Professor Ten, but I don't think that the moon will have changed its course one iota. But my reasons for believing that the moon cannot change its heavenly path are, I believe, quite different from the reasons that your colleagues might put forward for their pessimism. You see, I have done research on self-determining active agents all my life. Frankly, if we were interested in whether or not a particular person was self-determining, no group of psychologists would assent to the sort of test we put to the moon as being an adequate test of a person's agency. Think about it! 'Hey fella, make a ninety degree turn and triple your speed, then in two hours return on a diagonal to the spot you would have been at, had you maintained your original course. If you are able to do so, we would be willing to believe that you can self-determine.' The only hard part about that task for a human would be to compute the directional calculations! The only reason that our test of the moon could convince your colleagues is because after long years of study, each is completely convinced that he or she *knows* exactly what path the moon would have taken had we not intervened to put the test of self-determination to the moon. The power of the experiment, to shake up your colleagues' beliefs regarding the forces that produce the motion of the heavenly bodies, rests on the absolute predictability of the motion of the heavenly bodies under normal circumstances.

"But when you make a career of studying active agents—like human beings—you quickly come to realize that prediction of an individual human's behavior by a scientist is almost impossible. There is simply no way that an auditorium full of psychologists could have come close to agreeing to what a person was going to do under normal circumstances, as we easily did with the predicted path of the moon. Thus, you can see that if a person followed our instructions, like Professor Ten is hoping the moon is now following our instructions, all other psychologists would be unimpressed with that demonstration because (unlike you astronomers) they have no strong belief that the person was going to behave differently had their agency not been challenged experimentally. So you see, while it is much more likely that any person is an agent than is the moon, it is much more difficult to demonstrate this fact experimentally. But the bottom line is that the moon thus far has not acted at all like the other active agents we have studied over the years. Thus, I don't believe the moon is able to self-determine, and so I think its course will be unchanged."

Your curiosity has been aroused by this excursion into experimentation with humans, and you ask, "Well, then, is there no way in which a social scientist can ask a subject to perform a particular pattern of actions that will furnish evidence of their ability to self-determine their actions? I mean, if you really believe that humans can self-determine their behavior to some degree, then you should have developed some research techniques or methodologies that would demonstrate this ability."

"Well, yes, we do have some techniques that accomplish

precisely this task, but they are far more complex in nature than the experimental task that we put to the moon to prove its ability to self-determine its behavior. In short, these methodologies ask humans to embark upon a pattern of actions that we know in advance cannot be produced by any mechanistic cause or set of causes. Now, there is a complex set of methodological arguments necessary to justify my last claim—and I suspect your minds are on other topics—like what the moon is now doing. Thus, I'll spare you that line of reasoning for now."

Cal looks at his mentor sadly. "Well, old friend, it has been about an hour since the moon should have begun its new, self-determined course. If it veered, it will surely be obvious to us by now. I guess it's time to face the music."

You and Cal instinctively drape your arms around your mentor's shoulders and the three of you walk in synchrony toward the door. "Cal, Ivy, I can't tell you how happy I am to have you with me for my Presidential Address. Friendship is a very important part of life."

Santa Barbara picks up the bill and watches the trio head for the door. How odd, he thinks, to have three world-class scientists marching out together, each hoping desperately to see the evidence that will completely undermine the contributions of their long careers. Was this a tribute to scientists' lust for Truth at all costs, or an indication of the power of friendship?

Well, did you like the story? This was my way of highlighting the profound differences between psychology conceived of as a natural science and psychology conceived of as a human science. Did you notice that I told you a lie at the beginning of the story about the moon and Professor Big Ten? I told you at the outset that the story was impossible—that it couldn't possibly happen. That prediction was incorrect! The story could easily occur—and might yet.

In the telling of the story, it became clear that the points that I wanted to make could be done with fiction alone. It was unnecessary to resort to science fiction to make the points regarding methodology in science, putting theories to a fair empirical test, and important differences in prediction and/or explanation for a science where self-determination is central (like psychology) as opposed to a natural science (like astronomy). In fact, much of what this book offers is an elaboration of how important story telling has become in science (such exercises are often referred to as "thought experiments") and how absolutely vital stories will be for the science and practice of a psychology of the future.

CHAPTER 7
BOURBON AND ME

The medical literature has many examples of heroic researchers who performed extremely dangerous experiments on themselves rather than endangering others' lives. For example, when a drug is discovered that has potentially great medicinal value, its safety can be probed with studies using animals. But there still remains some danger in being the first human to take the drug. Rather than expose another person to the possible dangers associated with being the first human to ingest their new drug, some researchers felt it was more ethical that they bear that risk. But note, if the researcher did not die from the drug, no one questioned whether the researcher's investment in the drug's being effective had contaminated the finding that the chemical appeared to be non-lethal. Let me describe an experiment that I performed upon myself which was totally unheroic—but informative nonetheless.

Have you ever driven during rush hour in Houston, Texas? Believe me, it's no picnic! Several years ago I was on the faculty at the University of Houston. My home was on the opposite side of the city from the University. By the time I arrived home from work each evening I was coiled as tight as a spring. Having a drink as I read the newspaper served to help me unwind from the pressures of the day—and the drive home. I had the good fortune to take a job at the University of Notre Dame fifteen years ago, and now there are few traffic jams in my life—but my habit of having a drink after work each day remained.

My wife, Nancy, is a therapist in private practice whose work day typically starts and ends a few hours later than mine. Like all good spouses, she often comments about what she feels I am doing well, and what I might do differently. One day she mentioned that she would like it if I did not drink when I was alone—having a drink at home or out with others was fine. Since I enjoyed my end-of-the-work-day drink, I demurred. Being persistent, she challenged me by noting that since I urged others to gain volitional control over their behavior in my research, then why was I reluctant to test my own volition in this domain? I assured her there was no need to undertake the exercise. Knowing me as she does, and being the skilled clinician that she is, she settled the issue by hurling the one challenge that every true scientist is incapable of ignoring, "It's an empirical question, Sweetie! Prove it !!!"

Being hopelessly outwitted, I began designing my personal experiment on the volitional control of my after-work drink. I first suggested a one-year baseline period during which we could assess the stability of the behavior in question. Nancy objected, and asserted that we had very stable behavior indeed, and that I had my drink on about 90 percent of my work days. She was right, of course, so I determined that my "try not to drink" condition would begin the next day. I maintained this condition for a month and I was able to reduce my after-work drinks to about 30 percent. Of course, I was happy (with the reduction from 90 to 30 percent) but rather surprised that I had been unable to stop it totally. One day I had an interesting insight (Are research subjects allowed to have insights? They are in first-person research!) that suggested a way in which the study might be modified.

Bourbon is my favorite drink. It occurred to me that if there was no bourbon in the house, I might be less likely to have my after-work drink. This new phase of the study began when my last bottle of bourbon at home ran dry. I continued to keep ample supplies of other types of liquors, and drank them when friends visited, and so forth. I also continued drinking bourbon at restaurants, parties, and on other occasions. Well, my hunch was correct; not having bourbon at home decreased the frequency of after-work drinks. What shocked me was the magnitude of difference it made—the frequency of after-work drinks went from 30 to 0 percent! While I enjoy several types of liquor, I do not prefer any of them to cranberry juice, soda, or orange juice. But for me, bourbon is different.

The next interesting insight came several months later when I became convinced that the 0 percent in the "keep bourbon out of the house" condition would be maintained. The methodologist in me kept insisting that I reverse the condition by buying bourbon but still trying not to have my drink after work—or even a reversal to a "try to drink after work" condition. But somehow I couldn't bring myself to perform either of these reversals. Consequently, I am sorry to inform you that this personal experiment had an incomplete design. While I considered my personal experiment completed, it's funny how life goes on!

A little over a year after I began my personal experiment I read an intriguing little article entitled, "The beneficial side of moderate alcohol use," in The Johns Hopkins Medical Journal (Turner, Bennett, & Hernandez, 1981). I immediately "became able" to reverse to a "bring bourbon back in the house" condition, and my best estimate is that I now have an after-work drink on about 20 percent of my work days. Whenever I "catch myself" getting close to the 100 percent level of having a drink after work over a period of time (such as during tenure review, interviewing job candidates, and so forth), I "become concerned" and "force myself" to have a drink after work less often.

I used "scare quotes" liberally in the preceding paragraph to highlight the fact that a final cause (Rychlak, 1989), or phenomenological (Giorgi, 1970), or active agent (Harré & Secord, 1972), or volitional (Howard, 1984) explanation seems a more plausible (at least to my ear) interpretation of my action than any mechanistic, or psychodynamic, or biopsychological, or sociobiological account of my actions. The reality that you might find a different explanation more compelling highlights the fact known to every philosopher of science (e.g., Hanson, 1958; Kuhn, 1977; McMullin, 1983) and most psychologists (e.g., Cronbach, 1982; Howard, 1984; Gergen, 1982; Rychlak, 1989; Weimer, 1979) that the theoretical meaning of our data is never self-evident. Explaining the meaning of one's findings is an interpretive act that always involves a leap of faith which is underjustified by the data.

My personal experiment with bourbon perhaps should not be considered a proper experiment at all. I did not systematically alternate the various conditions in an experimentally appropriate manner. Additionally we might have observed a phenomenon that is unique to me: I refer here to the problems involved in generalizing from a single case study. Although my personal experiment fails to pass muster as a rigorously controlled investigation, I believe that it tells us a great deal. The personal experiment might be viewed as the analogue to how each of us obtains personal knowledge in our everyday lives. And while it resembles individual behavior-change problems sometimes encountered in clinical practice, strictly speaking, it is not a clinical demonstration. However, it serves as a simple introduction to first-person experimental research. Chapters 8 and 9 will present more sophisticated and methodologically compelling designs for first-person research.

Of greater importance is the fact that the bourbon experiment casts the issue in a different light than would traditional psycho-logical experiments (i.e., those that employ only the third-person perspective). It is clear that whatever changes occurred in the personal experiment were due to my wish to change. In the terms presented in Figure 4.3, personal agency (the middle oval) was primarily responsible for the reduction in the frequency of my after-work drinks. However, the personal experiment revealed that I did not have complete control over my after-work drink. The presence or absence of bourbon in my home represented a nonagentic, environmental factor that moderated my ability to exhibit complete volitional control of my after-work drinking. But rather than this environmental condition being in control of me, the personal experiment revealed that this was a nonagentic circumstance that I also could tailor to aid me in achieving my volitional goals [In the experiment, bourbon was removed to exhibit 0 percent drinking. After the experiment bourbon was returned so that I would drink moderately (about 20 percent).]

They say that imitation is the sincerest form of flattery. A sophomore flattered me greatly by imitating my bourbon study with her own critical self-experiment. What do you think of her efforts?

A CRITICAL SELF-EXPERIMENT
A Sophomore

All my life, I have suffered from the bad habit of being very negative toward myself and critical toward others. In the past few years, I have been working to decrease my negative attitude. That is, I want to become more positive about my life, and my work has been very successful. My work on my "criticisms of others" has been a much harder habit to break. Thus, it still has not been broken.

In the spirit of the bourbon self-experiment, and because of my interest in psychology, I decided to run an experiment on myself with regard to my habit of being critical of others. I wanted to see how much control I had of my habit, or rather, how in-control of me was my habit?

My experiment required me to record daily the number of times that I was critical toward other people. I allowed myself to think these critical thoughts, but every time I opened my mouth to say something critical, I had to record it. I would set goals for myself daily that I would try to achieve. On some days, my goal would be to not make any critical comments, on other days the goal would be one of various numbers of comments, and on still other days, I would simply observe my natural number of critical comments. My goals and actual data are presented below.

```
GOAL/DATA
Day 1: Just Observation/ 14 comments
Day 2: Just Observation/ 10 comments
Day 3: Just Observation/ 3 comments
Day 4: Goal, 0 Comments/ 1 comment
Day 5: Just Observation/ 7 comments
Day 6: Just Observation/ 11 comments
Day 7: Goal, 0 Comments/ 7 comments
Day 8: Goal, 3 Comments/ 6 comments
Day 9: Goal, 5 Comments/ 7 comments
Day 10: Just Observation/ 20 comments
Day 11: Goal, 1 Comment/10 comments
Day 12: Goal, 2 Comments/ 4 comments
Day 13: Goal, 0 Comments/ 3 comments
Day 14: Goal, 0 Comments/ 0 comments
Day 15: Goal, 0 Comments/ 5 comments
Day 16: Goal, 5 Comments/ 6 comments
Day 17: Goal, 3 Comments/ 5 comments
Day 18: Goal, 0 Comments/ 2 comments
Day 19: Just Observation/ 5 comments
Day 20: Just Observation/ 4 comments
Day 21: Goal, 0 Comments/ 1 comment
```

As can be seen from my data I am not completely in control of my habit. Although I seem to be more in control of it than I thought I was. On some days, my goals seem to be of no consequence. These days correspond to days on which very stressful events occurred. Thus it seems to me that the more stress I have in my life, the less I am in control of my habits and the more negative and critical I become. On the average, though, my critical comments tended to sway in number toward my goal, though not always matching exactly.

As a result of my experiment, I have learned to control my habit more. As with my negativity, my tendency toward being critical has come more under my control. Now, knowing that I have control over my habit, I will hopefully be able to make this habit a relative thing of the past as is the case of my negativeness toward myself.

In light of this experiment, I am now working on my criticalness of others. I am consciously working on controlling my habit, in hopes that one day I will no longer have to work at it—the critical habit will be a thing of the past.

Combing the data of "A critical experiment"

I was delighted that this sophomore conducted a self-experiment on her criticism of others, in the spirit of my bourbon self-study. Her data were marvelous—although their beauty was difficult to appreciate from her spartan write-up of the findings. Data are sometimes like a head of hair—at times it needs to be combed and coifed to appreciate its beauty. The student's data is like a beautiful head of hair when one wakes up in the morning. Now watch as I do a bit of combing to properly present the data's beauty. Of course, being a sophomore psychology major, the student can't be faulted for having no experience in combing data sets. I, on the other hand, have been at this data-presentation game for twenty years—I'm expected to be able to make findings much clearer to readers than is a sophomore.

A hairstylist first steps back to get an overall picture of a person's face and hair before beginning ("Let me see, darling, what do we have to work with here?"). I tried to get a sense of the overall picture of the data by creating Figure 1 from this student's observations.

The essential research question posed is, "Can one lower the number of critical comments one makes each day by setting lower (numerically speaking) goals for oneself." As a hairstylist might first wash, dry, and comb the hair, I'm going to determine whether these data are generally in agreement with that research hypothesis. I'll calculate the average number of criticisms per day for each of the six goal conditions (See Table 1).

TABLE 1

Goal	0	1	2	3	5	No Goal
Mean criticisms	2.7	10	4	5.5	6.5	9.25
Number of observations	7	1	1	2	2	8

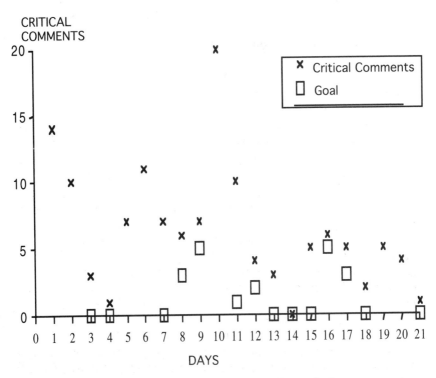

FIGURE 1: Goals and number of critical comments each day

In general, as the goals get higher (the highest being no goal at all) the mean number of criticisms seems to increase. However, that mean of 10 criticisms—when the goal was 1—seems out of place. The key here is that this offending mean is based upon just one observation. This highlights a bit of a weakness in the sophomore's study: four of the measures are based upon only two observations or one observation. This represents a design flaw in this self-experiment. Chapter 9 presents a general model for designing and running self-experiments. The general model precludes the "too few observations per goal category" problem and many other potential design problems. So be sure to read Chapter 9 before you design your own self-experiment.

With the hair now wet, and all the clumps out, it is now ready to be styled. One way of understanding the magnitude of her results would be to investigate whether or not there exists a significant difference between those days where the sophomore set a goal (regardless of the specific number) and those days when no goals were set, where she simply observed the number of critical comments she made. In order to do this, we might average over all the goal conditions and compare this mean to the mean of her observation-only (i.e., no-goal days) condition:

Some-Goal Days: 1, 7, 6, 7, 10, 4, 3, 0, 5, 6, 5, 2, 1   Mean: 4.38
No-Goal Days: 14, 10, 3, 7, 11, 20, 5, 4   Mean: 9.25

A t-test can compare these two means to see if the number of critical comments typically made on the goal days is significantly lower than the number of comments typically made in the no-goal days. If this is the case, we have some evidence of the student's ability to use her volition (via specific goals) to control the habit. It turns out that this is the case, with the actual analysis yielding a significant difference $t = 3.24$, $p < .01$.

The next four chapters will suggest why first-person research is essential for a proper (i.e., complete) understanding of human nature. Further, the reasons that first-person research is impossible for sciences other than psychology will be highlighted. Psychology has often been called a "soft science," and indeed it is. However, some think "soft" suggest the immaturity, imprecision, or inadequacy of psychological research. Such interpretations are wrong—pure and simple—and reflect an ignorance of the enormous problems and potential that agency (or self-determination, or volition, or freedom of the will) creates for a science of human nature. These are problems that no other science ever had to face. The next chapter suggests some of psychology's unique potential of first-person research to demonstrate a view of human nature that is unlike the scientific vision of any other object ever studied. That is, humans create their own destinies while simultaneously being subject to the hand of nonagentic causal influence in their lives.

CHAPTER 8
A POUND HERE, A POUND THERE

"It's a sad tale but true. The time demands upon me grew slowly at first: work on another committee; supervise another thesis; develop a new course; take part in a faculty reading group; and so forth. Then the cataclysmic events began to occur: taking the director of graduate studies job; the birth of my son John; chairing the psychology department; and the arrival of John's brother Greg. Even as we talk, my mind wanders back to a simpler, less frantic time—to those pastoral days when I was an assistant professor. Oh, I was busy back then—and pressured too. What assistant professor isn't? But it is almost literally true that apart from meeting two classes each week and getting some sleep, my time was my own. Lots to do—but 168 hours each and every week in which to do it.

Life was good back then. I was bursting with energy, enthusiasm and bright ideas. Life is good now too. The pleasures of family and career are difficult to describe, but real nonetheless. And while I've got no complaints overall, I do have a few regrets about my life as I now live it. For example, I finally forced myself to step onto a bathroom scale several months ago. I knew the news would be bad—after all I'm not blind. But I was not prepared for news quite that bad—210 pounds! For roughly a fifteen-year period (age eighteen through thirty-two, or from the beginning of college through assistant professorship) my weight had plateaued between 180 and 185 pounds. But those were the good old days—plenty of time to exercise. If my memory is accurate, I averaged about fourteen hours per week of strenuous exercise during that fifteen-year period. But I must admit that several old friends claim that my estimate is unrealistically low. In any event, it was heaven compared to what's happened to me in the last three years. Most weeks I do nothing—and a padded estimate would be two hours per week of exercise overall. But don't get me wrong, I've tried to exercise regularly. I even succeed for short periods of time. But I always backslide. The time demands on me are just too great. Something important always comes up to break my exercise schedule—and then I can't get back into it again for months. Doc, you've got to help me."

"What exactly happened three years ago that caused you to stop exercising regularly? Did you stop suddenly, or did you slowly decrease exercising?"

"Well, I was playing basketball and I tore my achilles tendon. I was on crutches for three months, and I couldn't do any strenuous exercise for ten months. During that time my wife and I had our first child and I became involved in the administration of the department. But by the time my leg was healed, I was completely out of the habit of exercising and the number of hours I could spend at work was greatly reduced because of my parenting responsibilities. Plus, I was just busier at work. But my injury does remind me of Bandura's (1982) article on the effect of unexpected events on a life course. In a certain sense, that was a thirty-pound injury! And my problem is compounded now by my personality. I am too impatient and competitive. Instead of slowly getting back into an exercise program, I jump right in, push myself too hard, and wind up hurting myself. Usually my feet or legs will give out—that thirty-pound increase takes its toll on the legs, plus I'm getting older. I could avoid injury by swimming—which I used to do—but frankly, I don't like the way those thirty extra pounds look in a bathing suit."

"Vanity, thy name is human!"

"Point well made, Doc. But that doesn't make it any easier for me to go swimming! However, I will tell you what I did do. There were two students, Mary DiGangi and Andy Johnson, who wanted to do a volitional study of exercise behavior for people who want to increase exercising. I agreed to be a pilot subject for them. The study ran for 112 consecutive days and was conducted in four phases: baseline, coin toss, choose, and maintenance phases. In the coin toss and choose phases, I tried to exercise as much as I could on half the days, and I tried not to exercise at all on the other half of the days. In the coin phase, the subject flips a coin 28 times and records the results on the data sheets. Thus, both the experimenters (Mary and Andy) and the subject (me) knew at the outset the exact pattern of "try to exercise" and "try not to exercise" days for the next four weeks in the coin phase. Conversely, in the choose phase, the subject could wait until the day before to decide and record whether the following day would be a "try to

Figure 8.1: Number of aerobic points earned each day in the four conditions, and subject's weight at various points in the study.

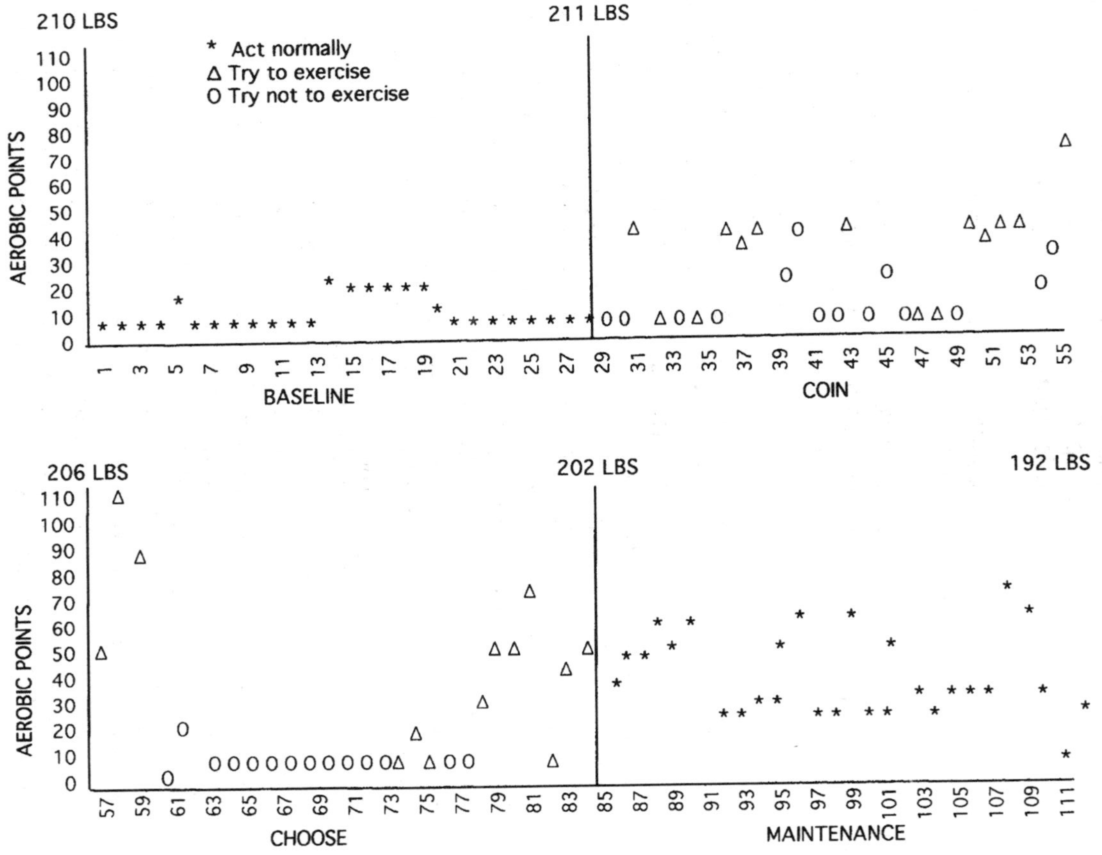

exercise" or "try not to exercise" day. Finally, in the maintenance phase I simply tried to maintain a steady daily exercise program. Previous studies (Howard & Conway, 1986; Steibe & Howard, 1986; Howard, Youngs, & Siatczynski, 1989; Lazarick, Fishbein, Loiello, & Howard, 1988) have documented the ability of this volitional approach to demonstrate the degree to which an individual's behavior is under his or her own control. Figure 8.1 presents my data for the pilot study. I've also indicated what my weight was at the beginning and end of the pilot study, as well as at the introduction of each phase of the study.

"Those are pretty interesting data, George. You got very little exercise during the baseline period. Then in the coin toss phase you exercised quite a bit more on 'exercise' days than on 'not exercise' days. In fact, the average number of aerobic points (Cooper, 1970) on 'exercise' days (20.28) is about five times the average number of aerobic points on 'not exercise' days (3.96). That seems like pretty good volitional control to me. Then, in the choose phase, you were even more successful. The average aerobic points on 'exercise' days was 21.21, while you never exercised on 'not exercise' days. That's pretty impressive control, I think. Apparently you are in control of how much you exercise."

"Perhaps the choose phase results appear more impressive than they really ought to be. I feel the coin phase was good for me because it urged me to take off from exercising every so often. Those periodic rests probably helped me to not overdo it and injure myself. But let's look more closely at individual days in the choose phase. I started out like a shot—on four of the first five days I chose to exercise and was quite successful. But on the fifth day I hurt the arch of my foot while playing basketball. I didn't twist it, or anything like that. It just gave out on me. I guess I just pushed too hard too quickly once again. For the next sixteen days I couldn't exercise much (whether designated 'exercise' or 'not exercise' days) because my foot hurt. In the last week of the choose phase I got back into an exercise routine of walking and jogging that my foot could take. In the maintenance phase I kept walking, jogging, and even swimming when my foot began to hurt. In that maintenance phase I simply tried to do a little bit of exercise every day. I feel that I was pretty successful at it."

"I'll say! You lost ten pounds in less than a month of maintenance. Your data in the choose phase have a very different meaning, when we talk about them as a client and therapist would, than they would appear to have if they were simply analyzed, presented graphically, and reported as a research report. I think

data would be richer and more helpful to practitioners like me if researchers discussed their findings with subjects and then not only presented the results in the traditional manner, but also presented a 'subject's-eye-view' of why the results came about. Clinicians often assign homework tasks to clients and then get a report from the person not only of how successful they were, but also why the client thought he or she was successful or unsuccessful. That's the kind of feedback that helps me to do a better job with my clients.

"George, in spite of the fact that we practitioners hate to correct the logic of you researchers, I feel compelled to note that just because you hurt your foot doesn't necessarily mean that people generally can't demonstrate greater volition in the choose phase than in the coin phase."

"Good point, Doc! I was concerned that I might infer that I had greater volitional control in the choose phase than in the coin phase, when in reality the data were artifacts of an unexpected injury. But the traditional experiment is not without resources in this regard. Specifically, groups of subjects, rather than simply one subject, are typically run. If the average effect size for volition is greater in the choose phase than in the coin phase, it is extremely implausible that this difference is due to subjects being injured in the choose phase more often than in the coin phase. As I indicated earlier, Mary and Andy conducted this study on thirty-five adults who wished to increase the amount they exercised. The methods employed in the study were identical to my pilot study except that each subject was randomly assigned to either the choose or coin condition in the second phase of their program, with the nonassigned condition becoming that person's third phase. This was done to balance the choose and coin conditions for sequence effects. (Mary and Andy's data can be found in Figure 8.2.)"

"There are several interesting findings here, George. First, in the choose phase, the 'exercise' days are higher in aerobic points than: a) the not exercise days of the choose phase ($F(1,34) = 37.70$; $p < .001$); and b) the baseline data $F(1,34) = 10.82$; $p < .01$. Similar comparisons of the 'exercise' days in the coin phase showed their superiority when compared with the 'not exercise' days of the coin phase $F(1,34) = 7.84$; $p < .01$). When one considers the magnitude of control (i.e., $\overline{X}$ 'exercise' days minus $\overline{X}$ 'not exercise' days) in the coin versus choose phases, a significant difference also emerges $F(1,34) = 9.12$; $p < .01$. Thus, subjects demonstrate an impressive ability to separate 'exercise' days from 'not exercise' days in both the coin and choose phases, and subjects

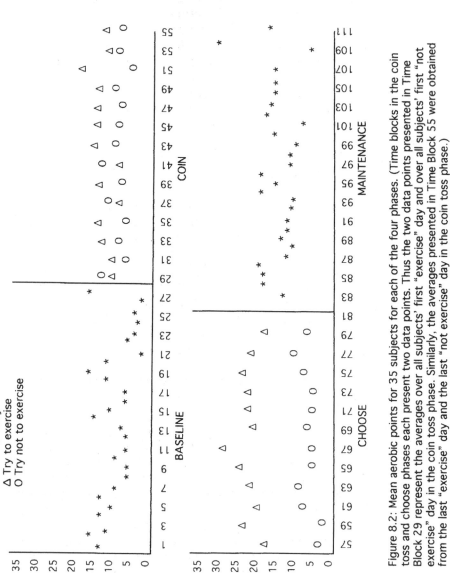

Figure 8.2: Mean aerobic points for 35 subjects for each of the four phases. (Time blocks in the coin toss and choose phases each present two data points. Thus the two data points presented in Time Block 29 represent the averages over all subjects' first "exercise" day and over all subjects' first "not exercise" day in the coin toss phase. Similarly, the averages presented in Time Block 55 were obtained from the last "exercise" day and the last "not exercise" day in the coin toss phase.)

are significantly better at separating 'exercise' from 'not exercise' days in the choose phase than in the coin phase."

"That's an important point, Doc. The operational definition I propose of a person's degree of volitional control over a particular behavior is the mean difference on the dependent measure between days on which the person 'tries to perform the behavior' and days on which the person 'tries not to perform the behavior.' In the conceptually cleanest case, days are randomly assigned to 'try to____' or 'try not to____' conditions, as in the coin phase of the study above. To date, there has been only one methodological critique of this operational definition: the problem of subject conformity to the experimenter's commands. That is, perhaps subjects are compelled to obey the experimental instructions because of their need to behave as 'good subjects' (Orne, 1962; Weber & Cook, 1972). If such a critique is valid, then mean differences between conditions would be caused by the pressure of the experimental situation (à la Milgram, 1974) and should not be attributed to the subject's power of self-determination, as the volitional interpretation implies. First, let me say that a number of studies (Howard & Conway, 1986, Study 2; Howard, Youngs, & Siatczynski, 1989, Study 2) have specifically tested the plausibility of the compliance interpretation and found it implausible. Additionally, a quick thought experiment might highlight the compliance explanation's implausibility nicely, and in the process also demonstrate some of the conceptual limitations of our operational definition of volition.

"Imagine that my pilot data on exercise enhancement had been collected in a slightly different manner. Suppose Mary and Andy had chosen a multiple baseline design to test their hypothesis. They not only would have collected exercise data, but might also have asked me to track the amount of time I spend reading professional books and journals each day as a second measure, and to record the number of times I slap my fifteen-month-old child, Gregory. As you may have guessed: a) I wanted to increase the amount I exercised; b) I was quite satisfied with the amount of time I read, not particularly caring to increase or decrease it; and c) I am ethically opposed to striking my child unless I feel it is absolutely necessary. Well, it's a matter of record that there was good separation between conditions in the coin and choose phases for my exercise data (see Figure 8.1). I really don't know how the data on reading would have come out: there may or may not have been some evidence of volitional control. But I can assure you that there would not be an iota of separation between 'hit Greg' and 'not hit

Greg' days. Now if the separation between 'try to _____' and 'try not to _____' merely reflected a subject's compliance to the experimenter's commands, one would be hard pressed to explain the extreme reactions in the three domains in our thought experiment given the same experimenter gives the three sets of instructions to the same subject at the same point in time.

"But our thought experiment also highlights a potential weakness of our 'try to _____' versus 'try not to _____' operational definition of volition. In many important domains of life I believe that I have volitional control of my actions, and I choose my actions carefully because they have important moral and/or practical implications. In these cases (such as beating my child; lying to friends; ingesting dangerous drugs; etc.) I believe I exert self-control over these actions. However, I believe it would be unwise of me to engage in any of these actions simply to demonstrate that they are under my volitional control.

"Remember that until recently it was impossible to unequivocally attribute a proportion of human behavior to volition (or self-determination, or behavioral freedom, or will, etc.). However, an enormous amount of research findings in psychology are best understood from this active agent, self-determining perspective. Rather than the present operationalization being the final solution to the problem of the empirical specification of the effects of volition in human behavior, it is but a first step toward an adequate solution. We still have a good bit of basic instrumentation work yet to be done in this area, Doc."

"*George, your point about active agents exerting volitional control in their lives reminds me of an article by Stanley Schachter (1982) several years ago where he claimed that the majority of people who maintain substantial losses in weight don't typically achieve weight losses through formal therapeutic interventions. Rather, they simply initiate weight reduction programs on their own. That finding plus the data above, suggest that a number of people might wish to lose weight and simply say to themselves something like, 'I'm going to exercise as much as I can.' To the extent they are successful, and our data suggest they often can be successful, that might reflect part of the way in which Schachter's subjects achieved their success. Of course, Schachter's subjects might also have told themselves to 'try to eat less fattening foods' and perhaps they were also successful in volitionally achieving a reduction in caloric intake, which would also help them to lose weight. You simply looked at one factor in the present study—exercise. But I suspect that individuals would be even more successful in volitionally attacking the weight loss problem from as many angles (e.g., diet, exercise) as possible—unless, of course, trying a lot of things leads one to be successful at none of them. But there are no studies on that possibility of which I am aware. That would make an interesting study.*

"George, I'm suddenly getting real nervous about the direction in which this conversation is going. It seems both your data and Schachter's findings suggest the importance of self-change, and in the process downplay the importance of psychotherapy. I hope you are not trying to put me out of a job."

"No, quite the contrary, I am trying to help locate the role of the therapist in individualized self-change efforts. I haven't yet told you about the last phase of our study. Remember, the thirty-five subjects represent a heterogeneous group, only a few of whom were considering seeking professional help for their exercise and/or weight control problems. Now our findings indicate that many in this group were able to achieve their goals by volitional, self-intervention efforts. But what about the subjects who were unsuccessful with these self-help approaches? Are they not likely candidates for therapy?

"Mary, Andy and I identified the fourteen least successful subjects as indicated by the mean difference between their baseline and maintenance aerobic point levels. We randomly selected seven of them to be offered therapy (all seven accepted the offer) while the remaining seven people continued collecting maintenance data (i.e., try to exercise as much as possible) in order to serve as a control group. Mary saw the seven treatment subjects for about one hour a week for four more weeks. She also called them periodically to assess progress, discuss strategies, and encourage them to exercise as much as possible."

"Did it work? Was the therapy successful?"

"It sure was, Doc! Figure 8.3 presents data on mean aerobic points for the old maintenance phase (now called maintenance phase one) data and treatment phase data (now called maintenance phase two) for the treatment and control group subjects. A significant group effect [$F(1,11) = 8.86$, $p = .013$] was found on maintenance phase two mean aerobic points covaried by mean maintenance phase one aerobic point levels. As can be seen in Figure 8.3, treatment subjects gained an average of 7.3 daily aerobic points from maintenance phase one to maintenance phase two, whereas control subjects only increased an average of 0.4 daily aerobic points from maintenance phase one to maintenance phase two.

"We'd like to suggest that people can periodically lose their

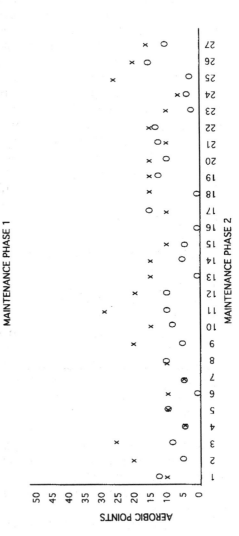

Figure 8.3: Mean aerobic points for treatment (7 subjects) and control (7 subjects) for the two maintenance phases.

degree of volitional control over some domain of their life (e.g., their weight, smoking, how depressed they feel, etc.). Many are able to reestablish this appropriate degree of control (such as the successful subjects in the early stages of the study above, or Schachter's self-helped subjects). But for whatever reasons, some people are unable to reestablish their normal degree of control, and thus are candidates for professional assistance.

"Sometimes a little professional help can get us back on a more even keel. Obviously, I am not saying that a person can (or should desire to) *completely* control his or her actions in any domain of life. But what most clients want from therapy is a greater or growing control over their problem. Perfect control is generally impossible because there are many other causal factors at work on us (such as biological, developmental, environmental, psychological, and social factors) that also influence our actions. The type of self-control desired in any domain probably should not fall outside the normal range of control that people of a similar stage and state in life exercise. For example, if a client is chronically depressed, the therapeutic goal would not be to completely eliminate depression from the individual's life. Rather, one might strive to have the client experience depression to the degree most people normally do. I mean, do you never feel depressed, Doc? Aren't there unavoidable experiences in life that would (and perhaps even 'should') depress anyone?"

"Since you bring up depression, let me ask you how you would conduct a 'volitional' treatment of a hypothetical depressed man, to be sure I've got this approach straight. After all, I work with depressed clients all the time, but I don't remember ever getting one who simply wanted to exercise more—such people usually go to a health club, not a psychotherapist."

"Fair enough! Let's assume that I encourage this client to monitor his mood at two or three points in each day, and that the client produces a reasonable amount of baseline data while I am getting background information and developing the therapeutic relationship. Now let's make the case a bit tougher by assuming that my intuition suggests that direct volitional control (i.e., 'try to feel less depressed' versus 'act normally') would be completely ineffective—so I would bypass it completely. Then I'd ask myself, 'What does the research literature suggest might be the possible causes of depression?'"

"Oh, lots of things might produce depression: disruptive life events (like losing a job, a divorce, a death in the family); biochemical imbalances; overgeneralized negative view of the world (as Beck

suggests); dysfunctional family systems; lack of response-contingent reinforcement (as Lewinsohn believes); life style problems (like exercise or diet); or, lastly, a general life style high in punishers and lean in reinforcers might be implicated. Really, almost anything might be a factor in someone being depressed."

"OK! Now my first move would be to view all of your suggestions *not* as causes of depression, but as *conditions* that might increase or decrease the client's volitional efforts to become less depressed. Since we've assumed that 'direct' volitional control will be ineffective, I would then test the client's ability to volitionally control the conditions that may aid him in his volitional efforts to become less depressed. Some of your suggested factors fit nicely into this model (e.g., cognitions, exercise, diet, antidepressant medications, who one interacts with, etc.) whereas others do not appear to fit (e.g., How would one volitionally control a disruptive life event or a dysfunctional family system?). Suppose we decided to concentrate on two conditions: a) exercise; and b) people with whom the client interacts. The levels of these independent variables might be: a) 'try to exercise' versus 'try not to exercise'; and b) 'try to spend as much time as possible with people you like and as little time as possible with people you dislike' versus 'act normally.' Research designs currently exist that enable me to assess my client's ability to volitionally control the conditions (i.e., how much he exercises, or his ability to manage how much time he spends with certain 'types' of people) and the 'spillover' effect this control has on his ongoing level of depression. For example, one study (Howard & Conway, 1986, Study 3) considered the ability of forty-five interpersonally shy college students to (both directly and indirectly) volitionally increase the number of heterosexual social interactions in their daily lives. Subjects were able to directly control (i.e., 'try to initiate as many conversations as possible' versus 'act normally') their interactions quite well (effect size: Partial Eta Square = .65). Indirect control of their number of interactions was also achieved. This was accomplished by subjects directly controlling a *condition* related to the desired target behavior, and having this control of a secondary variable 'spill over' to the target dependent measure (i.e., total number of heterosexual social interactions). For example, the effect size for the instruction to spend time in social places on the amount of time actually spent in social places was .46 with a 'spillover' effect size on total interactions of .19. Similarly, the effect size for the instruction to make as many positive self-statements as possible on number of positive self statements generated was .32 with a 'spillover' effect size on total interactions of .18. Thus, there is strong evidence that people can modify their behavior by exerting volitional control 'directly' to the target area (as was also the case in the exercise study above), as well as indirectly by volitionally controlling the conditions associated with success in that behavior.

"Thus, my work with the hypothetical depressed client might include helping him to gain greater volitional control over his overgeneralized negative cognitions, his support structure, his exercise regimen, and perhaps even his diet. I wouldn't work with him from a family systems perspective, nor would I use anti-depressant medications—but that's primarily because of the limitations of my professional background. If family work or antidepressant drugs seem indicated, consultation with other professionals or a referral would probably be advised. The volitional perspective sketched here makes many of the same recom-mendations as does Arnold Lazarus' Multimodal therapy (Lazarus, 1976, 1985). I think Lazarus has hit the nail right on the head with his recommendation that therapists initiate work through multiple modes of influence (all directed toward a common multifaceted goal), and that this process be coordinated from a unitary, coherent theoretical perspective. Both Lazarus' Multimodal approach and the volitional perspective I've outlined seek to tap multiple channels of influence to help clients regain control over their lives."

"*I just had a flash! You see therapy as an aid to individuals in their efforts to reestablish a normal degree of control in some domain where they are a bit out of control. Volition involves being as free as most people to act, think, or feel as one wishes in some domain. That sounds like an issue of freedom of the will—or one's range of behavioral flexibility. Are you really performing studies on free will?*"

"Gee, I'd hate to turn this into a discussion of philosophy of science—but a few basic points might be made. Free will-determinism debates have raged for several millennia. And, in fact, there are several quite different free will conceptions that have run through these discussions. For example, Mortimer Adler (1958, 1961) sees three different conceptions of freedom. First, free will represents instances where one is not physically coerced to behave in a particular manner. Second, freedom is the state one achieves when one frees himself or herself from internal handicap or weakness, and thus he or she is better able to achieve his or her desired goals. Third, free will involves instances where individuals make choices and act on those choices, *when in fact they might have done otherwise.* Our research on volition has nothing to say to Adler's first two meanings of free will. But the research speaks clearly to the third conception. If all other factors had been exactly the same in a particular instance, might a person have actually chosen to behave in a way other than he or she did? Or, as the determinist suspects, wasn't the person's course of action determined all along—and people's ubiquitous perception of freedom of choice and action merely an illusion? Briefly, I believe that the random assignment of days to conditions (e.g., 'exercise', 'not exercise'), and the strong evidence (four studies and the 'thought experiment' above) against the 'conformity to the experimenter's command' interpretation, represents the methodological analogue of the conceptual premise 'if all other factors had been exactly the same.' The logic of random assignment is that two groups are created which are equal (on the average) on *all possible* factors save the independent variable (and any variable inadvertently correlated with the independent variable, such as, conformity). Thus, differences on the dependent variable (e.g., food consumed, amount exercised, etc.) can be unequivocally attributed to the influence of the independent variable, namely, volition. The huge differences we've found on the various dependent measures demonstrate that people can indeed choose to do otherwise, even if all other factors are held the same on the average. Thus, our findings furnish crucial empirical support for what heretofore was only an assumption by free will advocates. Those data should be welcome support for free will advocates, who have grown accustomed to having scientific evidence always appear to support their antagonists' position."

"Oops! I see our fifty minutes is about up. Before we close, let me ask one more question. Remember that speech that you gave at the beginning about not exercising because you were so busy. Now that you are exercising regularly, does that mean your schedule is less demanding?"

"Be serious, Doc! I really did think that those time demands represented the primary cause of my inability to make myself exercise. Like you, I am a victim of the cult of psychological, non-agentic mechanisms. We are trained to look for the 'causes' of our own, and other people's, behavior. I think we would all do better to heed the wisdom of Shakespeare's claim that, 'A man is the cause of his actions.' Time demands, the presence or absence of exercise facilities, physical injuries, societal attitudes toward exercise, and many other factors might be better seen as enabling or restraining conditions that either increase or decrease the likelihood that we will achieve our desired plans, goals, intentions, and so forth. But, clearly, time pressures should not be viewed as 'the cause' of my problem with exercise since the solution to the problem (namely, an hour or two of exercise daily) serves to exacerbate this putative cause greatly (i.e., it creates even greater time demands on me). And in spite of this seeming paradox, I happily go on exercising. But you know better than I, Doc, that life involves choices—all of which result in trade-offs. That's what therapy is often all about. Namely, helping clients to: realize their choices; make healthy decisions; and live with the consequences of those choices."

"*One final question, George. What have we been doing here? Have we been engaged in science or in therapy?*"

"It's all a matter of money, Doc. If this is research, you should pay me for agreeing to be a subject in this study; if it is a therapy session, I should pay you for letting me talk through these issues. Do you take personal checks?"

"*Sorry, George, I don't. Do you take Mastercard?*"

CHAPTER 9
HOW DEPRESSING

To this point, you've watched me engage in self-experiments with bourbon and exercise and seen a sophomore conduct a self-study on her tendency to make critical comments. Perhaps you've even conducted a self-experiment on one of these or on another topic of relevance to you. The purpose of this chapter is to take you step-by-step through an elaborate self-experiment on depression. While one's level of depressive affect can become a clinical problem, for most of us it is simply an occasional annoyance. If depression might represent a clinical problem for you, please seek professional help to assess the severity of this difficulty before embarking upon this self-experiment. However, even for people with clinically significant levels of depression, the procedures of this self-experiment can provide help in the primary task of therapy—namely, for a person to find some way of dealing with his or her problem.

"Depression" is a lot like "cancer" in that a single term is used to cover a multitude of problems of vastly different origins that are amenable to a wide range of remedial efforts. Depressed people are those with an inappropriately low affect level. Low affect is usually associated with symptoms like sadness, moodiness, feeling tired all the time, enjoyable activities are no longer fun, disturbed sleep patterns, trouble concentrating, giving up too easily, pre-occupied with thoughts of failure, excessive self-blame, appetite disturbances, sluggishness, and others. For many people, important elements in their depression are that their lives possess little or no meaning, they experienced traumatic events in their life histories, and they have little or no hope for the future. While working to minimize the influence of such factors on our present level of affect is best approached through psychotherapy, one's affect level also can be improved by the types of exercises (i.e., autobiographies, teleographies) recommended in other parts of this book. However, there are still other causes of our depression—causes that can be understood and manipulated in the present.

You can't now change traumatic childhood events whose influence still leads you to be depressed. However, as discussed in the last chapter, you can modify other current factors that increase the likelihood that you will become less depressed. For example, getting enough exercise, or enough time with people you enjoy, or enough sunshine might have a marked uplifting effect on your spirits. What we'll do next is to outline a general format for studying your ability to indirectly control your mood by manipulating the conditions (e.g., amount of exercise, body potassium levels, number of positive self-statements, time spent with enjoyable people) that are related (in all likelihood) to your mood state.

Affect level is different from other target actions (like drinking and exercising) in that more positive affect is the generally preferred condition, rather than moderate levels of the action (as in the case with alcohol consumption and exercise). That is, for most people never drinking, never exercising, always drinking, and always exercising are all undesirable states of affairs. Moderate levels of drinking and exercise are generally the preferred levels. [Although some argue that no drinking is the preferred option.] However, with our level of depressive affect, less is usually better. Have you heard anyone seriously claim that their problem is that they are just too happy?

The importance of this point for our self-experiment is that people are generally trying their best to be happy (i.e., not to be depressed). Thus, I would not be surprised if we instructed people to "try to be happy" on some days and to "act normally" on other days, that there would be no difference on depressive affect on these two groups of days. This is because when told to "act normally," people are "trying to be happy." However, for ethical reasons, I would not want to instruct myself (or anyone else) to "try to be as depressed as possible today." Thus, I would not expect to find any direct effect for volitional control over depressive affect (i.e., no difference between "try to be happy" and "act normally" days). Therefore, I won't make direct volitional control over depressive affect a part of this study, and will, instead, concentrate on indirect volitional effects. See Studies 2 and 3 of Howard and Conway (1986) for designs that assess both direct and indirect volitional effects on subjects' eating and socializing actions.

A GENERAL MODEL FOR ASSESSING
DIRECT AND INDIRECT VOLITIONAL EFFECTS

All measurement in psychology is approximate, and so we must realize that all studies merely suggest causal relationships that might exist. While we believe the causes and effects we study (e.g., depression, level of potassium in our bodies, amount of exercise) are real, science cannot know (i.e., measure) these constructs perfectly. Donald Campbell (in Brewer & Collins, 1981) makes this point best when he claims that scientists are ontological realists but epistemological falliblists. Measurement imprecision is a fact of scientific-life. While one constantly strives to perfect measurement strategies, one is not paralyzed to inaction because our measures are inevitably less-than-perfect.

With that caveat in mind, I'll now suggest some extremely simple measures of the sort of variables we'll consider in our self-experiment on depression. Your measure of depression can be extremely simple. For example, you might rate yourself each evening on a 1 (this was the saddest, most depressing day of my life) to 10 (this was the happiest day of my life) scale. In contrast, if you wished to publish your self-experiment, you might complete a psychometrically more sophisticated measure of state of depression questionnaire, such as the Multiple Affect Adjective Checklist (Zuckerman & Lubin, 1985), each evening. For the purpose of enhanced self-understanding, the simpler measures are remarkably valid and effective (see Howard, 1993b, 1994). Similarly, a very rough approximation of your level of body potassium is obtained by noting the number of bananas you eat each day. While this is a crude measurement device, it has great potential as an easily manipulated nonagentic causal factor. Simply estimating the number of minutes you exercise each day will serve as a satisfactory measure of exercise as a potential causal influence on depression. Each evening, you can also easily estimate the number of positive self-statements (e.g., "Your performance is good, given the restrictions under which you work, George"; "You always try to be fair and pleasant with coworkers"; "You always try your best, George") that you made that day. Finally, you can make a list of the five to ten people whose company you enjoy the most and estimate the amount of time you spent with them (in person or on the telephone) each day.

To begin the self-experiment, simply monitor your behavior

for a week (Baseline Days) on the target dependent measure (e.g., depression) and the nonagentic causal factors (e.g., amount of exercise, time spent with positive people, potassium consumption) to be studied (see Table 9.1).

Table 9.1

Baseline Days	Intervention Days									
1 2 3 4 5 6 7 Depression	8 9 10 11 12 13 14 15 16 . . . 28									
Potassium	H	T	T	H	H	T	H	H	T ... H
Exercise	T	H	H	T	T	H	H	T	T ... T
Positive People	H	H	H	H	T	H	H	T	T ... H

Next, flip a coin 63 times to determine the order of manipulation of each of the three (in this case) nonagentic causal factors that may indirectly influence your level of depressive affect. Assume that "heads" indicates that you should "try to increase" a nonagentic factor as much as is reasonable for that day. Then on Day 8 (the first day of the intervention phase) I would try to eat a banana or two that day (i.e., increase potassium), visit colleagues that I like several times during the day, telephone a few ex-students and colleagues in other cities, and invite someone whose company I enjoy to join me for lunch (i.e., increase time spent with positive people). However, I would not make a special effort to try to exercise on Day 8 (because the coin came up tails) unless not exercising would produce negative consequences. For example, three other psychologists and I play tennis each week. If Day 8 happened to be our tennis day, I'd play. Table 9.1 could now serve as my data sheet. If I began my self-experiment on (for example) a Wednesday, then Days 1, 8, 15, and 22 would be marked W. Days 2, 9, 16 and 23 would be marked Th, and so forth.

In Table 9.2 I've generated some hypothetical data for this study in order to show you how to analyze your data. To conserve space, I've simply collapsed the baseline days and represented these data by the average on each measure over the seven baseline days. Thus, in the Baseline week this hypothetical person's level was quite near the midpoint of our 1 (best day) to 10 (worst day) depression scale; he or she ate one banana during the entire week of baseline (1 banana in 7 days = .14 bananas / day); he or she exercised a little over 30 minutes a day; and finally the person spent almost 2 1/4 hours per day with positive people.

Table 9.2

Baseline Average		Days												
	8	9	10	11	12	13	14	15	16	17	18	19	20	21
Depression 5.14	5	2	3	6	4	2	6	9	4	8	5	9	1	3
Potassium .14	1	0	0	1	2	0	1	0	1	2	0	0	0	0
	H	T	T	H	H	T	H	T	H	H	T	T	H	T
Exercise 31.38	10	80	90	0	30	70	50	0	30	0	0	50	90	70
	T	H	H	T	H	H	T	T	H	T	T	T	H	H
Positive People 133.51	300	350	250	300	200	300	250	40	180	20	180	100	300	220
	H	H	H	H	T	H	H	T	T	T	H	T	H	H

During the two weeks of intervention (in our example) the self-rated level of depression averaged 4.78, which while close to the person's baseline level, does show a slight improvement. The next logical question would be, "What might have produced this small decrement in depressive affect?" The mean number of bananas changed from .14 in baseline to .57 in the intervention phase. Similarly, mean number of minutes exercised increased from 31.38 in baseline to 40.70 in intervention. Finally, time spent with positive people increased from 133.51 minutes per day in baseline to 213.57 minutes in intervention. Thus, the increase in any of these three nonagentic factors might have been responsible for the person's lessened depression in the intervention phase. A more fine-grained inspection of these data are required to determine which (if any) of these nonagentic factors might have caused the observed decline in depression scores.

Let's consider the hypothesis that increased potassium

levels (due to eating more bananas) is an appropriate explanation for the reduced levels of depressive affect. First, reorder the data in Table 9.2 in the following manner. Compare the mean number of bananas consumed on "try to eat bananas" days (i.e., "Heads" days) with the number of bananas consumed on "try not to eat bananas" days (i.e., "Tails" days). Exactly 1.14 bananas / day were consumed on "try to eat bananas" days (i.e., $1 + 1 + 2 + 1 + 1 + 2 + 0 = 8 \div 7 = 1.14$ bananas / day). Conversely, no bananas were consumed on "try not to eat bananas" days. Thus, one can conclude that this person's potassium level was in all likelihood higher on "try to eat bananas" than on the "try not to eat bananas" days.

In Chapter 7 we spoke of "direct" volitional control of the nonagentic conditions that may (or may not) be related to the primary variable of interest. The above procedure shows how such direct control can be measured. With a few additional statistical procedures (that we will not elaborate) this direct effect for manipulating this person's potassium level can be precisely quantified as an effect size. Because the mean "try to eat bananas" days (1.14) is much greater than the mean "try not to eat bananas" days (0.00), we know the direct effect size would be substantial in this case.

However, one might ask, did the direct control of daily potassium level produce any "spillover" effects onto the dependent variable of interest (depression)? To answer that question, return to Table 9.2 and reorder the *depression* scores on Day 8 through Day 21 according to whether they were "try to eat bananas" or "try not to eat bananas" days. Mean level of depressive affect on "try to eat bananas" days (i.e., Days 8, 11, 12, 14, 16, 17, and 20) was 4.85, whereas on "try not to eat bananas" days it was 4.71. These means are very close to one another, and one would conclude that having eaten many more bananas on "try to eat bananas" days had no appreciable impact on the person's level of depressive affect. In fact, what little differences there are in depressive affect seem to be in the *wrong* direction. That is, slightly lower levels of depressive affect are found on days when bananas are not consumed. The proper conclusion would be that while the person could volitionally increase her or his intake of potassium, such changes did not produce substantial decreases in depressive affect. However, one does not know exactly why this failure to find a "spillover" effect to depression occurred. For example, it might be that potassium levels in the blood are not related to level of depressive affect; or perhaps this person receives ample amounts of potassium from other food sources and increased consumption of bananas is unnecessary; and so forth.

Let us now consider the similar questions and conduct similar analyses on the "Time spent exercising" and "Time spent with positive people" variables. Table 9.3 reveals that the subject was able to exert direct volitional control over both the amount of time the subject exercised (65.7 minutes for "try to exercise" days versus 15.7 minutes for "try not to exercise" days) and the amount of time spent with positive people (272 minutes for "spend time" days versus 108 minutes for "spend little time" days). However, unlike the circumstance where we found no spillover effects of potassium levels influencing depression, the mean depression levels reported in Table 9.3 suggest rather substantial spillover effects (in the predicted direction) on levels of depression when both exercise and time spent with positive people are volitionally manipulated.

Table 9.3

Days	Exercise Means	Depression Means
Try to Exercise	65.7	2.7
Try Not to Exercise	15.7	6.8

Days	Time with Positive People Means	Depression Means
Spend Time with Positive People	272	3.7
Spend Little Time with Positive People	108	6.8

Remember, these data are hypothetical. This demonstration was undertaken to show you exactly how complex self-experiments, where one attempts to volitionally control target constructs (e.g., depression, drinking, exercising) both directly and indirectly, can be conducted and the data analyzed. I urge you to initiate a self-experiment wherein you consider your degree of both direct and indirect volitional control over some domain of your life. The procedures described herein can serve as a general model for multi-factor self-experiments in a wide range of domains. For example, Study 3 of Howard and Conway (1986) studied shy Notre Dame students' ability to increase the amount of time they spent in social interactions with members of the opposite sex. If instead of measuring level of depressive affect in Table 9.2 you measured the amount of time you engaged in social conversations, and replaced the three nonagentic factors (i.e., potassium, exercise, positive people) with other factors (e.g., initiate conversations ["try to initiate" days versus "socialize as you normally would" days]; amount of time spent in social places ["try to go to social places" days versus "go where you normally would" days]; positive self-statements ["make frequent positive self-statements" days versus "conduct normal self-talk" days]), you could then follow each of the procedures detailed above to conduct and analyze your ability to directly and indirectly control your time spent socializing. Our experience is that people generally become confused when given more than three instructions to follow per day, so more complex studies might prove unfeasible. Generally speaking, simpler self-experiments (such as the example found in Chapter 8) work better. The lone drawback to very simple experiments of self-determination is that they hide in the background the numerous nonagentic factors (as depicted in Figure 4.3) that generally play some role in our actions. Thus, while simple experiments (of both the first-person and third-person variety) can depict accurate pictures of relationships among variables in our lives, of necessity these pictures cannot be complete, as other important causal factors are left unmeasured and therefore unavailable for analysis.

Students often report that they are surprised by what they learn about themselves through the writing of their autobiography. Similarly, the results of self-experiments are often both surprising (in some ways) and unsurprising (in other ways). A very important realization that students often come to through their self-experiments is that there are no divinely ordained, unchangeable sets of relationships among variables that must emerge from their self-experiment. Because they know everything about the design and analysis of their self-experiment, students can "see" relationships among these variables strengthening and weakening day by day. Students then quickly realize that they are often able to "make or break" these relationships among variables in their lives—if they want to do so. This is a remarkable discovery! It would be like the moon "realizing" that it generally travels along the path determined by all the gravitational forces acting upon it, but that it is also able to act in opposition to (or without regard to) gravity's dictates. But powers that would be extraordinary for the moon (such as self-determination and consciousness) are commonplace for human beings. The important insight here is that our actions are not completely determined by the nonagentic forces at work upon us. We play an important agentic role in the genesis of our actions (i.e., there is some degree of freedom of the will, active agency, self-determination).

And lest there be any doubt in anyone's mind, I do *not* believe that the moon is either conscious or an active agent. I simply used the moon story as a rhetorical device to show why a completely mechanistic (and third-person) analysis—while appropriate for understanding the moon's behavior—simply will not adequately appreciate human behavior. The moon is like a rudderless ship—the helpless pawn to the nonagentic, gravitational influences acting upon it. Humans are like piloted ships—whose life-courses are purposely charted out and self-determined, but still influenced by the nonagentic, human equivalents of winds and tides.

An undergraduate turned in a paper reporting the self-experiment described below.

EXPERIMENT AND IMPROVE YOURSELF

Continuous self-improvement is the key to success. After reading Chapter 9 of Dr. Howard's manuscript, I was inspired to perform my own self-experiment in imitation of his hypothetical study. I chose eating fruit and doing something nice for other people as the causal factors that might improve my mood. For the first seven days (Baseline) I simply acted normally, eating and going out of my way for others as I usually would. I also rated myself each day on the degree of my mood (10 = great mood, 1 = very depressed). I then flipped a coin to determine whether or not, for the next fourteen days, I would consciously try to increase each factor for that particular day. Beginning with Day 8, for example, the coin came up tails for both fruit and being nice, so I continued with my normal routine. However, on the days on which the coin came up heads, I made a special effort to eat a piece of fruit or do a good deed as was applicable.

Each night of this study, I recorded the amount of fruit I had eaten that day, the number of times I had done nice things for people, and the level of my mood that day. In order to protect myself from being considered a "scrooge," I would like to clarify that, in rating myself (from 0 to 100) on the level of charitable works that I did, I only considered those that required special effort and are not done on a regular basis. For instance, on Day 16 I rated myself at 70 because I made dinner for a friend who was celebrating her second year off chemotherapy. In contrast, I gave myself a 10 on Day 14 when I simply helped a secretary at work carry some boxes to her car.

At the outset of the experiment, I was confident that there would be a tremendous improvement in my overall attitude as a result of eating fruit and performing good works. Although there was only a slight improvement in my mood (4.43 average during the baseline period, compared to 5.14 in the two trial weeks), improvement was obvious on each of the two controlled variables. The average amount of fruit I ate increased from .14 to 1.07, and the magnitude of good works I did jumped ten points (from 5.71 to 15.71).

Intervention Days

Baseline average	8	9	10	11	12	13	14	15	16	17	18	19	20	21	Intr. avg.
Positive Mood 4.43	3	5	4	6	5	9	7	3	8	5	2	7	5	4	5.14
Good Deed 5.71	0	20	0	10	0	50	10	0	70	0	0	60	0	0	15.71
	N	T	N	N	N	T	T	N	T	N	N	T	N	N	
Fruit .14	0	0	1	2	1	1	3	1	0	2	0	1	2	1	1.07
	N	N	T	T	N	T	T	T	N	T.	N	T	T	T	

N = act normally (Days when the coin came up tails)
T = try to increase (Days when the coin came up heads)

I think that these changes definitely influenced my attitudes as I have made a more conscious effort to continue the two activities since the end of the experiment. For the past two weeks, I have found myself choosing fruit as part of my meals and being more considerate of others more often than before. Although I am not certain that I will be able to continue these behaviors, their effect so far has been positive and I hope that they will become part of my daily routine.

TEACHER'S REPLY TO "EXPERIMENT AND IMPROVE YOURSELF"

You did a pretty good job in conducting and writing up your self-experiment. I'm simply going to suggest a different analysis. As it turns out, your data are even more exciting and revealing than you realized. Your baseline averages looked fine to me, but it is a bit misleading to simply compare the intervention data for good deeds and for fruit with the corresponding baseline averages. This is because on many of those intervention days you were simply "acting normally" (i.e., not consciously trying to improve). If you look back in Chapter 8, you'll see that your intervention data should have been sorted slightly differently:

									Average
Increase									
good deeds:	20	50	10	70	60				42.00
(Positive mood):	(5)	(9)	(7)	(8)	(7)				(7.2)
Act normally:	0	0	10	0	0	0	0	0	0	1.11
(Positive mood):	(3)	(4)	(6)	(5)	(3)	(5)	(2)	(5)	(4)	(4.11)
Try to eat fruit:	1	2	1	3	1	2	1	2	1	1.56
(Positive mood):	(4)	(6)	(9)	(7)	(3)	(5)	(7)	(5)	(4)	(5.55)
Act normally:	0	0	1	0	0					.20
(Positive mood):	(3)	(5)	(5)	(8)	(2)					(4.60)

I've grouped data for the five days when you were trying to do good deeds on the top line. Immediately below are the mood ratings on those days in parentheses. Below these data are the nine days when you were following the coin's direction to "act normally" with respect to good deeds. Your mood ratings on these nine days are found below in parentheses also.

You had fantastic control over your good deeds (Average of 42.00 on "try to increase days" versus an average of only 1.11 on "act normally" days). This control over good deeds "spilled over" nicely to your mood (Average of 7.2 on "try to" days versus an average of 4.11 on "act normal" days). So taking part in good deeds had the hoped-for effect of improving your mood—not to mention the effect it probably had on the mood of the recipients of your kindnesses. What about the effect of fruit on your mood?

The bottom two panels of data present the number of pieces of fruit eaten on "try to" days (top lines, nine days) and the number of pieces of fruit consumed on "act normal" days (bottom lines, five days). The mood ratings for each day can be found (in parenthesis) below the fruit consumed. You were able to control the number of pieces of fruit consumed nicely (Average of 1.56 pieces on "try to" days versus an average of .20 pieces on "act normal" days). However, the number of pieces of fruit eaten did not appear to effect your mood very much (Mood average of 5.55 on "try to" days versus 4.60 on "act normal" days). Thus, while eating fruit might be good for your health in general, it didn't appear to effect your mood very much.

The only other point I'd make is that in each comparison of "try to" with "act normally" you had nine data points to compare with five data points. This situation is not ideal. For a fourteen-day intervention period, comparing seven days with seven other days would have been ideal. Thus, in setting up your study, for the good deeds assignment, when the coin came up as "act normally" on day #18, that put seven days in that condition. I would have automatically put the last three days in the "try to" condition. Thus, each condition would have had data for seven days. Similarly, when day #19 was assigned to the "try to" eat fruit condition, the remaining two days would have automatically designated "act normally," yielding two groups of seven days each.

You conducted a good study and obtained very interesting results. Keep doing those good deeds—both for your own sake and for the sake of others. While eating fruit is probably good for health reasons, it doesn't appear to be a very effective way to improve your mood—at least not as seen in these data.

The third part of this book will consider teleographies. Just as first-person self-experiments demonstrate how we "make or unmake" relationships among variables in our present behavior, a teleography is a strategy for "plotting a course" for the rest of our lives. Past experiences (as revealed in our autobiographies), current forces and factors acting upon us (as studied in self-experiments), and the slings and arrows of outrageous fortune (e.g., winning the lottery, getting hit by a bus, meeting your ideal mate, nuclear holocaust) will exert their never-so-little influences upon the remainder of our lives. However, it is one's imagined possible future (one's heart's desire, or one's dream) that all of us strive daily to create, that will be most responsible for reaching the shores upon which our lives eventually land. A good teleography can, I believe, help you to successfully pilot the course of your life.

CHAPTER 10
THANK GOD! PSYCHOLOGY IS A "SOFT" SCIENCE!

This chapter finishes the section on self-experiments. It does so by arguing for the absolute necessity that agency (or will, or self-determination, or personal causation) be included in psychological research, if we hope to achieve adequate explanations of human action. Parts of the present chapter might be tough-sledding for readers just beginning their study of psychology and/or readers who know little about philosophy of science. This chapter is a more technical follow-up to issues raised in Chapter 4, regarding the model of human nature found in Figure 4.3. However, not understanding parts of this essay will in no way lessen your understanding of the remainder of this book, as the final part of this book involves probing a fictional writing style called teleography. Thus, one should only read this chapter as closely and carefully as your background and interests allow. So let's begin.

Larry Hedges (1987) wrote an important and provocative article on the empirical cumulativeness of research in psychology. The article's title asks rhetorically, "How hard is hard science; how soft is soft science?" Given the measure of cumulativeness that Hedges employs, and the patterns in his data, psychology seems to be a cumulative enterprise indeed, and in this respect not unlike the "hard" physical sciences. But Hedges' point is subtle, and easily misinterpreted. For example, a leading statistician claims that, "... psychologists feel that our science has little power, even though Hedges has shown that our research studies produce the same size relationships that physics does" (Gorsuch, 1991, p. 1090). While Hedges does show that programs of psychological research can be as empirically cumulative as the physical sciences, he does *not* show (nor does he claim) that psychological research produces the same size relationships that physics does.

Hedges' points involve the replicability of effect size estimates, which is very different from the consideration of the magnitude of those effect sizes. Analogously, imagine two bowlers who each bowl five games. Bowler A obtains the following five scores 50, 50, 50, 50, 50. Bowler B scores 240, 220, 200, 180, 160. Who is the more reliable bowler? Who is the better bowler?

That we obtain different answers to these two questions does not pose a problem for our understanding of bowling. Bowler A is more consistent, while Bowler B is a better bowler. But consistency in estimating effects *does* represent an important value in science, and this is why Hedges is correct in claiming that it is significant that the reliability of psychological findings seems to approximate those of the physical sciences. Given the structure of the game of bowling, it is always preferable to obtain the highest scores possible. The same can*not* be said of all sciences. The question of the magnitude of effect sizes found in psychological research versus the physical sciences turns out to be a far more thorny issue than one would first imagine.

An important goal of the physical sciences is to predict and/or control the behavior of their objects of investigation (e.g., orbiting planets, combining chemicals) as close to perfectly as possible. Thus, if a theory of gravitational attraction (along with a calculational procedure that utilizes Newton's law of an inverse squared relationship that employs distance and mass) yields close to perfect prediction of planetary motions, we take this as evidence of the "hardness" or maturity of that discipline. On the other hand, if another theory only achieves about a 50 percent rate of prediction of planetary motion, one might see that theoretical explanation as inferior (i.e., "softer"). Greater skill in prediction in the physical sciences is like obtaining higher bowling scores. In both cases more is better. In fact, some philosophers of science (e.g., Hempel, 1965) have gone so far as to claim that there is a symmetry between prediction and explanation—the greater the degree of prediction, the better the theoretical explanation. While other epistemic criteria (fertility, internal coherence, external consistency and unifying power) are also invoked in the task of theory choice (Howard, 1985; Kuhn, 1977; McMullin, 1983), predictive accuracy is still the paramount criterion. If the "more is better" rule of thumb were true for psychological research, the question of whether psychology is as "hard" a discipline as physics could easily be answered with a resounding "no." Apart from a few individuals who misunderstand that Hedges' (1987) work deals with the consistency of effect sizes rather than the magnitude of predictive accuracy, I know of no one who seriously suggests that psychology's ability to predict and/or control human behavior is in any way comparable to the levels of predictive accuracy achieved in the physical sciences.

Meehl (1978) claims our use of group mean difference statistics results from psychology's lack of powerful *invisible hand theories* that allow for precise prediction.

> In my modern physics text, I am unable to find one single test of statistical significance. What happens instead is that the physicist has a sufficiently powerful invisible hand theory that enables him to generate an expected curve for his experimental results. He plots the observed points, looks at the agreement, and comments that 'the results are in reasonably good accord with theory.' Moral: *It is always more valuable to show approximate agreement of observations with a theoretically predicted numerical point value, rank order, or function form, than it is to compute a 'precise probability' that something merely differs from something else.* (Meehl, 1978, p. 825)

Cohen (1977) makes a similar point in a discussion of the use of proportion of variance estimates.

> The only difficulty arising from the use of PV [proportion of variance] measures lies in the fact that in many, perhaps most, of the areas of behavioral science, they turn out to be so small! For example, workers in personality-social psychology, both pure and applied (i.e., clinical, education, personnel), normally encounter correlation coefficients above the .50–.60 range only when the correlations are measurement reliability coefficients. In PV terms, this *effective upper limit implies something of the order of one-quarter or one-third of variance accounted for.* The fact is that the state of development of much of behavioral science is such that not very much variance in the dependent variable is predictable. This is essentially merely another way of stating the obvious: that the behavioral sciences collectively are not as far advanced as the physical sciences. (Cohen, 1977, p. 78 italics added)

Finally, Maxwell and Delaney (1990) note how our failures in predictive accuracy have conditioned us to accept nonspecific predictions from our theories.

> Naturally, theories differ in how well they achieve the desiderata of good theories regarding predictions—that is, they differ in how easily empirical predictions can be derived and in the range and specificity of these predictions. Unfortunately, psychological theories, particularly in recent years, tend to be very restricted in scope. And, unlike physics, the predictions that psychological theories do make are typically of a nonspecific form (the groups will differ) rather than being point predictions (the light rays will bend by x degrees as they go past the sun). (Maxwell & Delaney, 1990, p. 16)

Hedges (1987) shows that psychology might be considered a "hard" scientific discipline because the cumulativeness of our findings (i.e., the reliability of effect size estimates) appears to be comparable to the degree of cumulativeness found in the physical sciences. But the current state of psychological theorizing (in contrast to physical sciences) is such that we are able to predict *only a small fraction of human behavior in real-world settings*. From this perspective, psychology would seem to be a "soft" science. But keep in mind that all of the theoretical predictions discussed thus far involved the identification of *nonagentic, causal influences* acting upon the subject matter. Gravity attracts planets as peer pressure pushes adolescents. Scientific theories generally postulate the existence of nonagentic theoretical mechanisms (i.e., gravity, peer pressure, genetic endowments, personality traits, environmental presses, etc.) that allow for the prediction (*by the scientist*) of the behavior of the subject matter. If a "hard" science is one wherein scientists possess sufficiently strong theories that enable them to exhibit close to perfect prediction and/or control, then psychology appears to be a "soft" science. But several theoreticians (Harré, 1984; Harré & Secord, 1972; Howard, 1984) maintain that it would have been an absolute disaster had psychology actually achieved the levels of predictive accuracy (in human behavior) that are found in the physical sciences, because to do so might signal that humans are not free agents with some degree of ability to self-determine their actions.

Cohen's effective upper limit of prediction in real-world settings, which appears to be "something of the order of one-quarter or one-third of variance accounted for," is disappointingly small *only if one assumes* that a mature science of human behavior should allow for prediction (by the scientist) of 100 percent of the variance in human action. Why would anyone make such an assumption? Because that is precisely the goal that the physical sciences virtually achieve in many of their empirical efforts. Why should a psychological theoretician or researcher settle for anything less than that lofty ambition? Because there is good reason to believe that human beings are active agents with some degree of ability to self-determine their actions. To the extent that humans possess the power of self-determination, scientists will only predict a fraction (roughly, 1.0 minus the proportion of variance due to self-determination) of human behavior as an ultimate scientific ambition. Thus, Cohen's (1977) effective upper limit of prediction of 25 to 33 percent would not be at all disappointing if the circumstance were, for example, that self-determination accounted for 60 to 70 percent of the variance in a particular domain of human action.

Had nonagentic, psychological theories actually achieved the physical scientists' ambition, to predict successfully or control close to 100 percent of human behavior, there would have been no room left for self-determination (or the exercise of will) in the genesis of human action. Humans might have been found to be nothing more than pawns to nonagentic influences, as were orbiting planets, combining chemicals, evolving species, and the like. But psychology's inability to approach the levels of experimental predictive accuracy of the physical sciences (which in the eyes of some makes psychology look "soft") also suggests the possibility of a new capacity (or power, or ability) in humans to determine their own actions (all other nonagentic influences being equal).

Subsequent research has demonstrated that the causal power of self-determination (independent of all nonagentic, causal influences) in the formation of human action is great (Howard & Conway, 1986; Howard, Curtin, & Johnson, 1991; Howard, DiGangi & Johnson, 1988; Howard & Myers, 1990; Howard, Myers, & Curtin, 1991). We are now in a position to study how agentic self-determination achieves its effects in a world of nonagentic causal influences. This comprehensive science of human action (that utilizes both agentic and nonagentic predictors) has already demonstrated levels of predictive accuracy that far exceed Cohen's (1977) effective upper limit of prediction. Such empirical demonstrations suggest that psychologists may soon achieve heretofore unrealized levels of predictive accuracy to go along with the empirical cumulativeness suggested by Hedges' (1987) work. If one's definition of a "hard science" demands close to perfect prediction or control solely via nonagentic, causal influences, then perhaps psychology is doomed to be a "soft" science. Instead psychology should adopt a more comprehensive (and reasonable) definition of predictive accuracy—one that will appreciate agentic and nonagentic factors in tandem.

Hedges (1987) shows that empirical cumulativeness is important in any science. He then addresses another form of cumulativeness, noting that, "One might also argue that theoretical cumulativeness is really the important issue" (p. 454). What, then, keeps psychology from demonstrating theoretical cumulativeness? Its nonagentic theories appear to possess empirical cumulativeness, but weak levels of predictive accuracy. Recent research suggests that comprehensive theories of human action (employing both self-determination and nonagentic influences) yield superior levels of predictive accuracy of human behavior. Our hope is that such comprehensive theories will, in time, also yield a more theoretically cumulative psychology. Thank God, we now seem able to understand both the "soft" and "hard" aspects of humans—from both first-person and third-person scientific perspectives. Scientific psychology now appears to be on the verge of a complete understanding of human nature in all its richness and complexity.

Reader: Excuse me, George, did you say it would have been a disaster if psychologists had developed powerful theories of human behavior that predicted and/or controlled human actions to the degree that the natural sciences have achieved that scientific ambition with their subject matters?

George: Yes, it would have been a disaster if that level of control had been achieved solely through nonagentic theories—as is the case in the physical sciences. If psychologists had achieved extremely high levels of predictive accuracy in experiments, then people like Skinner (1971) would have been correct in claiming that concepts like freedom and human dignity were merely illusions and thus should be banished by a science of human behavior. But the necessary levels of such predictive accuracy in real-world human behavior were never approached by the behavioral sciences. Rather, the studies of self-determination demonstrate a high level of agency that is independent of any nonagentic causal influence. Because self-determination is a fact, human freedom and dignity are again safe from a completely adequate mechanistic explanation of human action.

PART III
TELEOGRAPHIES

By now you've noticed that I enjoy experimenting with unusual writing styles. I find a steady diet of standard academic prose unappealing. An innovative writing style (e.g., autobiography, fiction about issues in science) is better able to hold my attention. Further, I find myself thinking more daring and provocative thoughts when I couch them in nontraditional writing styles. Others might not need an assist from a writing style to be original, but I find it difficult to think creatively when I'm trapped in traditional writing styles. The final part of this book will suggest yet another nontraditional literary style called a teleography.

As we begin the final part of this book, we might take a moment to reflect upon its structure and (dis)organization. Part I focused upon autobiographies—a technique for appreciating one's past. Through autobiographical reflection each of us can learn how we became the sort of person that we now are. The second third of this book focused upon self-experiments—a first-person technique for discovering the causal force of our agency, while also discovering how our present circumstances cause us to act in the manner that we do. The final one-third of this text will study teleographies—an imaginative technique wherein possibly true stories about one's future are constructed in the hope that the future that actually occurs might come to resemble these hoped-for stories. Metaphorically, a teleography is like a climber's grappling hook. The hook is thrown to a point higher on the mountain that the climber hopes to scale. Once secured on some distant point, the grappling hook serves as an anchor that the climber uses to close the distance on her or his desired goal. Similarly, I would like you to write a creative fiction about the future of your life—that's a teleography. Some people focus only a few years out in their teleographies (as you'll soon see in "Ecology and me" and "My wife"). Other writers extend their horizon to the imagined end of their lives—and beyond (see "Two steps forward, one step backward").

CHAPTER 11
IMAGINE!

Why did George Orwell write the futuristic novel 1984 (Orwell, 1949)? Orwell painted a worst-case scenario in extrapolating several trends that he saw in society at that time. Why does one tell a horrific tale of the future? Undoubtedly, it is done to jolt readers into the realization that unless determined action is taken in the present, the future could be nightmarish. Not only is this an important fictional style, the genre is growing in importance as a strategy for scientists concerned about the future of our planet (e.g., State of the world: 1991 by Lester R. Brown, 1991). Such studies extrapolate present trends in an array of issues of global ecology (e.g., pollution, population growth, ozone depletion, non-renewable energy use, food production, deforestation, desertification) and demonstrate precisely when (at current rates) the planet will become uninhabitable due to each of (and a combination of) these problems. Such objective, dispassionate predictions of apocalyptic consequences represent (in my opinion) a related rhetorical style to the 1984-type futuristic, fictional, horror tale. But these State of the world projections (Brown, 1991) are not fictional—they dramatize the reality that we are not now a sustainable global society. As these trends become more compelling with each passing year, the chances grow slimmer that humanity will exert the sorts of herculean efforts necessary to reverse the trends, in order to avert catastrophe. Obviously, we will all watch in horror as each of these particular dramas play themselves out over the next three or four decades. Recalling the 1960s slogan, "If you are not part of the solution, then you are part of the problem," one might wonder what positive role (if any) psychology is playing in this worldwide, ecological drama.

Telling horror stories of the future represents a strategy that first seeks to identify a value with which we can all agree—such as a habitable world where there is still a place for human dignity. The futurists then point to current trends which, if sustained, seriously endanger that value. Therein lies the horror—a future devoid of a current "good" (such as living space, sufficient nourishment, clean air, human freedom, etc.). But before saying more about psychology and problems of world ecology, I should remind you that activist scholarship can occur in many different domains. All one need do is to identify a domain where there is disrespect of important human values (e.g., instances of sexism, racism, economic repression, etc.) and one has fertile soil for the seeds of activist scholarship.

BETWEEN NOW AND THE TWENTY-FIRST CENTURY: A TELEOGRAPHY FOR COUNSELING PSYCHOLOGY

It is difficult to get oneself to write grandiosely, as it goes against one's natural inclination toward modesty and conservatism. But since fantasy teleographies are meant to spur us to action, one is encouraged to aim high in his or her teleography. Then even near misses could produce marvelous results.

"Ecology and me" was my first published teleography. It was part of an invited paper commissioned to celebrate the centennial of the American Psychological Association that was to deal with the future of counseling psychology (Howard, 1992a).

ECOLOGY AND ME

I fire off a draft of the centennial article to the editors in early December 1991. After wrapping up a tough semester, my family and I have a great Christmas vacation—but my mind keeps returning to the coming ecological catastrophes, the fate of lifeboat earth, and counseling psychology's role in this life-and-death drama. I return to South Bend on January 3, 1992, back-burner all my writing commitments, and push forward my thinking on the world's ecological mess. The resulting essay, entitled "On a certain blindness in human beings: Psychology and world overpopulation," gets published. In subsequent interactions I become aware of an enormous groundswell of passion among counseling psychologists for improving the planet's status in many ecological domains (e.g., global warming, deforestation, ozone depletion, erosion and desertification, wars for scarce natural resources such as water, famine and starvation) by controlling a common cause of these difficulties—overpopulation. A figure from that essay (Figure 11.1) startles many psychologists to the enormity of our population problem.

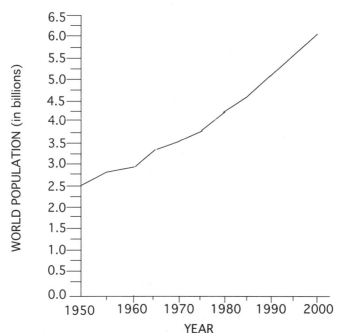

FIGURE 11.1. World population at five-year intervals from 1950 to 1990 with a projection for the year 2000 (Data are from United Nations Demographic Yearbook, United Nations, 1989, p. 117)

Note that the origin of Figure 11.1 represents an absolute zero value for world population, but not for time, as it required perhaps a million years of growth for the world's population to reach 2.515 billion in 1950. The average year of birth of my generation—the Baby Boomers—is about 1950. Thus, the world population had doubled by the time the "typical Baby Boomer" had reached the age of thirty-seven (in 1987), and at least another 1.2 billion person increase will have occurred before this hypothetical boomer turns fifty years old—that is, unless the human race is overtaken by catastrophic events.

Perhaps you feel that I've become a bit melodramatic and that I am, like Chicken Little, running around yelling that "the sky is falling." Perhaps. But before dismissing the gravity of the threat of overpopulation, take a step back to view population trends in larger perspective. Rather than the thirty-year span in Figure 11.1, consider the 1,025 year span in Figure 11.2. The threat is clear and present.

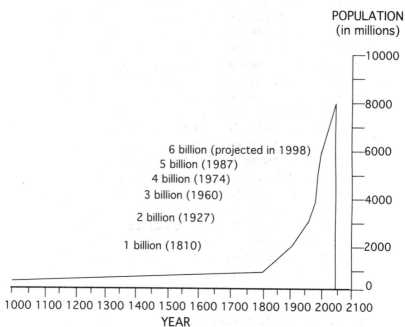

FIGURE 11.2. World Population 1000 AD to 2025 AD (Data are from Population Reference Bureau, 1989).

A person on the East coast points out that our religious and political institutions both actively and passively stand in the way of progress in curbing world population growth. She drafts model letters to government and religious leaders, and sends these models to hundreds of counseling psychologists. Over fifty percent of us send letters to our representatives. For my political leader, I choose United States Congressman Tim Roemer:

Dear Congressman Roemer:
I am a 43-year-old professor of psychology at Notre Dame who is so apolitical that I have never had any contact with a politician in my life. But my concern over the world population crisis has grown so acute that I must break my self-imposed silence. I address my thoughts to you, as our South Bend branch of Planned Parenthood claims that among my elected officials you are the only one who will give me a fair hearing. I have enclosed a paper exhorting psychologists to awaken to the apocalyptic threat of world overpopu-

lation, which is a common cause that contributes to all the other ecological problems we now face.

I urge you to endorse the principle that abortion and population control must be kept as completely separate issues. While reasonable people can hold opposing views on the morality of abortion, world overpopulation represents a clear and present threat to all humans. The Reagan/Bush abandonment of world leadership on population control because of their opposition to abortion demonstrates the myopia of their political vision, and constitutes a colossal disservice to humanity. In my judgment, world overpopulation will be the central issue of the twenty-first century. I urge you to consider becoming the political voice that leads a thirty-year campaign to stabilize world population. Unlike other issues you face, world demographic trends will not be altered without sustained efforts over decades—not years. This issue will not go away with time and inattention. Failure to arrest current population trends *dooms* our world to a series of ecological catastrophes (such as, global warming, nonrenewable resource depletion, wars over resources such as water, desertification, famine, etc.). The only gift that we *must* give to our children is a habitable world. But no one in our country seems to possess the vision, the political position, and the time required to begin the crusade against the effects of a million years of human evolution (since the only goals of evolution are adaptation and reproductive efficiency). Will you consider championing sanity, and offer a ray of hope to those of us who fear we may have already caught a glimpse of our children's fate?

My apologies for becoming melodramatic at times in my plea. But I'm enough of a psychologist to know that I have to catch your imagination, as much as your mind, to stand any chance of tempting you to seriously consider something greater than a perfunctory response to my concerns. I hope you will give the greater challenge, that you spearhead our government's efforts in this domain, your serious attention.

Sincerely,

My choice of a religious leader is easy: Father Edward Malloy, C.S.C., President, University of Notre Dame.

Dear Monk:
I'm sending along an essay on psychology and world overpopulation that you may find of interest. There are several reasons that you may choose to read it. First, it's as close to your interests as an ethicist as anything I do. Second, it takes me into topics (e.g., contraception, abortion) about which the Catholic church and Notre Dame care. Third, I hope to show that psychology has something to offer to issues of global ecology. Fourth, I hope you will agree with me that abortion and population control ought to be kept completely separate issues. And finally, since you command large audiences in the church and in higher education, I hope to encourage you to make responsible population practices an even larger part of your message.

Thanks for your attention. I think the essay makes good airplane or bedtime reading. The paper is directed to psychologists, and hopes to show specific ways in which their efforts can make a difference in what will likely be our most difficult problem of the twenty-first century—world overpopulation. I'm sorry I couldn't be a bit more hopeful in the essay, but my research suggests that the situation is far grimmer than I'd imagined.

Warmly,

Father Malloy responds enthusiastically, but I never receive a reply from Congressman Roemer. But many other counseling psychologists receive enthusiastic replies from their elected representatives. Heartened by this response, a group of counseling psychologists from the University of Maryland, in conjunction with the Worldwatch Institute (located in Washington, D.C.), sponsor a day-long seminar on the politics of population control that is attended by six U.S. senators and twenty-three members of the House of Representatives. The unanimous conclusion of the seminar is that abortion and population control must be kept as separate issues. Identical bills are introduced in both houses of Congress by this coalition that quickly result in the dismantling of the "Mexico City Policy." This Reagan-Bush policy had (for seven years) forged a linkage between abortion and population control in our foreign policy—and galvanized the link with dollar bills. The policy states that any country that supports abortion would no longer receive AID (Aid for International Development) money from the United States. AID money is used to support family planning initiatives throughout the world. Thus, in an attempt to force our abortion agenda upon other countries, our government undermined other countries' self-initiated efforts to deal with their own population explosions. But, thanks in part to the efforts of a group of counseling psychologists, that Kaffkaesque foreign policy has now been reversed.

In the June 1992 Catholic Conference of Bishops, the anti-abortion position is elevated to the conference's top political issue. Realizing their untenable position, the pro-choice bishops work to obtain a separation between the abortion and population control issues. In his speech welcoming the bishops to the conference at Notre Dame, Father Malloy drops the bombshell that refocuses the entire conference—Malloy suggests that in the face of terrifying world overpopulation, to oppose abortion, while remaining unmoved on serious measures of population control, constitutes a moral outrage. After extensive turmoil and debate, the conference urges Rome to rethink its prohibitive stance on contraception in light of the clear and present threat of world overpopulation.

Many other local, national, and international movements toward responsible reproductive practices are pushed forward in part through the efforts of thousands of counseling psychologists. But in the end, counseling psychologists' greatest impact in this crusade for ecological sanity results from the one-on-one changes in attitudes of their clients, students, colleagues, families, and friends. Once sensitized to the population problem, counseling psychologists use their considerable listening skills and powers of persuasion to influence the attitudes of millions of citizens. Counseling psychologists again play important behind-the-scenes roles in this sea-change in public consciousness.

Will this fantasy become true? Since I possess no crystal ball, it surely will not become completely true. But by the time you read the fantasy, parts (perhaps the majority) of it will have already become fact. But unless someone first dreams it—and then works diligently in the service of that dream—little or none of what is contained in the fantasy will become real.

The next teleography is by a Notre Dame sophomore who reflects upon the role that a mate will play as a most significant coauthor of his life story.

MY WIFE
Andrew Deitch

Things are always foggiest when I first open my eyes and try to comprehend the world around me. I can neither see the alarm clock on my bedside table nor understand why one should be there at all. There is a cloud of grey mist over my eyes and my mind. A faint smell of cedar confuses me and the soft plaid paper on the wall seems foreign. Gradually however, as I squint to see the clock through my 20/400 vision, things come back to me. I recall that the aroma of cedar comes from a chest at the foot of the bed which was a wedding present to my wife from my mother. I recognize the wallpaper as the pattern which my wife picked out and had hung regardless of the fact that I liked the stripe pattern. I remember in quiet succession everything about my life and no longer feel like an intruder to the realm of consciousness. Rather, I feel like a thirty-four–year–old husband/father of three, family practitioner who lives in a modest house in a modest town and derives a certain perverse pleasure from watching my favorite baseball team lose night after night. I would rather watch them win, but some things just aren't possible.

"Sweetheart, you'd better hurry. You have the clinic this morning at 8:30," whispered a soft voice in my ear.

Suddenly I remembered my wife sleeping next to me; my wife of ten years who has loved me through my struggles with Physiology in medical school and my difficulties in setting up practice; my wife who has always been a constant in my life. Rolling over on my side I see the woman whom I met so many years ago at a New Year's Eve party and remember how she broke the table she was standing on to see the ball drop, falling on top of me. Funny how chance, or just bad furniture, throws people together sometimes.

Looking at her with her slept-on blond hair and reddened morning face, I realize that I didn't marry this woman for her startling good looks. This is not to say that my wife Lucie (maiden name is Manette) is a Broom Hilda look-alike. It is only to say that it was her soul and mind that first caught me, rather than her hips or bust. It has always been her ability to love and to express that love that has warmed me and made me feel safe. Her somewhat curly blond hair, light blue-grey eyes, button nose, and soft smile have taken on this quality of commitment over the years and now when I look at them I am aware that this woman represents all that I want in a loving relationship. I am likewise aware of the fact that I have fifty minutes to get to the courthouse for free clinic.

"Gotta go, hon. Can't be late for court," I joke as I hurry to the bathroom.

I jump in the shower and grit my teeth until the ice cold water running over my shoulders warms up. There should be a name for people who are too foolish to check the temperature of the shower before they jump in; hydrofools, perhaps. While I contemplate this I can see through the steamed glass that Lucie has a suit set out for me on the dressing stand. This is typical and one of the reasons that I love my wife so much. She has a view of love and of relationships that matches my own that is visible when she sets out my clothes or whips up a bowl of shredded wheat on my way out the door. It has nothing to do with white slavery or chauvinism because I put the kids to bed and do the dishes when she is harried after a rough PTA meeting. Rather, it has to do with seeing love and the marriage relationship as one of loyalty and giving.

The other day I read a headline in a checkout line which read, "Woman files for divorce after hubby loses job. . ." Pretty mundane for the checkout line, I thought. Upon closer inspection, though, I saw, ". . . and marries Bigfoot." The disturbing realization came to me, in that aisle, that these days many people marry for gain and self-promotion instead of for love. My wife married to become one with her husband and while that may sound corny it is how she looks at it. She cares deeply for her marriage and does not see divorce as a possibility. I found this refreshing when I met her and still do today. She would no more divorce me after a failed promotion than she would. . . well, marry Bigfoot. Her gentle, constant love even in the heat of an argument is the reason that Lucie means the world to me.

I put on my suit and then changed my tie because no matter how loving and loyal Lucie is she can't match a tie to save her life. Halfway down the stairs I hear what sounds like a demolition derby coming from the kitchen. Entering the room I find that it's only Lucie and our three kids and not several beat-up Ford Mustangs making all the noise. The TV blares *Tom and Jerry* for all of the neighbors to hear, Josh and Zack are flipping corn flakes at each other and Abby, the youngest, simply sits in her highchair and screams. Maybe she doesn't like this episode of *Tom and Jerry*. Lucie is obviously overmatched. Hoping to remedy the problem I pick up the remote to the TV and hit the button.

Click!

Suddenly Lucie is gone and standing in her place is Rosanne Barr. "What the hell is going on here," I demand.

Following a brief comment about her being a domestic

goddess Rosanne answers, "That remote, sweetums. Dinja know it changes who yer married ta?"

As shocking as the concept is I press the button again and I hope Rosanne will turn into someone acceptable, perhaps Bigfoot.

Click! Edith Bunker . . . nah, I can't stand the voice.

Click! Claire Huxtable . . . now this has possibilities, I think.

Quickly my wife Claire whom I've loved dearly for ten years and has loved me in return through the birth of three children gains control of the situation and quiets the madhouse down. She sternly reminds Zack that he is already grounded for driving a ball to deep left field and through the living room window and suggests that it may not be a good idea to get in more trouble. One look at Josh and a simple shake of the finger shuts him up. He knows that mommy can be pretty disagreeable when her finger starts shaking. I'm sure he'll wonder later in life if finger shaking and sharp mood swings are medically connected. She then walks to Abby and soothes her with a couple of clucks and chirps while picking her up and going on with whatever she was doing before the eruption took place.

"You'll be sent to the minor leagues for good if you toss that flake, Zack." She warns as my overzealous son prepares to flick another piece of cereal.

This is what I love about my wife; her ability to love her children more than anything in the world and yet be stern with them. She strikes a perfect balance which lets our children know that they are unconditionally loved and yet their behavior is important to their status in the family and indeed, the world. I think of several of my nurses who complain daily that their children run roughshod over them and complain about their parenting responsibilities. They are afraid to use a stern word or a quick spanking to send a message to their children for fear of conveying a message of a lack of love. After seeing some of their children on the examination table I have decided that some of them could use a spanking or two. Hell, a few of them would probably benefit from a swift kick to the teeth. My wife feels that it is possible, and in fact necessary, to convey a deep sense of worth and love early in life and then to discipline from that foundation of love.

Several weeks ago, for instance, Zack put our cat Snuffy in the dryer to make it fluffier and Claire walked in with the whites to find him and a very dizzy, but fluffy, cat. She knelt on the floor, held Zack's hands, looked him straight in the eye and sternly told him that it was wrong to treat the pets like that and explained that to get the point across she was going to spank him. It was quite evident to Zack that the spanking was not a removal of love but a reminder of the correct way to act. Claire told me about this later when we were settling into bed and I couldn't help laughing about it.

"Did he use fabric softener so Snuffy won't stick to the drapes?" I asked.

"You're sleeping on the couch tonight, Mr. Comedian." She replied,

Luckily there were no crises this morning and after my coffee and bagel I was ready to go to work. I had twenty minutes and offered to take the kids to school. Needless to say Claire didn't argue. I've long had the feeling that taking the kids to school is not one of her cherished activities. As Zack, Josh, and I pile into my Nissan Maxima, Claire waves and gets into her Audi to go to work at the law office.

Wait a minute . . . what about Abby? Who's taking care of her? I realize that for some unknown reason I still have the remote control in my hand so I give it a quick punch.

Click! The Little Mermaid . . . no can do, she wouldn't last long out of her tank.

Click! Mrs. Finch . . . impossible! Atticus was a widower before the book even started.

Click! My mother . . . conjures up images of a blind guy in a toga, but it could work.

With a jolt, my mother, Sue, stops the Audi, waves, and re-enters the house. The door slams behind the wife I have loved for ten years and reflects the eastern sun sharply into my eyes. I chuckle when I remember Sue trying to explain to her college roommate that she really didn't want to enter the work force and wanted to raise a family. The slamming of the door reminds me because her roommate slammed the door on her foot in exasperation. I chuckle again and probably raise a serious question in my children as to the sanity of their father who laughs at nothing.

"You only want to raise a family?" asked her roommie in disbelief. "What a waste! Why don't you join the Peace Corps or become active in NOW?" Sue just shook her head and simply replied that family is more important to her than all of that. Having a family with me was more important to her than a paycheck every week. That is what I love so dearly in my wife; her realization that family is important and that having a parent home to tend bruises, praise accomplishments, and explain beehives is invaluable to a child.

I've received quite a bit of ridicule for my family situation from my colleagues. They accuse me of chaining my wife to the stove and handcuffing her to the blender. They are far from the truth but are entertaining nonetheless so I go along with their humor. In actuality Sue and I sat down before we were married and told each other what was important to us in raising children. I explained that it was important to me to have one parent at home. If the father was better at raising children and the wife pulled in more money then it only seemed logical to me that the man should stay at home. If the roles were reversed it only seemed right for the woman to stay with the children. Sue agreed and said quite plainly that she was looking forward to raising our kids.

Perhaps the most attractive aspect of my wife in this regard is that she doesn't see her workplace in the home as a limiting factor and certainly doesn't raise children by default. She is not a college dropout who only knows how to change diapers and run the vacuum. Quite the contrary, she graduated with honors in Elementary Education and beats the pants off of me whenever we play Trivial Pursuit. Without a doubt, she is my intellectual superior. She simply sees child rearing as the most prestigious and rewarding occupation. Zack bringing home an "A" in phonics after she helped him understand the confusing concept of the schwa, or Josh painting a train in kindergarten after she taught him how to keep paint off his clothes is every bit as rewarding to her as delivering a breech birth is to me. Sue just loves her family and loves working with her children. Either that or she just doesn't trust me to be with them all day unattended.

After a relatively long and tedious day I return home. I missed dinner because I had to cover for my partner and deliver one of his OB's. It's 10:00 and raining heavily out of the dark sky. I have to dash up the walk to the front door where I proceed to drop my keys into the rain gauge on the walk. There must be a law somewhere that prohibits getting home dry in a rainstorm. Anyway, I stumble through my darkened house up to the bedroom with a minimal amount of collisions with hidden end tables. I strip off my coat and the rest of my damp clothes, throw them in the hamper, and climb in bed. My wife is already there and mumbles a sleepy welcome. Reaching over to kiss her goodnight I realize that my wife is still my mother.

"Yipes!" I shout while groping for the remote. "How can I possibly go to sleep with my mother next to me in bed."

Click! Barbara Bush . . . no way! Sleeping with my grandmother is no better than my mother.

Click! Martina Navratilova . . . I think that she is in the wrong bed! Not to mention being on the wrong side.

Click! Christie Brinkley . . . the only word that fits here is goodnight.

"Goodnight."

Things are always foggiest when I first wake up. Everything seems foreign and strange until my brain has a chance to digest all of my surroundings. The cedar smell in the air and the pattern on the wallpaper confuse me until I remember that both are my wife's. I kiss my wife quickly on my way to the shower and then call to her from out of the steam.

"Honey! Could you bring me that remote control on the bedside table?"

"Sorry, Andy, there's nothing there but your class ring. What suit do you want today? I have to go down and get Zack and Josh ready for school and then take Abby to the doctor . . . a doctor that I trust with my little girl . . . at 11:00. By the way, make sure you are home by 8:00 tonight. I've got a surprise for you."

Scratching my head I realize that the remote control was just a dream. My real wife has all of the attributes and plays all of the roles which I love and no channel switching is needed. What a relief! Now I don't have to worry about Rosanne Barr showing up in my kitchen again.

Mr. Deitch is examining the crucial role that his future wife will play in his life. But his writing style resembles pure fiction or even science fiction. It reminds me that while most of us get to live but one life, writers of fiction—those lucky dogs—live many lives.

The choice of a spouse is a very common theme in students' teleographies. And why shouldn't that be the case? Your choice of a spouse could well be the most important decision you'll ever make. In "Dirt roads, jeeps, and slow pacing" another student reflects upon the characteristics she would like in her spouse.

DIRT ROADS, JEEPS, AND SLOW PACING
Joy Germundson

I feel the pressure on the sole of my right foot. It is an annoying throbbing that seems to coincide with the rhythm of my footfalls. It is only a dull ache at first, but as I shift my weight I feel the immediate searing pain that I had feared. I try not to slow my pace, but I find myself wincing with each step. I look to my left and see Christopher roughly three full strides ahead of me. He doesn't look back, but I am convinced that he knows that I'm here. I see the trickle of sweat forming on the pink flesh of my husband's back. I wonder if he can sense my gaze as I let it rest on the number he has pinned to the back of his shirt. Seventy-nine. I look down at my own number, eighty. We worked as a team when we registered this morning, not allowing anyone to get in between us in line. This is the same philosophy that we carry over into our racing. At times this is very difficult because Chris is clearly the better runner. I can usually hold pace in the 5 Ks and 10 Ks we often run, but anything longer and my performance plummets. I simply run out of gas; my endurance is not as developed as his. Today is different. My feet have decided to give out before my lungs. It seems so unfair, as if my body is playing out some cruel joke.

I begin to drop back further and further from Chris as I let other runners pass me. He is at least ten strides ahead of me now. I wonder if he has looked back yet and noticed that I have faded. I decide that he has, but his explanation is that my lungs have given out once again. He can't know the agony that I am really in. Or does he feel it along with me? As another shooting pain spreads through-out the surface of my foot, I imagine that this is what child birth must be like. Then I scold myself for being naïve. I have about as much knowledge of childbirth as Chris does. At forty I resigned myself to the thought that children would never be a part of my life. Chris kept hoping that it still would occur. He joked that if he lost his faith in my getting pregnant, then he would lose his faith in many other things of meaning as well. At the time I secretly believed not father-ing a child was a strong threat to his masculinity, but as with a lot of spontaneous thoughts I decided against sharing that one.

I am walking now. I come down heavily on my left foot so that I can favor my right. The jeep we loaded our gear in seems a million miles away parked in the ramp at the University. I try to compute in my head the number of steps it would take for me to get back to it by my own volition. I give up because the number seems astronomical, and besides Chris has the keys.

The throbbing in my foot is now echoed in my head. It isn't painful, but the pressure seems suddenly overwhelming. I see the green of the grass beside the race route and quickly let my weight fall before my legs can give out on me. My vision clouds and there is a roar in my ears. I lift my hands to my head and grab on, trying to control what surely must be a small explosion commencing from within. I sense rather than see in my mind's eye, orange, and then yellow, and then just black . . .

The path was 8.4 miles. I know because I measured it with my Chevy Nova roughly seven times. I kept hoping that each time I got in the car somehow the distance on the odometer would increase, because it sure felt like more than 8.4 miles. I really enjoyed running this trail because it was gravel and hilly and my legs didn't suffer at the end of every workout. Chris would meet me at about the four-mile mark and pace ahead. He was a solitary stranger at first who despite our lack of knowledge of one another had a very consistent part in my life. He would run up ahead and I would watch him from behind every day. I could tell by his gait that he was a competitive runner and this intrigued me. I had always run for pleasure, never summoning the courage to enter any road races. Here was my chance to meet Chris and take my running to the next level. I stopped him the next day, and it wasn't long before we were running side by side each evening sharing our experiences and insights concerning that day.

We ran like that for months without ever seeing each other outside of our designated exercise time. My initial attraction to him was still there, but it had grown into so much more. He was my friend and I didn't want to risk that by diving into a relationship that neither of us was ready for. He arrived one day at our meeting place on the route with a rose between his teeth. He ran that way, and only after we had finished our jog did he allow me to take it from him. He insisted that I carry it between my teeth so that we could share in the same experience. I was hooked.

The path before us would be rough for many years, so we decided not to get married right away. We lived together in a small, older home pooling our incomes and supporting two spirited yellow labs. He was a high school chemistry teacher at the time, and I was a licensed psychologist working for a small private practice. We were financially stretched and at times living beyond our means. Life never felt extravagant to me, but we did devote a reasonable portion of our income to our leisure pursuits of running, cycling, and downhill skiing. Our relationship had its disappointments, but it has been a wonderful companionship. Chris could be very demanding, and extremely competitive. I, on the other hand, am stubborn and very defensive. Our arguments are heated and sometimes I hold grudges, but I enjoy the time that we spend together. I learned so much about myself in the process of relating to him. Although we don't often discuss it, I believe that he feels the same way.

I am often injuring myself due to the repetitious nature of running. I usually just suffer from blisters, or strained and overused muscles. Yet once I fractured one of the bones in my foot and was instructed by my physician to stay off it for a number of weeks. This kind of a recommendation has an extreme impact on anyone who prides themselves in their daily run. I moped around the house and whined words of self-pity. Chris was patient, but I could tell that he was getting frustrated. Despite his own feelings, Chris made the experience memorable by the level of support he offered. I was most touched by the fact that he would sit me down at our running time and read to me from old Disney comics. He had found them in one of the unpacked boxes in my closet and assumed that they must have held some meaning for me. Donald Duck and Uncle Scrooge were never so endearing as when Chris propped up my foot and gave me the attention that I really needed. I have done my share of things for Chris as well, but I wonder if any of what I have done has measured up to that one simple gesture he made for me.

Shortly after we married we fell into a period of unhappiness that ended in a temporary separation. Chris claimed that I never shared any of myself with him. I believed that he was smothering me in his efforts to do everything as a pair. We approached intimacy differently, a struggle we had encountered when we lived together, and it became more apparent now that we were married. We lived independently for awhile, but it wasn't long before Chris was dropping by frequently to pick up something he had left behind. We began to talk. Many of the ways that we were hurting each other were brought to our awareness and discussed. I learned to feel comfortable saying what I needed because there was an openness and sense of quiet desperation in our interactions. It was an urgency in our relationship that was never there before.

During that time I missed our running together. I was of the mind that even though Chris had moved out of our home he would still show up on the dirt road at the appointed time and race ahead of me. It was the one stable aspect of my life, and somehow I felt less secure now that it was gone. It felt like a punishment, and I became frustrated and angry. It wasn't that I couldn't exercise alone, but rather this was the first time that I realized that I didn't want to. I told Chris this when he moved back in and he reached over and playfully hit me with one of the dog's rawhide bones. He tried to make light of the situation, but I could tell that what I said meant a lot to him. He didn't say anything back. He didn't need to now. He would when he was ready. That was enough for me . . .

The black faded into a warm inviting green that felt almost fluid-like beneath my arms and the backs of my legs. The warmth in my head expanded to the rest of my body and the throbbing began again in my foot. I had to push the sweat and the hair out of my face before I remembered where I was. The line of people before me blocked the paved race route, but I could still see the bright colors of the runners as they passed by. I was sitting alone on the grass. Funny how no one had noticed me and offered to help. I thought the pain I was feeling must be evident on my face. Maybe they mistook my stillness as the serenity that comes with replenishing sleep or meditation. I became aware of the pressure of something on my shoulder and looked up to see Chris standing behind me. There was a look of concern on his face, but also a sense of levity in his eyes. He prodded me with his well-worn running shoe and chuckled, "Where were you, honey? You know that I can't run without you. Well, actually it's not that I can't, it's just that I don't want to."

In her Presidential Address to the Division of Counseling Psychology of the American Psychological Association, Janice Birk (1994) responded to my teleography on ecological psychology by telling a teleography of her own—on rural psychology. Unlike traditional third-person scholarship, first-person scholarship (such as teleographies) often draw responses that can be a bit unsettling. [I attended Dr. Birk's Presidential Address in Toronto. But since I am not very interested in rural psychology, I'm afraid I was day-dreaming when I suddenly heard her say my name. I was immediately transported backward in time to the fourth grade. In my panic I almost jumped out of my seat and shouted, "No, Sister Stella Regis, I wasn't daydreaming! I was paying attention! I'm a good boy!" Fortunately, I kept my cool and did nothing. Here's what Dr. Birk said.]

George's Challenge
Janice M. Birk

At this point, I would like to tell you about a very provocative article I read by George Howard (1992) that was part of the *Journal of Counseling Psychology*'s centennial issue. Those of you who also read George's article will appreciate the fact that I am not going to formally cite the reference, and simply, refer to George. Among many other provocative twists and turns throughout the manuscript, George speaks to the reader in the first person intending, through that personal voice,

> to demonstrate how my life has led to the ways in which I think; how as counseling psychologists our lives and thoughts form counseling psychology; and

how our imagined possible futures (our hopes, dreams, and ambitions for the remainder of our life stories) can serve as springboards that might be used to create our personal futures and simultaneously—brick by brick—construct the future of counseling psychology. (p. 419)

Using himself as a model, George converses with the reader about what he sees as the contribution we can all make by writing in the first person—in our subjective and personal voice rather than our typical mode of scholarly discourse. I decided to take up the challenge and have delivered my comments this afternoon within the context of my personal experiences. I have tried to express a new professional purpose I feel because of experiences connected to my farm in rural Virginia. I can perhaps expand the context by mentioning that I did not grow up in a rural area; I grew up on the Northside of Chicago. I lived in a Catholic ghetto of German families. I rode streetcars and the "L," not tractors and trucks. My eventual journey to rural American is as fantastic as it has been deeply satisfying to me.

I will end with a "teleography"—something else that I learned from George. As he explains it, in a teleography I would turn toward my future and tell a possibly true story of the rest of my life. Not, George says, to predict the remainder of my life but to attempt to have you understand the constellation of values that energize my life. The particularly significant feature of a teleography is that by constructing a fantasy of the future, formed by personal and professional commitments, the fantasized image might serve as a projector into a future different than what might have been without the dream.

Beginning of a fantasy

After a surge in the real estate market and a welcome shift from a buyers' market to a sellers' market, my home in Silver Spring, Maryland finally sold. The significance of that is that then it became possible to have a home built on the new farm I co-purchased. Unlike some people's experiences with having a home built, this experience was, of course, hassle free. In what seemed like a matter of days, rather than the actual months, the buildings and fencing were completed, and I now can walk each morning along the Robinson River, which is the back boundary of the farm.

I particularly like the walks around the farm and have become an expert at this point on fauna and flora—due in large part to weekly meetings of the organization I joined in town. Its members share the common goal of becoming expert in the wildlife and wild-flowers in the region. Our underlying agenda is environmental conservation and preservation. After my first meeting, I was a little apprehensive about returning to the group because, as it turned out, the current coordinator of activities was a client's wife. Ultimately, that turned out to be a good thing because, in her professional role, she later became director of the drug rehabilitation center in the next county, and I have found my contacts with that center, and with her as director, to be very helpful resources in my practice.

My practice takes up three days of the week. I am successful in maintaining that limit because I value the other activities in my life, such as riding, hiking in the nearby Blue Ridge Mountains, volunteering at the women's shelter and at the AIDS clinic in Charlottesville, speaking on mental health issues at local church and group meetings, and of course, being present for the many friends who spend long weekends at the farm. Also making it possible for me to practice limited hours is the fact that many of my friends followed me to this rural area and have joined me in developing our community counseling center. The great need for psychological services characteristic of this and surrounding counties has been greatly alleviated by our presence. One of the ways we quickly distinguished ourselves from the other mental health providers in the area was by our consultative and preventive efforts and our advocacy for disenfranchised groups within the community. Just recently, we organized a meeting of multidisciplinary providers in the area to talk about ways we can support one another, learn from one another, and try out additional ways of making a difference that go beyond direct service.

From what I have said, you can see that we are a diverse group, thus enabling us to offer a wide range of services to the community, including consultation, brief therapy, sport psychology, career counseling, and psycho-educational programming. A few of us teach part-time at nearby University of Virginia. That is something we all profit from because of the intellectual stimulation rechanneled into our staff meetings and case conferences.

Because we are diverse and because several of us have former or current lives on graduate training faculties, we were instantly successful in developing an internship training program and getting it accredited by the American Psychological Association.

Recently we heard from three of our former interns. One practices in a small community in Louisiana and works mainly with very poor African Americans. The other two both relocated to rural North Dakota, and although they are several hundred miles from one another, they have frequent phone contact to get the support they need to help counter the isolation. Soon we will have enough interns to arrange the first annual "intern return." We take no small amount of pride in being the first accredited internship site in a rural community that is preparing counseling psychologists specifically for rural practice.

And that, friends, is my fantasy

I do know that Dr. Birk's home is now on the market. Wouldn't it be nice if her teleography turns out to be prophetic?

May I remind you that you should begin writing your teleography as soon as possible. You might find an attractive idea or theme by focusing upon an important upcoming event (e.g., "Does everyone approach college graduation with mixed emotions?"); your career (e.g., "Even as a child, teaching was in my blood. But as I begin my first teaching job . . ."); future relationships (e.g., "The birth of my daughter was to be the greatest day of my life. But I almost fainted when the doctor chirped, 'It's a boy!' "); or an important life transition (e.g., "Death comes like a stranger in the night . . ."). However, since school rarely prepares us to write fiction, you might have some problems in finding a writing style that serves to free your imagination. Don't worry about your style. Just begin writing about your future and eventually you'll find a style that fits.

Have you noticed that I've modeled a wide range of writing styles in this book. My thinking is that some atypical writing style might actually capture a few readers' imagination, melt their writer's block, and enable them to begin writing their life stories. However, I have avoided one writing style "like the plague"—poetry. The reason for my poetry-phobia is simple—I have no talent in that domain! While it might prove therapeutic for you if I demonstrate total incompetence in the poetry domain—and God knows you would certainly enjoy the laugh—I really ought to resist the temptation to share my poetry. Happily, as I was about to insert one of my poems, I was saved by a wonderful student paper by a sophomore entitled "The playwright."

THE PLAYWRIGHT
Brandi Coyner

Scene One:
Eye enter,
Stage left,
Being pushed onto the stage,
Others guiding my steps,
Eye watch others,
Taking note of their stories,
Their roles,
Trying to find my own.

Scene Two:
Eye now begin to take my own steps,
Trying out stories,
Eye begin to write my own,
Taking lines from this,
Lines from that,
Borrowing characteristics from one,
Making sure to avoid those from others.
Eye begin to gain confidence,
Strutting across the stage.

Scene Three:
My story takes form,
Pulling together the stories of others.
The plot begins to unfold,
Slowly,
A little behind schedule,
The story begins,
Finally my own.

Scene Four:
The climax
Still testing the waters of other stories,
Always giving them a flavor of my own.
No other is quite like mine.
All encountered have a part in my story,
My play.
Some only a brief appearance.

Others come . . .
And stay,
Playing major roles
    in my work of art.

Scene Five:
A look back.
Eye see the effect of my story,
The story Eye told myself,
The story Eye lived by.
Eye see the effects of the stories of others.
The effects of the stories Eye tried,
The ones Eye did not choose.
Each has shaped me,
Leading me down a different path,
Toward a different outcome,
For my character,
The lead in my play,
My story.

Eye have made my life,
Shaping it from experiences,
From encounters.
Influenced by each story
    that Eye chose to play.

In the next chapter I started a teleography where I was trying to appreciate what was important in my life. I wound up explaining the meaning of death for myself. As you write teleographies, you also might find that you begin your story in one direction, but it quickly takes you somewhere else entirely. I'm happy I allowed my muse to reroute "Two steps forward, one step backward." I hadn't even realized that I was struggling with death until I found myself writing my way through a mid-life crisis. This teleography was a writing experience that was as cathartic and therapeutic as any I have encountered. I hope your writing efforts are similarly rewarding.

CHAPTER 12
TWO STEPS FORWARD, ONE STEP BACKWARD

This teleography deals with the psychology of patience. I believe that the practice of the virtue of patience will pay dividends— patience well placed will work to the benefit of any person. Thus, I come to praise patience—not to bury her. My optimistic title ("Two steps forward, one step backward") also reveals something about me. I still believe in the idea of progress; I've never yet seen a half-empty glass; and I believe all's well that ends! A virtue that I possess in abundance is optimism. Patience, on the other hand, is but a dream for me.

Did you know that patience is a member of the band of traditional virtues? Its brothers and sisters being justice, temperance, wisdom, charity, agreeableness, constancy, fidelity, fortitude, tactfulness, hope, mirth, and many others. With that many siblings, patience would never want for backups if she found herself sucked into a brawl. By the way, that list of virtues was gleaned from a bevy of writers as diverse as Homer, Aristotle, the New Testament, Jane Austin, Benjamin Franklin, and Alisdair MacIntyre. I left off virtues like faith, piety, and fear of the Lord so as not to overemphasize one important cultural strain in my background; and, similarly, I omitted thrift, industry, acquisitiveness, and cleanliness in order to downplay yet another important developmental influence upon me. But, alas, somewhere along the line—I missed out on patience. For all the good work done on my behalf by John and Sis Howard, by Our Lady Star of the Sea Roman Catholic Church, by the Boy Scouts of America, by the Bayonne New Jersey Police Athletic League, by the Marist Brothers of the Schools, by the sons and daughters of Hibernia, by the counseling psychology program at Southern Illinois University, and by the usual Saturday night crowd at the Dewdrop Inn—in spite of their herculean efforts in the formation of my character—I never got patience. "So what?" you might ask.

So what, indeed. You see I am telling myself an important story about what's going on in my life—a story about what the meaning of my life is. And the virtue of patience is a crucial, but missing, part of that story.

Suppose I asked you, "What's your best guess as to how you will die?" Tell me what is the most likely candidate to be your killer—please force yourself to give a specific answer. Although no one knows for sure, I think I'll die of a heart attack or a stroke. As you may have already noted, I have more than my share of Type A characteristics—and a lack of patience is one of those characteristics.

When I try to think objectively about my life, I think of the important people in my life—first, I think of my sons. I know that they're doing fine, so I can't be screwing up too badly as a parent. But with a little more patience on my part, my sons would be a little bit better off. I'm a good-enough husband—but I push myself to be a little better nonetheless. My wife Nancy and I have an equal marriage—but it is an exhausting task to see to it that I always do my fair share in every domain. My track record as a researcher and writer is nothing to be embarrassed about. But I press myself daily to do more writing and better research. I'm surely an adequate teacher and advisor, but I press myself not to rest on my laurels. Finally, I am a good friend. I urge friends to call on me whenever I can be of assistance—and they feel comfortable enough to do so—often. Talk about multiple-role strain, you don't have to be a woman to experience that—as any true Type A knows all too well.

So, now I ask you, what kind of a life-story am I creating here? What tale will be told of George Howard once he's dead and buried? Well, that depends, in part, on whether I died of a massive heart attack five minutes after I finish this chapter (even God wouldn't dare take an academic in the middle of a paper) or if I have a busy, productive life and slip away peacefully at the ripe old age of one hundred. Scholars in the humanities have been telling us for years that endings are by far the most important parts of stories. And this perspective is very different from what has been believed to be true by mainstream psychology. People like Freud told us that the past was the most important part of our lives; people like Skinner focus upon the ways in which the present controls us. But thanks to the constructivist revolution, we now realize that our lives can be understood as if we were being drawn forward by the future—the future as each of us now imagines it. This shift in temporal emphasis does not demand that we denigrate the importance of the past and the present in the formation of human action. Rather, it simply offers the possibility of influencing human actions by altering a person's imagined futures. We can now rewrite life-stories by focusing the storytellers on different imagined possible futures. [This is, of course, exactly what I am doing in telling this teleography—playing with possible futures.]

So what does the future hold for me? If I am called to my final reward immediately after this chapter is completed, then the recounting of my life-story might go something like this: "At age forty-five, he left Nancy and the young boys to fend for themselves. In spite of his degrees in psychology, his articles and books, he showed about the same amount of insight into self-destructive life styles as did Janis Joplin. What a waste!"

But if in the year 2008 I watch my youngest son graduate from Notre Dame, and if twelve years later I retire after a forty-year career of productive scholarship, then my epitaph will read quite differently. It might say something like this: "He retired with a TIAA-CREF total accumulation value of $1,742,388—which at that time, coincidentally, was the exact price of a Chevy Nova."

So, now you can see that the meaning of my vice of impatience looks quite different depending upon how my life-story ends. But no one knows how their life is going to end! So, our lives represent acts of faith, made in the hope that something like our desired, imagined futures might actually occur. [This assumes, of course, that fate will be charitable to us for the remainder of our days.]

I should say something about the role of humor in my life and stories. Miller Mair set up my explanation by noting that our lives are told (in part) by the great stories of our race and culture. As I said earlier, I grew up in a ghetto—but a ghetto of a peculiar sort—it was really a warm, Irish-Catholic cocoon. All of my grandparents' relatives (who were also our neighbors) grew up in Ireland and immigrated to Bayonne as young adults. Any group that referred to Bayonne, New Jersey as "The Promised Land," and "The Land of Milk and Honey," or "God's Country" either experienced ghastly childhoods, or they had extraordinary senses of humor. I can assure you that it was the latter. In our crowd, one of the ways you prepared yourself to face any terror—whether unemployment, or surgery, or failure in school, or even death—was by cultivating friendships. The most important tools in building friendships are virtues like honesty, warmth, fidelity, and compassion. Our crowd also emphasized the importance of songs, story telling, a shared drink, and a shared joke in friendship-creating. While I haven't yet offered to buy you a drink, please don't give up hope, for the chapter is not yet ended. As you probably already know, humor is under attack these days—and I think that's sad. We interviewed a young woman for a job a few years ago, and she began her colloquium with the following joke:

"Did you hear about the tremendous breakthrough by a dyslexic theologian? He proved there was no dog!"

She did not get a job offer from us, in part, because of that joke. People argued vociferously that it showed her insensitivity toward the handicapped. It mattered not a whit that the two dyslexics in our department thought it was a great joke, and not at all offensive. The chair of psychology at Vanderbilt, Howard Sandler, is a good friend of mine, who constantly jokes with friends. But Howard advises me to not joke in professional papers. Howard chooses not to joke in professional settings because he says jokes are always at someone's expense. I've told a number of jokes here, and if anyone has been offended by them—I am truly sorry. I consider all readers to be friends, and I have no desire to hurt any of you in any way. As I said earlier, I joke about precisely those people and things that I care most about: my family, my friends, my profession, my heritage, my academic institution, my religion, and myself. Jimmy Buffett had it about right when he claimed: "With all of our running, and all of our cunning; If we didn't keep laughing, we'd all go insane."

Let's think of joking from a virtue perspective, as was discussed in the beginning of this teleography. Howard Sandler's advice—to not joke in formal settings—honors the ethical principle to do no harm. But there is another equally important ethical obligation, namely, to do good. My task in this chapter is to do some good for you. And when I think back on the most significant learnings in my life—humor has often been an important part of those insights. For example, one day in 1964, five of my sixteen-year-old male buddies and I were hanging around my family's kitchen one summer day. My mother was trying, unsuccessfully, to get some work done, and my Great-Uncle, Tom Mahon—our designated family philosopher—was just trying to be where the action was. You see, that was the job description for pensioners in Bayonne. Like most sixteen-year-old boys—we were "in heat"—and all we talked about was girls, girls, girls. Finally, my mother could take it no longer, and she blew up at us. She was far-less-than-thrilled with the attitudes toward women that were exhibited in our conversation. In the stunned silence, my Uncle Tom cleared his throat. Everyone knew that meant, "Shut-up! Uncle Tom's got some philosophizing to do." He slowly puffed on his pipe, and said "Laddies, do you know what's the most over-rated act in the whole world? The Sex Act." And then he cleared his throat again, and we all knew what not to do. Finally, he continued, "And do you know what's the most under-rated act in the whole world? It's a good shit."

Now if Tom had simply said "Sex is overrated, boys," who would have ever remembered it? Adults are always talking at teens like that. But because Tom wrapped it in a joke—none of us could ever forget it. [Although honesty demands that I report that Tom went to his grave, swearing on a stack of Bibles, that he wasn't joking.] I could go on and on with stories from my past of significant learnings where humor was an important element, but since space is limited, I must go on. For, as an old Chinese proverb says so well, "One who spends too much time living in the past, has no future."

Life stories aren't authored at one point in time, at a desk, by an independent author—as is fiction. At most, each of us is only a coauthor of our own life story. Miller Mair sees race and culture as significant coauthors; my earlier points about the importance of religion, academic psychology, and Notre Dame in my life-story hint that these institutions deserve coauthorship in my life story. And who can doubt that our parents, grandparents, and other forebearers from generations back, live on in us and our life stories. I am one acorn who would have considered it an absolute tragedy if I had fallen far from my family tree. That's why I spend so much time reliving and re-appreciating my roots. You see, what I've been doing up to now is constructing and reconstructing my life for you. Philosophically, I am a constructivist as well as an objectivist. Briefly, objectivism believes in a free-standing reality, the truth about which can eventually be discovered. The constructivist assumes that all mental images are creations of people, and thus speak of an invented reality. Objectivists focus on the accuracy of their theories, whereas constructivists think of the utility of their models. Watzlawick (1984) claimed that the shift from objectivism to constructivism involves a growing awareness that any so-called reality is—in the most immediate and concrete sense—the construction of those who believe they have discovered and investigated it. Objectivists are inventors who think they are discoverers—they do not recognize their own inventions when they come across them. Good constructivists, on the other hand, acknowledge the active role they play in creating a view of the world and interpreting observations in terms of it (Efran, Lukens & Lukens, 1988). I'd love to go on talking about constructivist metatheory and related epistemological issues, but I can imagine my readers' eyes glassing over, so I'll have to leave the topic with just these spartan comments.

But before we leave constructivism, imagine with me a Pantheon of Patron Saints of Constructivism—who would get on our all-star team of Constructivist Super-heros? Giambattista Vico and Immanuel Kant would be pioneer constructivist super-heroes. Jean Piaget and George Kelly are more recent stars who we psychologists know well. To this august list, I would like to volunteer a dark-horse candidate, another psychologist, the late, great Don Bannister. I never met him—as he died far too soon. But he lives on in me, through his writing. I only have time to mention one of his many, many great quotes. Don was worrying about the problematic relationship between experimenters and their human subjects in psychological research, when he told the following story:

> I am reminded of a recurrent theme in certain types of science fiction stories. The master chemist has finally produced a bubbling green slime in his test tubes, the potential of which is great but the properties of which are mysterious. He sits alone in his laboratory, test tube in hand, brooding about what to do with the bubbling green slime. Then it slowly dawns on him that the bubbling green slime is sitting alone in the test tube brooding about what to do with him. This special nightmare of the chemist is the permanent work-a-day world of the psychologist—the bubbling green slime is always wondering what to do about you. (Bannister, 1966, p. 22)

When I thought of writing a teleography for this book, I wasn't sure at first how to do it. And then the voice of my friend Don Bannister spoke to me—and he said, "Wake up, stupid! You're not just a chemist—you're also a slime!" And as I began to write this chapter, it came out as a semi-proper chemist-to-slime paper. At every turn in the writing, whenever I lapsed into scholarese, Don whispered: "'Cop-out', 'whitewash', 'academic bullshit.' Don't talk chemist-to-slime to them; talk to them slime-to-slime! They can take it!"

I figured Don might be right—so I just kept on writing. "Don," I said, "while I've still got you on the line, can you tell me, why I can't just let myself end this chapter?"

"Endings are always tough," Don replied.

"Don," I whispered, "tell me about death."

"Sorry, I can't," Don replied, "I'm a psychologist—a life expert. I'm not allowed to practice outside of my area of competence. Death belongs to the philosophers and theologians—not psychologists. But, you won't believe how lucky you got it, kiddo.

Guess who is the Dean of Theology and Philosophy up here? It's your Great-Uncle, Tom Mahon! George, Tom hasn't changed a bit. He's still joking, cursing, and smoking that smelly, old pipe. He's your friend, George, he'll tell you all you need to know about death. Just call on Him."

"Thanks, Don," I said. Then I whispered, "Tom? Uncle Tom, can you hear me?"

"Ara Georgeen (which is Gaellic for little-George)," Tom replied, "why would you be callin' on me now, after havin' missed my last twenty-four birthdays?"

"The birthday cards are in the mail, Tom," I replied.

"Ah, you still have a sharp tongue, Georgie-boy. Where'd you learn that?"

"At your knee, Tom," I replied.

"So you did. So you did. What can I do for you?"

"Tom, you gotta tell me about death. It's driving me nuts."

"'Tis a damn short drive," he teased. But when I didn't laugh, he knew I was serious, yet he still wouldn't budge. I decided to try flattery.

"Tom," I said, "I hear you're the Dean of Philosophy and Theology up there. That's quite a feather in your cap—and you, who never set foot in high school."

"Oh, things are much different up here, Laddie," Tom replied. "Degrees don't mean a thing. Advancement is based solely upon competence and hard work."

I was impressed! "Tom, now that you're the head man, I'll bet you're giving a real hard time to dogmatists, liturgists, logicists, and all analytic philosophers."

"Oh, none of them ever make it to heaven," he joked.

"Tom, I can't believe you'd leave them alone. You would never get off their case, here on earth."

"Sure, inasmuch as I'd like to, I give them no trouble at all," he replied. After a long, uncomfortable pause, Tom noted feebly, "Georgeen, did Don Bannister tell you that up here, a deanship is an elected position?"

"You won an election? You? A lousy politician? Tom, are you sure you weren't condemned to hell?"

"Be not too hard, Georgie-boy," Tom replied, "heaven's a lot like earth in that we all do what we must do in order to get by."

Now that was the Tom I knew and loved.

"Tom?" I asked, "Are you going to be able to help me on this death-thing?"

"Well, yes and no," he replied, "No because death and heaven are different for everyone. But yes because there are some things you can do to get ready for death."

"What can I do to get ready, Tom?"

"Well, you can lead a good life," he shot back.

"How do I do that, Tom?"

Tom thought for a moment, and then slowly replied, "Georgie, you might learn something about life and death by running yourself through a 'special nightmare' about death."

"Tom, if you think it might help, then I'll try it," I replied. "So, how do I do it, Tom?"

"Close your eyes, George. Imagine that you just died. Now open your eyes to being dead, and tell me what you see."

I opened my eyes and said, "Nothing! I see nothing when I'm dead. I no longer exist, so I can't even feel the biting cold or see the black nothingness."

"And how does that make you feel?" Tom asked, sounding for all the world like a psychologist.

"Awful!" I replied. "Absolutely terrible. I'm depressed and terrified at the thought of death being the end of everything for me. If that's the way it is, I see no good in life, and no point in going on."

"Right!" Tom shouted. "And right now, that depressive outcome seems to you like the most probable scenario after your death. But you now sound like a depressed, suicidal adolescent who can only see his or her life getting worse—becoming a tragedy. Life looks black—you have no hope. Now aren't you just-after-tellin' us that the future looks terrible until one begins to imagine a better, more hopeful, possible future? That's not the right ending for you, Georgie. Despair doesn't fit with the rest of your life. Don't settle for less from God and death than you've expected from yourself in life. Come on, kiddo, give us an ending fitting of your life—a proper ending for your life story. Georgeen, let me take the role of a therapist for a moment and help you to imagine a different ending to your death. When therapists rewrite clients' life-stories, they don't completely change good stories, they make small but important alterations—changes that make all the difference in a life. Go ahead, Georgeen, I"ll do the speaking for God."

"Okay, Tom," I replied. "I'm game!"

"Close your eyes," Tom whispered. "You die. Then you open your eyes, and you are staring face to face with God. Talk to Him, Georgeen. Work it out with Him. I'll answer for God. There He is, George—talk to Him—He doesn't bite. What would you say?"

"Well, God, what do you know, you do exist!"

"Yep," God replied. "Does that make you feel uncomfortable?"

"It does," I stammered, "because you could be pissed that for a long time I couldn't imagine you—I didn't believe in you."

"If I'd wanted you to believe in me down there, I'd have given you more faith. I'd have made myself more real to you. I'm not in danger of being forgotten down there—why a recent Harris poll shows that 94 percent of all Americans believe in God. But I had different plans for you."

"You did?" I asked excitedly. "How'd I do? Did your plan for me work out? Did I live a good life?"

"Slow down," God said. "That's not the way things work up here. You tell your life-story, and we decide from that story whether or not you honored the two commandments."

"Two commandments?" I queried.

"Yep!" God replied. "Do good! And do no evil! Now, George, where do you want to tell your life-story?"

"You wouldn't happen to have a pub up here, where they sing songs, tell jokes, and spin tall tales—would you?"

"I know just the place," God replied. "Come walk with me. It's just two clouds over." God looked at me sadly and said, "I always have such mixed emotions about Irish pubs. They're both a source of great joy and camaraderie, and the soil of the great Irish tragedy—the weakness—alcoholism."

"Yes—the weakness," I replied. "I remember my grandmother consoling a young widow at an alcoholic's funeral. His drinking buddies were standing around saying things like 'Poor Martin, he had the weakness,' 'Sure the poor devil had the weakness.' My grandmother thought they were trying to exonerate the deceased and themselves of their role in producing this tragedy. She gave them a withering glare and snarled, 'Tis a damn strong weakness ye all have.'"

God nodded his assent and asked, "George, who should we assemble to speak on your behalf at your final judgment?"

"I get to bring along friends?" I asked excitedly. "Okay! Let me see: my parents; my brother and sister, my wife Nancy; and our boys. They'll say that I did good. And my Uncle Tom Mahon—I want him there also."

"George, Tom Mahon would try even an all-patient God," the Almighty replied. "Are you sure you want him? Besides, he keeps grousing about how many of his birthdays you've missed."

"It's Okay, God," I replied. "You see, I wrote him this great part in this chapter I'm writing—it's the best role he's ever played. Don't worry, he'll forget the birthday cards. Besides, Lord, I'm assuming that we don't have to be perfect in this examination—we don't need to get a letter grade of 'A'. This is gonna be 'Pass-Fail' isn't it? I mean, my family is gonna bring up this patience problem of mine, so a grade of 'A' is absolutely out of the question."

"Sure! Sure, George! Relax! You don't have to be perfect. To err is human—to constantly err becomes a problem. That reminds me of a story, George, the guy who got the lowest passing grade ever on the final judgment is named Billy Bob Widebody. Do you know what we call him up here?"

"Saint Billy Bob," I replied, to God's dismay. And it made me feel better to know that even God—who is perfect—can't make every joke work.

"God," I asked cautiously, "are there many people in heaven?"

"Relax, George," God replied. "The greatest wisdom of all decreed that human lives would be graded 'Pass-Fail'—one doesn't have to be perfect. Just try your best to 'do good' and 'do no evil,' and that will be good enough. Heaven is mobbed! All my friends are here—and all their friends also. But, of course, there's always room for a few more."

"God, can you round up a bunch of my former students and faculty colleagues and my childhood friends and relatives to be there?"

"I know just the ones," God replied.

"I'd like Knute Rockne at my final judgment also," I volunteered.

That one surprised God a bit.

"The Rock? You never even met the Rock."

"It's this Notre Dame connection. Rockne loved Notre Dame, and I think I've represented Notre Dame well, so I thought . . ."

"Okay," God replied. "But I think you're reaching a bit."

"Well, how about Saint Patrick?" I queried.

Now the all-just God was clearly angry, "George, for someone who has never even set foot on 'The Old Sod,' you've soaked this Irish-thing for all it's worth."

"I guess so, Lord," I mumbled. "But now I'm worrying about the do no evil commandment. I have a pretty vivid imagination, and in angry moments I've imagined some pretty awful things occuring to people who have hurt me . . ."

"Two points you need to know," God explained. "First, we have a hard enough time dealing with the facts of things that actually occurred. What you imagined in your life is of no concern to us. That's called the 'Twain principle.' You see, Mark Twain's final judgment had to be held in a stadium—over 100,000 people attended. And Twain went on and on—'Oh, the tragedies I've seen in my life—Oh, the tragedies.' He had the entire house in the palm of his hand. At times you could scarcely hear what he said, for all the weeping and wailing. And then, at the end, he says, 'Fortunately, most of these tragedies never occurred!' So now we have the 'Twain Principle': Whatever goes on in your imagination is your own business! It's a good principle because people need some free space to plan out, test out and weigh the value of different possible life-stories. We only hold folks responsible for the story they actually chose to live.

"My second point," God continued, "is that you get to invite those who will speak on your behalf—those who will speak against you choose to attend of their own free will. When you die you have no means to influence what will be said by those who choose to testify against you. So you might want to do what you can about those matters, while you still have the chance. Oh, by the way, George, did I tell you that because of the number of people who'll be at your final judgment, we've had to reschedule it for the stadium?"

I clutched my chest and staggered backward in horror.

God, seeing my reaction, became extremely upset and blurted out, "Joke! Joke, George! It was meant to be a joke. Gee, I'm sorry! It was just a joke—I guess it was in bad taste. I didn't mean any harm by it. Everybody makes mistakes."

"Don't you know that jokes are always at someone's expense?" I fired back. "There's a time and a place for everything, and a joke like that is . . ."

"You're right, George!" God countered, "it was stupid of me—but not malicious. Everyone is entitled to their moments of stupidity—it goes along with being human. Don't forget that a part of me is human too. All I can say is that I'm truly sorry, and I assure you it was done without malice. If I could turn back the hands of time and undo that stupid joke, I'd do so immediately. But what's past is past—even for God—we can only strive to do better in the future."

We arrived at the pub, and could hear the singing, joking, and story telling going on within. But I was still frightened.

"Jude!" I blurted out. "I want St. Jude in there for me. Things might turn ugly, and St. Jude has lots of experience with hopeless cases."

"George," God replied, " you had no special devotion to St. Jude in life. You have to earn the testimony of people who'll speak on your behalf. Besides, you won't need Jude. Come on, George. Where's that old optimism? This is no time to turn cowardly on us. Do you think I've been stringing you along your whole life—just to pull the rug out from under you at the last moment? What kind of a God do you think I am? Now, you shouldn't keep your guests waiting. Let's go in."

"Would you mind if you went in first, Lord, and I took a moment to collect my thoughts?" I asked. God smiled, squeezed my arm reassuringly, and He went in. I felt alone and friendless as I summoned the courage to tell my life's story. Then I heard someone singing an Elton John song in an Irish brogue, as he hurried through the clouds. It was my Uncle Tom Mahon.

"Tom! You sing Irish rebel tunes—Clancy Brothers songs. You couldn't stand rock and roll. What are you doing singing Elton John?"

"Oh, that's the wonderful thing about heaven, Georgie-boy," Tom bellowed. "You're finally able to see beyond the petty biases of time and culture. Turns out, I love rock and roll."

Heaven was sounding more remarkable by the minute, and so I tried to press credulity. "Tom, tell me, do you now also like 'The Talking Heads' and 'The Sex Pistols'?"

Tom slowly removed the pipe from his mouth, cleared his throat, and whispered, "Georgeen, a lack of bias does not imply a lack of taste!"

Then, as he moved past me to the pub door, Tom said, "I'm glad I'm not late—I wouldn't have missed your final judgment for the world." Tom, seeing the worry on my face, asked, "Ara Georgeen, you're not still worried about those twenty-four birthdays of mine that you missed, now are ye? Sure, I've put them behind me long ago. And I sold my stock in Hallmark Cards back in the fifties. Have no doubt, sonny, I'm in your corner all the way. In fact, I need to thank ye for the part you gave me in that chapter on teleographies. Now you need to be followin' up on that character—write some more stories for me. Have me helpin' St. Patty drive the snakes out of Ireland; and I could be whisperin' in young Jack Kennedy's ear during the Cuban missle crisis. I tell you, Laddie, those stories have got great potential for a series on television . . ."

"Tom," I interrupted. "I can't do that. I'm a psychologist."

"Ah, Georgeen," Tom said softly as he patted my shoulder, "this is no time to be runnin' yourself down like that."

Tom reached for the door, stopped, and turned to me one last time.

"About that problem you've been having in ending that chapter," he began, "I think I've finally figured it out. Your teleography isn't about patience, or humor, or virtues, or culture, or friendship, or heaven, or any of those things. It's about human nature. End the chapter by thanking them kindly for their patience, and then tell them the nature of human nature."

"And just how might I be tellin' them the nature of human nature?" I asked, while also mocking his brogue.

Tom let the dig pass, and simply said, "Ye might try using that wonderful Gregory Bateson quote. You know, the one about stories."

"Oh, you mean the one that goes:

A man wanted to know about mind, not in nature but in his private large computer. He asked it (no doubt in his best Fortran), "Do you compute that you will ever think like a human being?" The machine then set to work to analyze its own computational habits. Finally, the machine printed its answer on a piece of paper, as such machines do. The man ran to get the answer and found, neatly typed, the words: THAT REMINDS ME OF A STORY. (Bateson, 1966, p. 8)

"No! No! No!" Tom said, "That's the story he used to tell back when he was a scientist, on earth. I mean the one he's using now as a philosopher-theologian up here in heaven."

Tom stuffed a piece of paper into my hand, grabbed the doorknob to the pub, and said, "And now you'll be excusin' me, as I have to be buying a pint of stout now. You see, they close the bar the moment a judgment begins."

Before entering the pub myself, I read Tom's gloss of Bateson's quote.

A man wanted to know about human nature, not through the eyes of a science, but through the eyes of human beings themselves. So he asked himself: Where did we humans come from? What is it like to have a human nature? and What is the meaning of life? And suddenly God appeared to the man to give an answer. And, God (looking for all the world like Charlton Heston) pointed to a rock, and a lightning bolt travelled from His hand to the rock. And one could see that some words were neatly emblazoned upon the rock. The man ran to the rock to find the answer to his questions. And the message was: GOD MADE HUMANS BECAUSE HE LOVES GOOD STORIES.
—Last line adapted from Robert Murphy

Uncle Tom opened the door to the pub and hissed at me, "Laddie, have ye gone daft? The grim reaper waits for no man.

Now get in here—for the mood of the jury for your final judgment might turn ugly."

"Tom," I sobbed, "how can I—how can anyone—justify their life? Help me, Tom."

"Georgeen, don't you know that everyone in that pub is exactly alike? Who among us is more than only-human? Just remind them of themselves—and they'll be your friends. And if your friends are there, then everything's alright. Why don't you start out by singing them that sad, lonely song by Neil Diamond? You know, the song that claims that the saddest thing about the death of people who possess great dreams (such as Jesus, Ghandi, Mozart, and Martin Luther King) comes from the fact that their dreams are incomplete. We weep when great lives are done—for they've been ended too soon."

Tom took my hand and slowly led me into the pub. He turned to me, winked, and said, "And when you're done tellin' your story, laddie, be sure to thank them for their patience."

[End of teleography!]

Well, that's my teleography—at least for now. You can see that I'm wrestling with the meaning of life and the meaning of death. That makes me quite similar to a great many other people in their forties. I guess I'll go to my grave reflecting upon my Irish-Catholic background. Like other psychologists, I'll wonder about the nature of human nature until I can wonder no more. And, when I reach the far-side of death, I hope to encounter a loving and understanding God—and lots of good friends who made safe the way before me. Until then, I'll teach, and think, and write—about science and about human nature. I'll also befriend and love a lot of people and institutions, and generally try to leave this world a better place than I found it. And in those respects, I'm not very different from any of you. Is that because my self-analysis was good? Or because we all share the same human nature? Or both? And, finally, I'll continue leading the life story that I've chosen because, frankly, I can't think of anything better to do between now and death.

How is your teleography coming? Please don't get discouraged if your first effort went nowhere. Try, try again. Eventually you'll catch your own rhythm, and then it will be easy to dance into your future.

Chapter 13
Pumping Karma

> What is real wisdom? It comes from life experience, well digested. It's not what comes from reading great books. When it comes to understanding life, experiential learning is the only worthwhile kind; everything else is hearsay.
> Erick Erikson (in Myers, 1990, p. 77)

Howard Sandler is one of the wisest people I know. We were on our way to the airport—

". . . you just do it, Howard. It doesn't matter whether you'll ever get repaid for it or not. It's 'the right thing to do', so you do it. Make it a conscious effort. You see an opportunity to do something—anything—good, kind, decent, or generous, and you do it. Bang! Just like that you do it. Don't think about it. Act now—think later. It becomes a habit—and a nice habit at that. And the amazing thing is, if you're good to the world—it will be good to you."

"Good karma!"

"What's karma? As old as I am, I don't know what karma is."

"Just that! It's exactly what you said. People have a running bank account with the Universe. Do something good or decent and you add to your store of good karma. Do something mean and you add to your bad karma. Keep piling up the bad karma—and you come back in the next life as a cockroach!"

"My God! We must have been terrible in our last lives—we came back as psychologists!"

"Right! And in Eastern thought, karma has nothing to do with luck. Do good all your life and the universe owes good back to you. Do bad and it'll come back to haunt you."

"While I don't believe in the reincarnation part, I think the 'running bank account with the Universe' part is a great strategy for life. I believe that all those karma bank accounts will get settled up right here in this life in the long run."

"I agree, George! Of course there is tremendous evolutionary validity to philosophies that have thrived for over 5000 years. Remember, this Christianity thing is just a new kid on the block."

"How old is 'Do unto others as you would have them do unto you '?"

"I don't know—but that's a handy way of knowing in which direction the good karma lies. If you'd like someone to treat you in a particular manner, chances are others will appreciate it if you'd treat them in the same way. Ditto if you wouldn't particularly like something else."

"Getting back to the point I was trying to make earlier, people should make a habit of working at building up their good karma. If you want a great body—you don't just sit around and wish you had a great body, you get on with the exercises—like pumping iron."

"So now you want me to think about 'Pumping Karma'."

"Yes! Exactly! Face it, in all other skill domains of our lives we don't leave things to chance. We work on skills by practicing. We concentrate on developing the right set of habits. For example, if you want to be able to hit a particular shot in basketball, you practice it over and over again until it's virtually automatic. It almost becomes second nature to hit it. You ought to work at becoming good, decent, fair, reliable, objective, understanding, tolerant, and all those other 'good karma' ways of living. But the problem is that in the hustle-and-bustle of everyday life we tend to get caught up in what's going on. We react in a knee-jerk manner, rather than stopping to realize that we ought to be structuring each interaction in the hope that good karma will come out of it. You know what I mean—you just know nothing good will come from an interaction with a member of your faculty which begins with him or her shouting, 'I can't believe that you actually wrote that memo on who may use the xerox machine!'"

"No! I don't know that to be true. Most of the time good things come from interactions that start out badly. I turn them around by employing a very simple strategy. I take everything as a compliment. That's because almost everything that is said has some degree of ambiguity in it which you can use to your advantage. To that faculty member you mentioned I'd quickly say, 'Thank you! I agree that a policy statement on the use of the xerox machine was long overdue.' Depending on what the person had on his or her mind, the conversation will either be constructive or destructive in tone. But I guarantee that it is off to a far better start than if I'd reacted negatively to the opening line."

"And do you keep up that strategy throughout the conversation? I mean—every subsequent statement will also be somewhat ambiguous. Do you keep trying to take every additional remark in the conversation as a compliment?"

"Within reason, yes! Some statements are so negative that they couldn't possibly be construed as compliments, but you can always receive and interpret them in the best possible light. For example, if our irate faculty member says that the new xeroxing rules will slow down the work of his research assistants, I'd respond by highlighting the positive value that prompted his criticism. Depending upon the circumstance I might say something like, 'Yes, you are always doing your utmost to facilitate your research program, and it's precisely that single-minded dedication that makes you as successful at research as you are. Now let's see if there isn't some small adjustment to my new system that will meet the department's needs, and still won't slow your research program one iota. Got any suggestions?' It takes a bit of effort, creativity, and practice, but I've found that the quality of my interactions improves dramatically when I am consciously looking to see compliments in whatever others say to me."

"I don't think most people tend to naturally 'accentuate the positive' the way you do, Howard. Let's think about strategies to help folks to get better at dealing more positively with others, and in the process perhaps pump more good karma. And before you answer, I must tell you that I'm real skeptical because I've seen too many cases of people who try to use psychological techniques on other people, and it comes off as phoney. The people they 'try them out on' resent it because it feels really manipulative. I can easily imagine somebody trying to see everything as a compliment and doing it badly. People would react to it like 'What a bunch of happy-horseshit that joker is throwing at me. It stinks!'"

"Well, I'd certainly never want to be downwind of anybody acting like that. But I think you touch upon the right place to start—relationships should always be viewed as give and take propositions. One should always look at relationships from two separate perspectives—from your perspective and from the perspective of the other. A friend told me an interesting way to think about such interactions. It's called the Win-Win box. Suppose you think of our relationship, George.

"I put your name at the top and mine on the side of the box. The left hand column depicts situations wherein you win, and similarly, the top row is my win area. The right hand column is your bad domain and the bottom row is my badland."

GEORGE

		Win	Lose
HOWARD	Win	A	B
	Lose	C	D

"Right, Howard, I think this box is called the Johari Window. Let's first label the boxes A through D. Now Box A represents the promised land. That's the goal for every relationship. In my opinion, both parties in any relationship should strive to have the relationship be in the A box. Some people have a bit of difficulty understanding how both members of a relationship can win. The problem stems from the fact that many games we designed and often play require that one team lose in order for the other to win. While this is a necessary requirement of most competitive games that we have created, it is not a necessary aspect of human relationships—even though some people see relationships as if there must be a winner and a loser. Many people who are clients in therapy view the world of human interactions in that way. Psychologically speaking, it is a very destructive way to lead one's life, and often leads to social isolation and/or asymmetric, unsatisfying relationships.

"But let's look at a Win-Win relationship to see how one can analyze relationships into quadrants. I'll begin by analyzing our relationship, Howard. For my part, the "costs" of our relationship are really minimal. Every once in a while I have to pick you up at the airport—which is really nothing. Sometimes, when you want to discuss some issue, it takes me away from other pressing work. But that's it! You are a wonderfully unobtrusive and self-sufficient house guest, and you have never imposed upon our friendship professionally. That's it. The "costs" to me of our relationship are minuscule.

"Now for the benefits. First, you sharpen my thinking. In our discussions you point out every weak point in my thoughts—that's a big help. But you challenge and correct in a most helpful way. By that I mean that you try to help me toughen up the weaknesses. It is clear you probe with the goal of shoring up the weak spots. You want me to be as good a scholar as I can possibly become. Second, you make me a better department chair. You've been at this administration game longer than I, and the seasoning shows! I feel welcome in running any problem past you and getting honest advice. Third, you fill in whenever our parenting system fails (e.g., babysit for a half hour; you care enough to correct our kids when we are not able to do so, etc.). Fourth, you have a great disposition and sense of humor. You're just fun to be around. I work too hard for my own good—but I don't work hard at all when you are around. That's good for me. Fifth, you know lots of things that I don't know—phenomenology, developmental psychology, Taoist philosophy, and so forth. I could go on with this list, but I think I've made my point. The benefits I receive from you so overwhelm the costs involved in our relationship, that if the costs would escalate enormously—like if something terrible happened to you and I jumped in to help—I would still be firmly in the Win side (left column) in our relationship."

"From my perspective the costs are minimal as well. Aside from having to get up a little earlier than might otherwise be the case and having to watch reruns of the Smurfs on the VCR, I have had a marvelous month visiting South Bend. You have gotten me back in the habit of writing again, which I greatly appreciate. You have made me walk two to five miles a day, which I greatly need. Our conversations during the walks are both enlightening and fun—I don't often get as sympathetic an audience for some of my strange ideas about the direction in which psychology is headed. Even the discussions about departmental matters have been very helpful to me. They have led me to rethink some of the things that I have been doing as department chair, things that weren't working as well as they might have. In short, the benefits to me of our relationship also far outweigh the costs. I will return to Nashville a better (and healthier!) person."

"Phew! How did we ever get along before we met? That little exercise should make two points clear: first, in relationships, somebody doesn't have to lose in order for someone else to win; and second, our lives are enriched by others, and thus we should seriously analyze and work toward making our relationships better. Have you been pumping good or bad karma so far today? What are you going to do about it?"

"George, let's look at other quadrants of your Win-Win box. Can you think of any relationship you now have which isn't Win-Win that we can analyze?"

"Unfortunately, I've got plenty of them. There's one I'd like to talk through, because I can't figure out if it's Win-Lose, Lose-

Lose, or Lose-Win. There is a graduate student named Dan who is well on his way toward getting thrown out of the doctoral program for not making progress on his dissertation. So now let's replace "Howard" with "Dan" in the box. He's supposed to be working with me—but he shows up every six to eight months to get some stupid form signed—and he never mentions his dissertation. So here's the problem with the analysis of the relationship, since he makes no demands on me, it's hard to say that I'm losing. Given my track record as a research supervisor, no one will think he failed to succeed through any fault of mine. So it's hard to say I'm losing anything. But you can tell from the way I'm talking about it that I feel badly about the situation. Thus, I'd say that I'm probably on the losing side of the box (right side, either Box D or B). Now Dan is probably losing in the relationship also (bottom row, specifically Box D) because he isn't making any progress toward achieving his stated goal of getting a Ph.D. But I highlighted "stated" because I'm just not sure that he still wants the degree anymore. He might have written off getting the degree long ago, and he might be effectively using this time to get ready for his next career move (top row, specifically Box B)."

"So you really don't know where you and he stand in your relationship. The next move is obvious, you should talk it over with Dan to find out where you stand with regard to one another. But George, you surely have figured that out. And yet, you haven't yet broached the topic with Dan. So more must be going on than you have let on."

"Yep! You are enormously insightful for a statistician. Oops, I hope I haven't damned you with faint praise? My problem in not talking to Dan falls under one of my rules of thumb (like your 'Take everything as a compliment'). My father told me this one: 'Never ask a question that you don't want to hear the answer to.' My father never minded ending sentences with prepositions—he said people remembered them better that way."

"OK, let me guess what you're thinking. If you have a conversation where you bring up the fact that Dan's not making progress, and he says, You're right! Help me do a dissertation. Then you've got an undermotivated student, with program deadlines staring him in the face, on your hands. That's not a happy thought for someone as busy as you are right now."

"That's right, Howard. And if instead he says something like, I'm just writing computer software now so that I can be well on my way toward opening my own business when I drop out of the graduate program, then I'm also in a jam. In that case, I would have some ethical responsibility to force his hand, since he is tying up University resources and has no intention of using them properly. So I'm having a hard time imagining a happy ending to this scenario. Thus, since the ball is now in his court, I'm not taking any action at this point in time. If I could imagine a possible happy outcome, I would act to bring it about."

"OK. I can see why your relationship with Dan isn't Win-Win right now. My problem involves a few people I must work with now who are acting really immaturely and it's driving me crazy. They are adults—they are faculty members—and they ought to think and act more maturely. If I think of it in Win-Win terms, will it help me to feel better about my job?"

"I think so. Let's think it through. I assume that you are successfully facilitating this person's work, and rather than being appreciative of your efforts, the person just makes your life miserable."

"Exactly. He acts like the entire world should be anxiously waiting to be of service to him and his needs. His attitude is really quite immature and frustrating. He should be grateful for all the University has done for him—but instead his needs seem insatiable. So, I guess it is probably a Win (for him)–Lose (for me) situation."

"The first step I'd recommend, Howard, is that you simply lay out the situation to him exactly the way you just did for me. Suppose he objects. Howard, you and I know that you go the extra mile for everyone. So I'd just say that if he will not be cooperative, you'll be forced to give him his fair share of departmental resources—no more, no less. Further, you will be forced (by him) to live up to the letter of the law of your job description—no more, no less. He makes you take this step because the present arrangement makes you feel ripped-off—so now you need to take measures to protect your feelings. How would he react to that?"

"Well, first we'd have to pick him up off the floor and revive him. He would starve if he only got his fair share."

"Precisely! Howard, you've been carrying this joker for too long already—and feeling miserable in the process. Either he takes the responsibility for doing whatever is necessary to move you from Win-Lose to Win-Win, or the relationship becomes purely formal and legalistic. That's not too much to ask of an adult—is it? Even if he forces you to the formal relationship, you'd probably feel fine about that. Let me make one other point. It wasn't a really risky guess on my part to suggest that he was already getting more than his share of the resources. In most organizations it is 'the squeaky wheel that gets the grease.' This guy has learned over the years that 'squeaking' gets results. You've got to send the message to your folks that squeaking gets you pissed—and gets them in trouble."

"I do! I even got a memo out on that. It's the people who work hard and are the good departmental citizens who get special treatment. The thing that makes it tough with the guy we're discussing is that he is a good scholar and teacher. If he were unproductive, I would have held his feet to the fire long ago. But it would be a real loss to the University if this guy took a job somewhere else. That's why I put up with a bit more crap than I would have for normal faculty members."

"Yep! That's going to make it a bit more difficult for you to negotiate a Win-Win situation with this guy. Both you and he know that he has a power base due to his competence. Fortunately, you are as competent as he; you have position power since you are the department chair; and, most importantly, you are right. He's needlessly making your life miserable. He should be expected to make reasonable efforts to make your job more bearable.

"But more needs to be said about the role of power in these attempts to bring about Win-Win relationships. As a general rule of thumb if you are in a position of superior power you need not seriously fear opening up a discussion aimed at reaching a fair (i.e., a solution both would endorse if there were no power differential) settlement. Since you do have the power—you could enforce an unfair solution. But that would be a mistake, from the good karma perspective. Thus, you must be very sensitive to the 'Do unto others as you would have them do unto you' perspective. Make sure that you haven't forced the other person into a bad deal that they are agreeing to only because you hold the power. After a good deal (Win-Win) has been struck, I take a moment to see if I can think of any 'pot-sweeteners'. Those are little add-ons that I can throw in to make it a better deal for the other person. I only suggest 'add-ons' that I feel good about. That is, things I don't mind doing for the other person that I know he or she will appreciate.

"If you are in a Win-Lose situation where you are losing and the other person is in the position of power—proceed with great caution. The best way to broach the issue is under the cover of pursuing ways in which the relationship could become more lucrative for the person in power (e.g., 'Howard, I might have the time to try for an NSF grant if I just didn't have so many teaching duties next semester'). Make that proposal if you want to reduce your teaching load—especially if you plan to try for the grant anyhow."

"George, I tell my faculty that work counts—it counts for a

lot! As long as that faculty member is willing to do an honest day's work, I'm convinced we can strike a Win-Win arrangement."

"There's no doubt in my mind that you're absolutely right on that score, Howard. In fact, you are precisely the type of boss for whom each of us would love to work. But that brings us to the most difficult—but by far the most important—concept of this entire conversation. It is absolutely essential that you assess the character of the person you are dealing with correctly. There are good people out there—and there are some mean, sick, bad dudes out there. You have to protect yourself from getting used by such individuals. Nothing can sour someone on people as fast as a series of relationships with mean, self-centered, egotistical, and selfish sleazeballs. Hope I didn't blow you away with all that psychological jargon. Wait a minute. I'm getting down-and-dirty a bit too fast. This crucial issue of assessment should be approached a bit more analytically."

"Aw nuts! I want to hear more about the 'egotistical sleazeballs!' Gimme names."

"Be serious! Howard, one of the reasons I like you so much is because of your attitude toward your wife and daughter. Soon after we met, you began telling stories about them, and gradually your relationships with them began to become apparent. Your love, support, and consideration for them tells us a lot about you—and how you view others in your life. Second, we have some mutual friends who consistently speak very highly of you. Finally, our early interactions had a good feel to them. I can't be specific as to what it was exactly, but my clinical intuition told me you were a good person—one who could be trusted. I put a lot of faith in my initial impressions of people. Fortunately, trusting my intuition almost invariably proves to be a good modus operandi for me.

"I can only remember two instances where my gut reaction was completely wrong. Once I got taken for a ride by a really skilled sociopath for whom I worked. It took me months to realize that he was only using me—and everyone else for that matter. Boy, that bugger was a dangerous person. He was unbelievably skilled at deceit—and deception. My other poor first assessment was a woman whom I disliked a lot when I first met her. Turns out she is a wonderful person. I still haven't figured out why I misread her so badly.

"Assessment is critical in pumping good karma because you need to protect your attitude toward others. Some people are good karma black holes. If you get taken advantage of often enough, you soon sour on people in general, and gradually you lose your will to trust others. That can lead to a death spiral of suspicion-isolation-depression that, in extreme cases, can completely destroy one's support system. Surround yourself with good people, and you'll become a much better person. Did you know that a key therapeutic strategy for depression involves helping the client to just spend more time with people they like and at the same time trying to minimize the amount of time they spend with people who 'bum them out'?"

"Yes, I heard about that approach. Tell depressed clients to 'cheer up' or 'become less depressed', and they can't do anything with that advice. In fact, that's why they came to therapy in the first place—they can't control their attitude as well as one would normally be able to do. But often they can follow their therapist's suggestion that they spend more time with Carol and Bob (who are people they enjoy) and spend less time with Mary and Mr. Jones (people who bring them down). They typically don't see how this will 'cure their depression', but when they do it, they almost always feel a bit better. Obviously, more is usually required than simply improving one's support system, but these improvements are important actions, and do help one's attitude immensely."

"So there might be real validity to the old saying 'Show me your friends and I'll tell you what kind of person you are.' It's good advice to actively seek out warm, wholesome, pleasant people because of the impact they will have on your attitude—and your life overall. So pick out the people that your intuition tells you will return your good will, and actively work at 'pumping good karma'. I think your life will be richer for having done so."

I would have loved to continue our conversation, but we had arrived at the airport terminal. Howard disappeared down the throat of our air transportation system. As I pulled away from the terminal, I thought . . .

In our conversation, Howard and I were getting close to some important issues that cut to the heart of human nature, and how one might lead a good life. Why is it that such conversations are all too rare between academic psychologists, and between teachers and students in psychology courses?

Jerome Bruner (1986) claims there are two kinds of thinking and knowing: paradigmatic (which seeks to locate the Truth about categories of things) and narrative (which seeks to determine the meaning and interconnections among things). When you are conducting science, you are operating within the paradigmatic mode and are constrained by the rules and regulations of paradigmatic thought. When you are telling your life-story in either an autobiography or a teleography, you are in the narrative mode of thought. Self-experiments are interesting because the person who serves as the narrator in her or his life story agrees to serve as both the experimenter and the research subject in a paradigmatic study of her or his life at one particular point in time. Figure 4.3 is a typical paradigmatic view of human nature, which is why it helps us to understand the results of self-experiments quite well. But that figure gives us little aid in understanding autobiographies or teleographies because it pays little attention to the roles of time, meaning, and intentionality (which are crucial to narrative thought). When things occur (or might yet occur) in an autobiography (or in a teleography) represents a crucially important consideration in the narrative mode of thought. Similarly, you now know the meaning of many events in my past (and my imagined future) in part because I have disclosed what it is that I intend my life to accomplish. Trying to understand a human's actions without any appeal to her or his intentions was a terrible intellectual misstep, advocated by scholars who assumed that the categories of causality that were sufficient to explain the behavior of objects in the physical sciences (e.g., the moon, see Chapter 6) would also be sufficient to understand humans. A century of scientific study has proven that appeal to solely nonagentic causes is insufficient for psychology. A first-person, narrative understanding is also required.

In reading my stories, readers might also feel that they know some other people (e.g., my wife Nancy, my uncle Tom) who have played important roles in my life story. But you don't know them as they really are, only as they are in my construal of reality. They are third-person actors who play roles in what is for me a first-person narrative. Nancy or Tom would have to agree to tell us their story for us to really know who they are and for what they stand.

Where does the narrative dimension "fit" in Figure 4.3, you may ask? The self is located in the central oval (labeled Personal Agency) in Figure 4.3. At least for me, the essence of my "self" appears to be linguistic. George Howard appears to be that "little voice" in my head that furnishes a running commentary on virtually everything that happens in my life. And talk he does! Sometimes I wish I could shut him up—or at least slow him down a bit. But I rarely can, as he seems compelled to try to understand almost everything and every one in his life. How did he get to be that way? That reminds me of a story. . . The story of how I came to be the way I am would have to be the sum of the stories of my life.

Like all scientific models, Figure 4.3 has adopted a number

of simplification strategies. For Figure 4.3 time is made to stand still. We are invited to analyze the effect of causal influences on a person's actions at one point in time. Imagine that a life is like a movie. Suppose you were given one, or ten, or ten thousand frames of the film of my life to analyze. [A two-hour film really consists of a sequence of hundreds of thousands of frames that are aligned on celluloid.] Analyzing single frames from the movie of a person's life is a lot like what Figure 4.3 asks the reader to imagine. A great deal can be learned from the intensive study of single frames of a movie— and analogously through self-experiments of the agentic and nonagentic causes of our actions. However, one would not have "seen the movie" itself through this sort of careful analytic study.

Reading autobiographies and teleographies (or discussing a person's life in therapy) is a lot like seeing a movie of the person's life. This perspective (first-person and narrative) is much closer to how the person experiences her or his life—and analogously how the director, producer, actresses and actors intend their movie to be experienced. Clearly, however, a complete scientific appreciation of human nature will come from careful scientific analysis and integration of various perspectives—first person integrated with third person, paradigmatic with narrative, and life-stories with self-experiments.

Properly understanding humans will require a far more complex and complete analysis than was satisfactory for understanding inanimate and insentient objects (e.g., planets, chemicals, plants). While our early forays have proven quite rewarding (e.g., Howard, 1993a, 1993b; Howard, 1994; Howard et al., 1992), this project of an integrated study of human action is still in its infancy. I believe we will be well into the twenty-first century before we have a satisfactory set of theoretical models and the methodological sophistication to adequately conduct such comprehensive studies of humans. But take heart! Even though scientific psychology is over 100 years old, that's still very young as sciences go. We've learned as much as we can from some of our older siblings (the natural sciences). But—Thank God!—our subject matter (human nature) is "softer" than their subject matters. Thus, we must strike off on our own to develop an appropriately soft science. However, we are not completely on our own in this adventure of discovery. Our siblings in the humanities will show us ways that will help us to appreciate the role of meaningfulness, language, story telling, intentionality, imagination, fiction, and so forth in human lives. Our challenge is to craft a discipline poised midway between the humanities and the sciences—a discipline that is just soft enough to get human nature right.

Every culture seems to produce a leading prophet—one who foresaw the critical issues and challenges long before they bubbled up to the level of consciousness for the rest of us. William James was scientific psychology's greatest prophet. With amazing prescience, and a stunning economy of words, he outlined scientific psychology's agenda for the future almost a century before the rest of us could appreciate it, claiming, "Let the science be as vague as the subject" (James, 1890, p. 19). It's clear from James' writing that he meant "vague" in the sense that I have been urging a "soft" science of humans. [To many scientists, an idea of a "soft science" sounds like an oxymoron. Appendix II represents cognitive therapy for people troubled by the notion of a "soft science," as it shows how all scientists have become victims of a linguistic structure that makes it difficult to imagine some desirable characteristics of an appropriate science of human nature.]

I was jostled out of my meditations on methodology to find I was parked in my garage. Somehow I had driven home safely from the airport—but I don't remember much of the trip. Aren't humans' multiple levels of consciousness wonderful! What am I supposed to do next?

Oh, I remember. The next page of the story of my life has me sending the babysitter home, taking my boys to the pool for an afternoon swim, cooking supper, and . . .

"Daddy! How come you're so late? We were supposed to go swimming ten minutes ago!"

Quick! Remember! What did Howard Sandler tell me to do? Take everything as a compliment. Work out a Win-Win situation. Stay focused and keep trying to pump good karma.

"Mr. Howard, something has come up and I won't be able to watch your kids tomorrow. The air conditioner stopped working about three hours ago—I have no idea what its problem is. Two people from work called. They both want you to call them back— one said it's an emergency. The phone messages are on the counter. Gotta run."

Thinking about scientific methodology is so easy and so much fun. It's living life that's tough work!

Chapter 14
Epilogue: Psychology in the First Person

[In July 1994, I gave the keynote address at a conference on constructivist psychology. This is adapted from that address.]

I recently finished writing a book entitled, "Understanding human nature: An owner's manual." The book is based upon a very simple premise; one's best shot at understanding human nature is to work toward understanding oneself. If this premise has any validity whatsoever, then it might be a devastating indictment of the last 100 years of psychological scholarship. For virtually all our scholarly efforts involve the study of some "other," be they research subjects, clients, members of another culture, and so forth. Did any of you ever read a scholarly report that claimed (in effect), "After extensive, careful study of myself I've reached the following conclusions about human nature . . ." ? But, fortunately, psychology's fascination with the study of "the other" rather than studying "myself" (or the fixation on third-person perspectives to the exclusion of first-person scholarly approaches) hasn't been that serious a liability. Here's the reason why.

One can come to a pretty good understanding of human nature using either third-person or first-person perspectives. Neither are "wrong," both are "right" but incomplete. A richer, more complete appreciation of our nature as humans comes from the combination of disciplined, scholarly investigations that alternate between first-person and third-person perspectives. The image I like to invoke is my binocular vision. Let me perform a quick first-person experiment. If I cover one eye I can still see everyone in the audience perfectly well—there's Greg Neimeyer, that's Larry Leitner over there, and Mark Wilson is in the far corner. But when I uncover my eye, I can now perceive depth, because binocular vision provides depth. By the way, Mark, have you been putting on some weight? If I lived with the use of only one eye long enough, I might almost begin to forget that my monocular vision is handicapped relative to our typical binocular vision. Of course, it was psychology's desire to become a science over the past 100+ years that led us to ignore first-person scholarly approaches.

Three approaches are recommended as promising, first-person scholarly endeavors: autobiographies, self-experiments, and teleographies. These techniques urge people to carefully analyze their pasts, presents, and futures, respectively. The basic wager in recommending these techniques is that since each of us is a human being, whatever we learn that is true about ourselves is true about (at least a subset of) humans. Recall that in Chapter 8, the self-experiment where I volitionally increased the amount I exercised, we immediately performed the same experiment on a group of people to find whether my ability to control the amount I exercised was unique to me, or if it was a capacity that many humans share—which of course it was. To my chagrin, these generalization studies always seem to suggest that I am simply an ordinary human being, nothing more, nothing less. Imagine my horror at finding that out. While generalizability is always a question for first-person research, it is also a question for third-person research. Generalizability won't be a problem in your self-experiments either, if you happen to be lucky enough to be as ordinary as I am.

But there are critiques of first-person perspectives that are more telling, and it is to one of these problems that we now turn.

AN INDIVIDUAL PSYCHOLOGY IN A SOCIAL WORLD

Undoubtedly, the greatest shortcoming of a psychology in the first person is that it will focus upon individual persons, and thus might slide to the background of our consciousness the roles that larger social collectives (of which we are a part) will play in the formation of our lives. Our families, neighborhoods, churches, businesses, nations, races, and other social groups profoundly influence the courses of our lives. One can do everything in his or her power to create a happy and healthy life story, but if all-out nuclear war breaks out . . . All bets are off! This, of course, has long been an important theme of great literature—Les miserables, Dr. Zhivago, Gone with the wind, Boyz in the hood, etc. The individual is often a pawn to social forces, over which she or he has little control (sometimes, no control). As always, William James gave what for me is the best answer to the problem of how one ought to view life's ultimate uncertainty, and why an individual might choose to live a virtuous life in the face of such uncertainty.

> What do you think of yourself? What do you think of the world? . . . These are questions with which all must deal as it seems good to them. They are riddles of the Sphinx, and in some way or other we must deal with them. . . . In all important transactions of life we have to take a leap in the dark. . . . Each must act as he thinks best; and if he is wrong, so much the worse for him. We stand on a mountain pass in the midst of whirling snow and blinding mist, through which we get glimpses now and then of paths which may be deceptive. If we stand still we shall be frozen to death. If we take the wrong road we shall be dashed to pieces. We do not certainly know whether there is any right one. What must we do? Be strong and of a good courage. Act for the best, hope for the best, and take what comes. . . . If death ends all, we cannot meet death better. (James, 1897/1956, pp. 30–31)

Larger, societal groups and issues were considered in my autobiography (e.g., the Catholic church, the Vietnam war, University of Houston departmental politics, cf. Chapters 1 & 3) and in my teleographies (e.g., global overpopulation, developments in narrative psychology, cf. Chapters 11 & 12). However, these four chapters focused primarily on the past development and possible futures of the life of a single person—larger groups and issues played only tangential roles in these stories. "But why is this a problem for first-person approaches?" you may ask.

Moving the personal and individual to the forefront (and thereby sliding the social and collective to the background) can lead us to see problems that are produced by social conditions (e.g., poverty, racism, violence) as being due to individual pathology—and thus in need of individual remediation. Clearly, both individual and social factors are implicated in human problems. Further, it is not that first-person approaches cannot consider social and collective factors, but the emphasis in first-person approaches tends to be placed upon the individual. What I am concerned about is a subtle shift in emphasis toward a perspective where a person's problem is seen as "a personal disease in need of individual remediation" rather than being seen as "a social disorder with primary prevention required." This preference for individual explanations over social explanations might actually be exacerbated if first-person approaches were to come to dominate our study of humans. [Obviously, this is not a problem for the near- or intermediate-future.]

The most effective antidote that I've found for the disease of "seeing the effects of social problems as individual problems in need of remediation" is a daily dose of the writings of George Albee (See Appendix III for a brief introduction to Albee's vision).

QUO VADIS?

"Quo vadis?" means "Where are you going?" The question was asked by St. Peter of Jesus, who was on his way to Jerusalem to be crucified. The story reports that when Jesus told Peter his destination and the purpose of his trip, Peter begged Jesus not to go. But, as we know, Jesus went anyway—for even God's gotta do what He's gotta do.

Parts of this book can be understood as my best guess as to where the science of psychology is heading—if "Quo vadis?" had been addressed to the discipline of psychology. But suppose the question, "Where are you going?" was asked of me personally. Other parts attempt to reveal as much as I am able (and probably as much as you can stand) about how my life has come to possess the trajectory along which it now travels, as well as a path it might yet traverse.

It is becoming much more commonplace to recommend that people consider writing themselves into significant life changes—to alter where they appear to be going. For example, sociologists Terry Williams and Ann Mische work on a project called, "The Harlem Writers' Crew" wherein people work with greatly at-risk teenagers from Harlem. Mische (1993) describes the project,

> Terry recruited young people from these neighbor-
> hoods to write about their experiences growing up.
> As the Writers' Crew developed, the young people
> began writing stories, poetry, plays, and autobiog-
> raphies. They also developed a support network
> among themselves and a relationship with Terry as
> an important role model. Since February 1991 I have
> been taking part in meetings of the Writers' Crew
> and interviewing its members. I have been examin-
> ing the impact that the young peoples' participa-

tion in the Crew has had on their process of mobilizing hopes. I'm very interested in how the process of writing about their experiences, and thus gaining a critical perspective on their past and present, affects their ability to think of and believe in possibilities both for themselves and for the larger community.

One of the fascinating things about working with the Writers' Crew has been exploring the creative dimension of street culture—music, rapping, poetry, graffiti, tee-shirt art, etc.—in which the kids assert in various ways that they're not just the passive victims of circumstances, although they may occasionally see themselves as such. A certain sort of creativity can be seen even in the choice of drug dealing or teen parenthood. We need to understand that these choices, however negative their consequences, are expressions of the hoping process. Although paradoxically such choices may end up further limiting the field of possibilities, they are still an attempt to create possibilities, to find a way out of an apparently no-win situation. In drug dealing, for example, young people definitely have a sense of seeking a future, involving ambition, role modeling, and all sorts of values and ideals. People don't go into drug dealing out of hopelessness. They may go into it out a sense of limited possibilities, but as I said earlier about despair, that's not the same thing as hopelessness. Rather, these choices must be seen as attempts to expand the field of possibilities, as part of the process of trying to give meaning to their lives and direction to their action.

The question becomes how you channel these various forms of creativity and hoping in constructive ways, and help them to avoid the dead-end, exploitative, and self-destructive possibilities that so often comprise the alternatives society offers them. In building alternative educational experiences for kids, we have to think of ways to help them to expand their fields of possibilities in directions that they can feel as being real and genuine, and then give them the support and the courage they need to turn their hopes into actions (pp. 23–24).

For members of the Harlem Writers' Crew, writing becomes a method for imagining and creating better possible futures than might have been the case had they not written these hopeful stories.

Another trend toward using writing as a self-change strategy comes from the narrative literature on psychotherapy (Parry & Doan, 1994; White & Epston, 1989). In these therapy strategies, both the client and therapist continuously write reactions about their therapeutic encounters to one another. Further, creative writing efforts pepper the course of psychotherapy. For example, the client is encouraged to "externalize" the problem (e.g., anger, overeating, drug abuse) and write a dialogue between the client himself or herself and the externalized problem. Thus, clients are instructed to write dialogues quite similar to the dialogue in Chapter 8, except that the fictitious partner in conversation is the client's problem rather than a fictitious therapist. These and other writing exercises are rapidly becoming important parts of therapeutic relationships as people are encouraged to write themselves into more satisfying futures.

So now we ask, "Quo vadis?" one last time. Where are you, the reader, going? If an ultimate goal of all education is to help you—the learner—to come to know yourself and your world better, then this book strongly recommends that you engage in first-person activities such as self-experiments and both autobiographical and teleographical story telling, along with third-person studies, to most effectively come to "know thyself."

Appendix I

Autobiographies, personal experiments, and teleographies are not the only means of gaining self-knowledge. The most important (and best-known) method is through serious conversations with friends, family members, school counselors, psychotherapists, pastoral counselors, and the like. Great care should be taken in selecting the correct partner for such exercises in exploration. Some combination of a subjective feeling that you would feel comfortable sharing your thoughts with this person, along with feedback from others that this person has a history of being a reliable helper, is ideal. Growth and development can be greatly enhanced through various forms of conversation. There are several informative books you might peruse (e.g., Martin, 1994) on how conversations can often achieve their educational and/or therapeutic effects.

Four other techniques that can lead to enhanced self-understanding will be described briefly. First, journals are close kin to autobiographies. Some people gain enormous benefit from the careful examination of their life and thoughts through the exercise of writing. Such people might choose among techniques like autobiography, teleography, and journal writing. Some individuals quite naturally develop their own style of diary or journal keeping, and need no techniques to enhance the benefits they obtain from their journal work. However, the examination of systematic ways of keeping a creative journal can provide a number of helpful suggestions that enhance the yield from one's journal. The creative journal: The art of finding yourself by Lucia Capacchione (1989) is a good example of creative ideas about how to keep a journal.

A second technique for enhancing self-understanding is a computer-aided exercise called I-Spi (Doan & Knight, 1995). Using Q-sort methodology, I-Spi offers eighteen adjectives to the user and asks her or him to select the adjective that best describes him or her (e.g., warm, ambitious), and then the adjective least like him or her (e.g., competitive, calm). Next, the two remaining adjectives most like the user and the two least like the user are selected. After all eighteen adjectives have been sorted, we have a distribution of characteristics that describes the user (Self sort). Sorts on the same eighteen adjectives are then conducted for other conditions of instruction (e.g., mother, wife, ideal friend, preferred self, greatest fear, love). I-Spi then notes patterns of strong similarity and dissimilarity between the various sortings of the eighteen adjectives. Users are then encouraged to explain in their own words the meaning of these patterns of similarity and dissimilarity between sorts conducted under different conditions of instruction. For example, my output indicated a correlation of .94 (i.e., extremely similar) between my "self" sort and my "father" sort. I can then tell the story of how my father and I are so similar. In another person's sort (by Rick Watson) there was a correlation of -.87 (i.e., extremely dissimilar) between "home" and "greatest fear." Rick would then give an explanation of this island of significance (i.e., the -.87 correlation of greatest fear with home). In describing what his greatest fear is, Rick would explain why this fear represents for him the converse of what "home" means to him. Successive iterations of this procedure develop more islands of significance and relationships between these islands of significance. Eventually, the collage of meanings and relationships that characterize each person's life can be built-up through the assistance of the I-Spi program. This objective, yet completely individualized and personal, analysis of your web of meanings and interrelationships can be extremely revealing and helpful. One might obtain the I-Spi computer program and user's manual by writing either Mike Knight or Rob Doan at the Department of Psychology, University of Central Oklahoma, Edmond, OK 73034.

A third self-exploration technique that many have found helpful is the Myers-Briggs Inventory. Responses to this inventory allow people to be placed with respect to four dimensions. The dimensions are Introversion-Extraversion, Sensation-Intuition, Thinking-Feeling, and Perceiving-Judging. Consideration of these personality-types brings one into the domain of Carl Jung's vision of personality. Many people find Jung's views on human nature quite provocative and appealing. A book by Keirsey and Bates (1984) entitled Please understand me: Character and temperament types gives a nice introduction and interpretation of the Myers-Briggs and Jung's vision of humans.

The fourth method of self-exploration can be found in a remarkable book by Dan McAdams (1993) entitled, The stories we live by: Personal myths and the making of the self. In Chapter 10 McAdams shows readers how they might explore the personal myth that energizes their life. A standard protocol has been developed for research interviews on personal myths that is presented on pages 256 through 259. One can read through this interview protocol and write answers to the questions posed. These questions are designed to elicit stories and explanations that can serve as the core of a good autobiographical sketch.

THE LINGUISTIC ASSASSINATION OF A "SOFT" SCIENCE

The Whorf-Sapir hypothesis (Whorf, 1958) claims that the content of our thinking is conditioned by the structure of meaning inherent in our language. Whorf maintains,

> that the background linguistic system (in other words, the grammar) in each language is not merely a reproducing instrument for voicing ideas but rather is itself the shaper of ideas, the program and guide for the individual's mental activity. . . . We dissect nature along lines laid down by our native languages. The categories and types that we isolate from the world of phenomena we do not find there because they stare every observer in the face; on the contrary, the world is presented in a kaleidoscopic flux of impressions which has to be organized by our minds—and this means largely by the linguistic systems in our minds. We cut nature up, organize it into concepts, and ascribe significances as we do, largely because we are parties to an agreement to organize it in this way—an agreement that holds throughout our speech community and is codified in the patterns of our language. (Whorf, 1958, p. 5)

I believe that some empirically determined relationships (such as, self-reports being more valid measures of behavioral parameter values than are behavioral measures) are very difficult for us to accept because these findings place a stress on the structure of relationships among meanings that are implicit in our scientific language. Let me offer one example of a "claim that strains our language." William James first made the delightful, normative claim, "Let the science be as vague as the subject matter." I maintain that there is a semantic tension embedded in this claim that strains our linguistic structure of meanings—regardless of whether you agree (like me) or disagree with the content of the claim. The following semantic exercise (suggested in Howard, 1984) might make this point clearer.

A SEMANTIC EXERCISE

Humans tend to think in semantic opposites. Therefore, when researchers are forced to make research choices, the choices represent, at least on an implicit level, a rejection of some alternative approach, method, or perspective. In what directions have these choices tended to be made in psychological research thus far?

Much of the research in mainstream, American psychology reflects our naturalist predilections. The accumulated influence of this systematic preference has resulted in a lopsided prevalence of method over meaning (Koch, 1959), manipulation over understanding (Kaplan, 1964; MacKenzie, 1977), certainty over authenticity (Gibbs, 1979), internal over external validity (Campbell & Stanley, 1963), rigor over sensitivity to human subtlety (Sanford, 1965), and narrow quantification over broad qualitative inquiry (MacLeod, 1965). When psychologists are presented with the numerous choices involved in conducting research, all too often they opt for more "scientific" solution.

Knowledge

Scientific		Nonscientific	
1) exact	13) unromatic	1) inexact	13) romantic
2) definite	14) faithful	2) indefinite	14) unfaithful
3) concrete	15) constant	3) ungrounded	15) changing
4) precise	16) unerring	4) imprecise	16) erring
5) well defined	17) particular	5) ill defined	17) particular
6) just	18) meticulous	6) unjust	18) sloppy
7) right	19) delicate	7) wrong	19) gross
8) correct	20) clear-cut	8) incorrect	20) confused
9) strict	21) fact	9) lax	21) fiction
10) rigorous	22) reality	10) approximate	22) dream
11) scrupulous	23) authenticity	11) unscrupulous	23) deception
12) literal	24) accurate	12) fable	24) inaccurate

TRUTH   ERROR

FIGURE A-1. Demonstration of the meanings associated with scientific knowledge

Perhaps a quick, linguistic exercise will suggest some reasons for this strong bias for scientific ways of knowing. In *Roget's Thesaurus,* the term "scientific" is found under the heading of

"Truth." Figure A.1 lists twenty-three of the synonyms grouped with "scientific" in the *Thesaurus*. I then generated antonyms for each of these twenty-three synonyms and listed them under what appeared to me to be the antonym for "scientific," namely, "nonscientific." Lastly, I located each of the twenty-three antonyms in the *Thesaurus*, and found that fifteen of these terms could be found under the heading "Error." The point of this exercise is obviously not to suggest that nonscientific approaches are fraught with error. Rather, it seems we might inadvertently be glorifying scientific ways of knowing, and in the process, linguistically devaluing alternative approaches. Would psychologists have arrived at a radically different conception of appropriate research strategies if they had analyzed the characteristics of human beings and developed research methods appropriate to these characteristics, rather than simply assuming that the methods of the natural sciences (properly modified for use with humans) would yield veridical knowledge?

The semantic exercise shines light on the seemingly oxymoronic feel to phrases like, "vague science" or "soft science". "Soft" and "vague" are kin to "imprecise", "incorrect" and "sloppy"— all being located in the domain of "Error". But "science" lives with "rigor", "accurate" and "reality"—all worthy offspring of the great god "Truth." Unfortunately, these semantic moorings pull psychologists in precisely the wrong direction, if human nature is the subject matter that demands the "softest" or "vaguest"of sciences in order to be properly appreciated (see Howard, 1986, 1989, 1991, 1993a for elaboration).

Linguistic traps are not confined to the semantic exercise above—where the poles of a hard science–soft science dimension are too closely associated (semantically) with the poles of more general, evaluative dimensions (such as good-bad or truth-error). The fact that humans tend to think dichotomously (Kelly, 1955; Rychlak, 1989) predisposes researchers to frame issues in "either-or" terms, when more continuous thinking might be appropriate. Thus, for long periods of time we tended to think in terms of "free will or determinism" (Howard, 1993a), "masculinity or femininity" (Constantinople, 1973), "nature or nurture" (Plomin, 1990), "innocent or guilty" (Howard, 1992b), and "cost-efficient or ecologically appropriate" (Gore, 1992). We now understand that in many instances the "or" in these dichotomies might profitably be replaced by "and." Dichotomous thinking can sometimes (although not always) be inappropriate, because it suggests that one must deny one pole (e.g., femininity, free will, cost-efficiency) in order to be able to champion the value of its (assumed) opposite pole. But why would scholars think in dichotomous (either-or, black-white) terms when the world obviously presents itself as a continuous, tapestry of greys?

This question brings us full circle to the Whorf-Sapir hypothesis that language structure determines human thought. Did you know that in all Indo-European languages (like English) verbs can only be expressed in two "voices" (i.e., active [I push] or passive [I am being pushed])? Other languages possess "middle voices" wherein various graduations of shared activity-passivity can be expressed in subject-verb relationships (Howard, 1992). The structure of our language itself, and the semantic web of meaning among words (like subjective, objective, self-report, behavioral, soft, hard, vague, etc.), condition us to inappropriately devalue certain research methods and simultaneously overvalue others. Thus, it is important to periodically review the evidence both for and against our options in science. Further, I have tried to explain why virtually all of us are suspicious when we hear phrases like "soft science," for such concepts tear at the semantic net of meaning that we think of as commonsense knowledge. I believe Alfred North Whitehead (1948) best expressed the proper relationship between science and common sense.

> Science is rooted in what I have just called the whole apparatus of common sense thought. That is the datum from which it starts, and to which it must recur. . . . You may polish up common sense, you may contradict it in detail, you may surprise it. But ultimately your whole task is to satisfy it. (p. 18).

Appendix III

Perhaps I can make partial amends for the emphasis in this book on individual over social perspectives by pointing to the work of George Albee—one of the most important psychologists of the twentieth century. Albee's work (1982, 1987) on psychopathology being seen as socially produced disorders rather than diseases caught by individuals, and on the importance of prevention rather than the treatment of problems in reducing the incidence of psychopathology, is monumental.

Albee points out that the incidence of a public health problem (whether an infectious disease or a psychopathological condition) has never been reduced by treating people *after* they contract the problematic condition. Only prevention efforts are successful in reducing the problem's incidence (the number of new cases) in a population. Albee and Ryan-Flynn (1993, p. 118) explain the factors related to a problem's incidence with the following formula:

$$\text{Incidence} = \frac{\text{Organic Factors} + \text{Stress} + \text{Exploitation}}{\text{Coping Skills} + \text{Self-Esteem} + \text{Support Group}}$$

Reducing the incidence of a disorder is accomplished by reducing factors in the numerator (noxious agents) and/or increasing factors in the denominator (strengthening the host). While a psychology in the first person can help to strengthen the host (e.g., increasing self-esteem and social skills), first-person perspectives' individualistic emphases will tend to minimize the importance of predominantly social factors in the formula (e.g., exploitation, support groups, stress). Thus, I must reemphasize that first-person psychology is meant to supplement (not replace) third-person perspectives. While individual issues and factors are important, one must never lose sight of the fact that social forces also mold and deflect the course of individual lives.

Despite the efforts of Albee and others, psychology remains much more focused upon the treatment of psychopathology after it occurs, rather than undertaking primary prevention efforts so that the incidence of disorders will decrease. This balance of professional efforts is sad, in that most of us would rather *not* experience a problem (due to effective prevention efforts) than to contract the disorder and then be effectively treated for the problem.

This odd professional (and societal) choice of treatment over prevention is better understood when we recognize who society deems to be its greatest heroes. Imagine that God said that he had a list of four candidates for sainthood, from which He could select two. If He asked your opinion of what each of the following four had done for humankind,

> Mother Theresa
> John Snow
> Ignatz Semmelweiss
> Albert Schweitzer

Which two would you endorse for canonization? Albee gives a compelling rationale for his two choices in a remarkable essay entitled, "No more rock-scrubbing." In the essay, we see the extent to which our society glorifies individual treatment, while group prevention efforts are banished to the background. In reality both efforts are important in their own right—just as it is important that both first-person and third-person research be used to complement each other.

No MORE ROCK-SCRUBBING
George W. Albee

Most people, if asked to rank order Albert Schweitzer, Mother Theresa, John Snow, and Ignatz Semmelweiss would put the first two names at the top and confess ignorance about the latter two. Yet in terms of contributions to humankind, like the number of lives saved, human anguish prevented, and of accomplishments for the betterment of people throughout the world, Snow and Semmelweiss tower over the other two.

It may seem subversive or mean spirited to fail to praise Schweitzer and Theresa as recent-day saints, but I greatly prefer the canonization of Snow and Semmelweiss.

As B. F. Skinner pointed out at his last public address at the APA Convention in Boston, Schweitzer was trying to save humanity one person at a time. Similarly, Mother Theresa, with a heart full of compassion and kindness is also trying to save the world one person at a time. It simply can't be done. By way of contrast, John Snow figured out that cholera was a water-borne disease long before the noxious agent causing cholera had been identified. He observed that the pattern of cholera infection was related to where drinking water can from; in the most famous act in the history of public health he removed the handle from the Broad Street pump and stopped a cholera epidemic.

Semmelweiss puzzled over the high rate of child-bed fever and death in women in the public wards of hospitals in Budapest. (In those days physicians didn't wash their hands, but wiped them dry on the lapels of their frock coats, so the more experienced physicians had stiffer and smellier coats.) Semmelweiss finally decided that somehow medical students and obstetrical trainees were carrying some poison from the dissecting rooms of the anatomy lab to the women giving birth. He ordered all of his medical trainees to wash their hands for ten minutes before they delivered a baby. Suddenly and precipitously the rate of child-bed fever and death dropped to almost nothing. Of course the great experts of the day did not believe either Snow or Semmelweiss. But fortunately, as Freud was wont to point out "The captains and the kings depart, truth remains."

The point here is that Snow's and Semmelweiss' work illustrates the truth of the dictum that "No mass disorder afflicting mankind has ever been eliminated or brought under control by attempts at treating the affected individual." These two public health saints have saved millions of lives while Schweitzer, full of heart and compassion, was treating suffering individuals in his jungle hospital in Africa and while Mother Theresa was administering to the poor and the hopeless in Calcutta. Individual treatment has no effect on incidence.

One cannot help but admire and respect those selfless people who reach out in humanitarian concern to support suffering individuals. But at the same time, if we respect evidence, efforts at primary prevention are even more humane and admirable if our criteria include the reduction of mass human suffering.

With the exception of a small number of community psychologists, prevention has not been the focus of current psychological intervention efforts. One need only read the divisional newsletters and the APA Monitor to see how important individual psychotherapy, delivered by individual practitioners, has become. The mission of this large group of psychologists has changed the structure of APA. While valiant efforts are being made by APA to keep science alive and content, a great many scientists are dissatisfied and the scientific training of applied psychologists has been put on the back burner in a great many clinical programs.

The field of public interest in psychology has also suffered an eclipse. Political conservatives rarely get involved in public interest issues unless they are forced to. Conservatives favor the status quo and resist social change. There has been a major move towards more conservative right-wing explanations of mental and emotional disorders for at least the past ten years. We are told by the American Mental Health fund (founded by Jack Hinckley) that "All mental illness is a medical illness." The Head Guru for psychiatry, E. Fuller Torrey, has said that nearly every mental condition is a brain disease or genetic defect. The American public is being educated to believe that anxiety, phobias, obsessive compulsive behavior, depression, bipolar disorders, schizophrenia, alcohol and other drug abuse, and juvenile delinquency are all caused by bad genes or bad brains. The advantage of this organic model is that it means that no social changes are required to reduce the stresses of sexism, racism, homophobia, and exploitation of the poor and homeless. Prevention efforts are opposed as woolly-headed idealism. In fact the National Alliance for the Mentally Ill publicly denounces efforts at prevention.

The prevention of mental and emotional disorders must involve social change efforts at creating a more egalitarian and just society. . . .

Last Spring I offered a couple of bright undergraduate students the opportunity to attend our annual conference on prevention, this one entitled "Improving Children's Lives: Global Perspectives on Prevention." After some agonizing they both decided that they would rather go to Alaska and volunteer to scrub oil off rocks on the beach. Somehow this symbolized for me one of the critical intellectual conflicts in our society. Should we sit around and scrub oil off rocks after the oil spill or should we demand that safer tankers be required by international law? Treatment or prevention? Schweitzer and Theresa, or Snow and Semmelweiss?

References

Adler, M. J. (1958, 1961). The idea of freedom. Garden City, N.Y.: Doubleday. Two volumes.

Albee, G. W. (1982). Preventing psychopathology and promoting human potential. American Psychologist, 37, 1043–1050.

Albee, G. W. (1991). President's message: No more rock-scrubbing. The Scientist Practitioner, American Association of Applied and Preventive Psychology, 1, no. 1, 26–27.

Albee, G. W., & Ryan-Flynn. (1993). An overview of primary prevention. Journal of Counseling and Development, 72, 115–123.

Alexie, S. (1993). The Lone Ranger and Tonto fistfight in heaven. New York: Atlantic Monthly Press.

Alexie, S. (1994). The business of fancy dancing. New York: Atlantic Monthly Press.

Angelou, M. (1969). I know why the caged bird sings. Toronto: Bantam.

Angelou, M. (1973). Gather together in my name. Toronto: Bantam.

Bandura, A. (1982). The psychology of chance encounters and life paths. American Psychologist, 37, 747–755.

Bannister, D. (1966). Psychology as an exercise in paradox. Bulletin of the British Psychological Society, 19, 21–26.

Bateson, G. (1979). Mind and nature: A necessary unity. New York: Dutton.

Berzins, J. I. (1977). Therapist-patient matching. In A. S. Gurman & A. M. Razin (Eds.), Effective psychotherapy: A handbook of research (pp. 222–251). New York: Pergamon Press.

Bettelheim, B. (1976). The uses of enchantment: The meaning and importance of fairy tales. New York: Knopf.

Beutler, L. E. (1981). Convergence in counseling and psychotherapy: A current look. Clinical Psychology Review, 1, 79–101.

Beutler, L. E., Clarkin, J., Crego, M., & Bergan, J. (1990). Client-therapist matching. In C. R. Snyder & D. R. Forsyth (Eds.), Handbook of social and clinical psychology (pp. 78–101). New York: Pergamon.

Birk, J. M. (1994). Country roads: Counseling psychology's rural initiative. The Counseling Psychologist, 22, 183–196.

Brewer, M. B., & Collins, B. E. (Eds.). (1981). Scientific inquiry and the social sciences. San Fransisco: Jossey-Bass.

Brislin, R. W. (1988). Increasing awareness of class, ethnicity, culture, and race by expanding on students' own experiences. The G. Stanley Hall Lecture Series No. 8. Washington, D.C.: APA.

Bruner, J. (1986). Actual minds, possible worlds. Cambridge, MA.: Harvard University Press.

Campbell, D. T., and Stanley, J. C. (1963). Experimental and quasi-experimental designs for research. Chicago: Rand McNally.

Capacchione, L. (1989). The creative journal: The art of finding yourself. North Hollywood: Newcastle Publishing.

Carkhuff, R. R., & Pierce, R. (1967). Differential effects of therapists' race and social class upon patient depth of self-exploration in the initial clinical interview. Journal of Consulting Psychology, 31, 632–634.

Cohen, J. (1977). Statistical power analysis for the behavioral sciences. San Diego, CA.: Academic Press.

Constantinople, A. P. (1973). Masculinity-femininity: An exception to a famous dictum. Psychological Bulletin, 80, 389–407.

Cook, T. D. (1985). Postpositivist critical multiplism. In R. L. Shotland & M. M. Mark (Eds.), Social science and social policy. Beverly Hills: Sage.

Cooper, K. H. (1970). The new aerobics. New York: M. Evans.

Cronbach, L. J. (1982). Designing evaluations of educational and social programs. San Francisco: Jossey-Bass.

Doan, R., & Knight, M. (1993). Psyching mental life. Edmond, OK.: University of Central Oklahoma.

Dougherty, F. E. (1976). Patient-therapist matching for prediction of optimal and minimal therapeutic outcome. Journal of Consulting and Clinical Psychology, 44, 889–897.

Efran, J. S., Lukens, R. J., & Lukens, M. D. (1988). Constructivism: What's in it for you? The Family Therapy Networker, 12, 27–35.

Frank, J. D. (1961). Persuasion and healing. Baltimore: Johns Hopkins.

Frazer, J. G. (1890). The golden bough: A study of magic and religion. London: Macmillan.

Fry, P. S., & Charron, P. A. (1980). Effects of cognitive style and counselor-client compatibility on client growth. Journal of Counseling Psychology, 27, 529–538.

Gardner, H. (1985). The mind's new science: The history of the cognitive revolution. New York: Basic Books.

Geertz, C. (1973). Interpretation of cultures. New York: Basic Books.

Gelso, C. J., & Carter, J. A. (1985). The relationship in counseling and psychotherapy: Components, consequences, and theoretical antecedents. The Counseling Psychologist, 13, 155–24.

Gergen, K. J. (1982). Toward transformation in social knowledge. New York: Springer-Verlag.

Gergen, K. J. (1989). Personal letter dated December 13, 1989.

Gibbs, J. C. (1979). The meaning of ecologically oriented inquiry in contemporary psychology. American Psychologist, 34, 127–140.

Giorgi, A. (1970). Toward phenomenologically based research in psychology. Journal of Phenomenological Psychology, 1, 75–98.

Gore, A. (1992). Earth in the balance: Ecology and the human spirit. Boston: Houghton Mifflin.

Gorsuch, R. L. (1991). Things learned from another perspective (so far). American Psychologist, 46, 1089–1090.

Hanson, N. R. (1958). Patterns of discovery: An inquiry into the conceptual foundations of science. Cambridge: Cambridge University Press.

Harré, R. (1984). Personal being: A theory for individual psychology. Cambridge, MA.: Harvard University Press.

Harré, R., & Secord, P. F. (1972). The explanation of social behavior. Oxford: Basil Blackwell.

Hawking, S. W. (1988). A brief history of time: From the big bang to black holes. New York: Bantam.

Hedges, L. V. (1987). How hard is hard science, How soft is soft science? The empirical cumulativeness of research. American Psychologist, 42, 443–455.

Hempel, C. P. (1965). Aspects of scientific explanation and other essays in the philosophy of science. New York: Macmillan.

Hillman, J. (1975). Re-visioning psychology. New York: Harper & Row.

Howard, G. S. (1984). A modest proposal for a revision of strategies in counseling research. Journal of Counseling Psychology, 31, 430–442.

Howard, G. S. (1985). The role of values in the science of psychology. American Psychologist, 40, 255–265.

Howard, G. S. (1986). Dare we develop a human science? Notre Dame, IN.: Academic Publications.

Howard, G. S. (1989). A tale of two stories: Excursions into a narrative approach to psychology. Notre Dame, IN.: Academic Publications.

Howard, G. S. (1991). Culture tales: A narrative approach to thinking, cross cultural psychology, and psychotherapy. American Psychologist, 46, 187–197.

Howard, G. S. (1992a). Behold our creation: What counseling psychology has become—and might yet become. Journal of Counseling Psychology, 39, 406–434.

Howard, G. S. (1992b). No middle voice. Theoretical and Philosophical Psychology, 12, 12–26.

Howard, G. S. (1993a). Steps toward a science of free will. Counseling and Values, 37, 116–128.

Howard, G. S. (1993b). I think I can! I think I can! Reconsidering a place for practice methodologies in psychological research.

Professional Psychology: Research and Practice, 24, 237–244.

Howard, G. S. (1994). Some varieties of free will worth practicing. Journal of Theoretical and Philosophical Psychology, 14, 50–61.

Howard, G. S., & Conway, C. G. (1986). Can there be an empirical science of volitional action? American Psychologist, 41, 1241–1251.

Howard, G. S., Curtin, T. D., & Johnson, A. J. (1991). Point estimation techniques in psychological research: The role of meaning in self-determined action. Journal of Counseling Psychology, 38, 219–226.

Howard, G. S., DiGangi, M. L., & Johnson, A. (1988). Life, science, and the role of therapy in the pursuit of happiness. Professional Psychology: Research and Practice, 19, 191–198.

Howard, G. S., Maerlender, A. C., Myers, P. R., & Curtin, T. D. (1992). In stories we trust: Studies of the validity of autobiographies. Journal of Counseling Psychology, 39, 398–405.

Howard, G. S., & Myers, P. R. (1990). Predicting human behavior: Comparing ideographic, nomothetic, and agentic methodologies. Journal of Counseling Psychology, 37, 227–233.

Howard, G. S., Myers, P. R., & Curtin, T. D. (1991). Can science furnish evidence of human freedom?: Self-determination versus conformity in human action. International Journal of Personal Construct Psychology, 4, 371–395.

Howard G. S., Youngs, W. H., & Siatczynski, A. M. (1989). A research strategy for studying telic human behavior. Journal of Mind and Behavior, 10, 393–412.

James, W. (1890). The principles of psychology. New York: Holt.

Kagitcibasi, C., & Berry, J. W. (1989). Cross-cultural psychology: Current research and trends. In M. R. Rosenzweig & L. W. Porter (Eds.), Annual Review of Psychology (Vol. 40). Palo Alto, CA.: Annual Reviews.

Kaplan, A. (1964). The conduct of inquiry: Methodology for behavioral science. San Francisco: Chandler.

Keirsey, D., & Bates, M. (1984). Please understand me: Character and temperament types. Del Mar, CA.: Gnosology Books.

Kelly, G. A. (1955). The psychology of personal constructs. New York: Norton.

Koch, S. (1959). Epilogue. Some trends in study I. In S. Koch (Ed.), Psychology: A study of a science, vol. 3. New York: McGraw-Hill.

Kuhn, T. (1977). The essential tension. Chicago: University of Chicago Press.

Landfield, A. W. (1971). Personal construct systems in psychotherapy. Chicago: Rand McNally.

Lazarick, D. L., Fishbein, S. S., Loiello, M. J., & Howard, G. S. (1988). Practical investigations of volition. Journal of Counseling Psychology, 35, 15–26.

Lazarus, A. A. (1976). Multimodal behavior therapy. New York: Springer.

Lazarus, A. A. (1985). Casebook of multimodal therapy. New York: Guilford.

LeVine, R. A. (1984). Properties of culture: An ethnographic view. In R. Shweder & R. LeVine (Eds.), Culture theory: Essays in mind, theory and emotion (pp. 67–87). Cambridge: Cambridge University Press.

Levy-Bruhl, L. (1910). Les fonctions mentales dans les sociétés inférieures. Paris: Alcan.

Lyddon, W. J. (1989). Personal epistemology and preference for counseling. Journal of Counseling Psychology, 36, 423–429.

Mackenzie, B. D. (1977). Behaviourism and the limits of the scientific method.. Highlands, N.J.: Humanities Press.

MacLeod, R. B. (1965). The teaching of psychology and the psychology we teach. American Psychologist, 20, 344–352.

Mair, M. (1988). Psychology as storytelling. International Journal of Personal Construct Psychology, 1, 125–138.

Mair, M. (1989). Between psychology and psychotherapy. London: Routledge.

Markus, H., & Nurius, P. (1986). Possible selves. American Psychologist, 41, 954–969.

Maxwell, S. E., & Delaney, H. D. (1990). Designing experiments and analyzing data: A model comparison approach. Belmont, CA.: Wadsworth.

McAdams, D. (1985). Power, intimacy, and the life story. Homewood, IL.: Dorsey Press.

McAdams, D. P. (1993). The stories we live by: Personal myths and the making of the self. New York: William Morrow.

McMullin, E. (1983). Values in science. In P. D. Asquith & T. Nickles (Eds.), Proceedings of the 1982 Philosophy of Science Association (Vol. 2, pp. 3–23). East Lansing, MI.: Philosophy of Science Association.

Meehl, P. E. (1978). Theoretical risks and tabular asterisks: Sir Karl, Sir Ronald, and the slow progress of soft psychology. Journal of Consulting and Clinical Psychology, 46, 806–834.

Milgram, S. (1974). Obedience to authority. New York: Harper & Row.

Mische, A. (1993). Hope and inner city youth. In L. Carter, A. Mische, & D. R. Schwarz (Eds.), Aspects of Hope (pp. 20–24). New York: ICIS Center for a Science of Hope.

Myers, D. G. (1990). *Exploring psychology.* New York: Worth Publications.

Nelson, N., Rosenthal, R., & Rosnow, R. (1986). Interpretation of significance levels and effect sizes by psychological research. *American Psychologist, 41,* 1299–1301.

Nisbett, R., & Ross, L. (1980). *Human inference: Strategies and shortcomings of social judgment.* Englewood Cliffs, N.J.: Prentice-Hall.

Orne, M. T. (1962). On the social psychology of the psychological experiment: With particular reference to demand characteristics and their implications. *American Psychologist, 17,* 776–783.

Parry, A., & Doan, R. E. (1994). *Story re-visions: Narrative therapy in the postmodern world.* New York: Guilford Publications.

Patton, M. J. (1984). Managing social interactions in counseling: A contribution from the philosophy of science. *Journal of Counseling Psychology, 31,* 442–456.

Plomin, R. (1990). *Nature and nurture: An introduction to human behavioral genetics.* Pacific Grove, CA.: Brooks/Cole.

Polkinghorne, D. P. (1988). *Narrative knowing and the human sciences.* Albany, N.Y.: SUNY Press.

Richardson, M. S., & Patton, M. J. (1992). Guest editors' reflection on a centennial series in process. *Journal of Counseling Psychology, 39,* 443–446.

Rosnow, R. L., & Rosenthal, R. (1988). Focused tests of significance and effect size estimation in counseling psychology. *Journal of Counseling Psychology, 35,* 203–208.

Rychlak, J. F. (1979). *Discovering free will and personal responsibility.* New York: Oxford University Press.

Rychlak, J. F. (1989). *The psychology of rigorous humanism* (2nd ed). New York: New York University Press.

Sacks, O. (1987). *The man who mistook his wife for a hat.* New York: Harper & Row.

Sahlins, M. (1976). *Culture and practical reason.* Chicago: University of Chicago Press.

Sanford, N. (1965). Will psychologists study human problems? *American Psychologist, 20,* 192–202.

Sarbin, T. R. (Ed.) (1986). *Narrative psychology: The storied nature of human conduct.* New York: Praeger.

Schachter, S. (1982). Recidivism and self-cure of smoking and obesity. *American Psychologist, 37,* 436–444.

Schank, R. C., & Abelson, R. P. (1977). *Scripts, plans, goals, and understanding.* Hillsdale, N.J.: Erlbaum.

Schneider, D. M. (1968). *American kinship: A cultural account.* Englewood Cliffs, N.J.: Prentice Hall.

Shweder, R. A. (1984). Anthropology's romantic rebellion against the enlightenment, or there's more to thinking than reason and evidence. In R. A. Shweder & R. LaVine (Eds.), *Culture Theory* (pp. 27–66). Cambridge: Cambridge University Press.

Simon, H. A., & Newell, A. (1964). Information processing in computer and man. *American Scientist, 53*, 281–300.

Skinner, B. F. (1971). *Beyond freedom and dignity.* New York: Knopf.

Spence, D. P. (1982). *Narrative truth and historical truth: Meaning and interpretation in psychoanalysis.* New York: Norton.

Steibe, S. C., & Howard, G. S. (1986). The volitional treatment of bulimia. *The Counseling Psychologist, 14*, 85–94.

Stein, M. L., & Stone, G. L. (1978). Effects of conceptual level and structure on initial interview behavior. *Journal of Counseling Psychology, 25*, 96–102.

Sue, S. (1988). Psycholtherapeutic services for ethnic minorities. *American Psychologist, 43*, 301–308.

Tanney, M. F., & Birk, J. M. (1976). Women counselors for women clients?: A review of the research. *The Counseling Psychologist, 6*, 28–31.

Triandis, H. C. (1972). *The analysis of subjective culture.* New York: Wiley.

Turiel, E. (1979). Distinct conceptual and developmental domains: Social convention and morality. In C. B. Keasy (Ed.), *Nebraska symposium on motivation* (Vol. 25). Lincoln: University of Nebraska Press.

Turner, V. (1967). *The forest of symbols.* Ithaca, N.Y.: Cornell University Press.

Tyler, E. B. (1871). *Primitive culture.* London: Murray.

Van Inwagen, P. (1983). *An essay on free will.* Oxford: Clarendon.

Watzlawich, P. (1984). *The invented reality: How do we know what we believed we know?* New York: Norton.

Weber, S. J., & Cook, T. D. (1972). Subject effects in laboratory research: An examination of subject roles, demand characteristics, and valid inference. *Psychological Bulletin, 77*, 273–295.

Weimer, W. B. (1979). *Notes on the methodology of scientific research.* Hillsdale, N.J.: Lawrence Erlbaum.

White, M., & Epston, D. (1989). *Literate means to therapeutic ends.* Adelaide, Australia: Dulwich Center Publications.

Whorf, B. L. (1956). *Language, thought and reality.* Cambridge, MA.: MIT Press.

Zuckerman, M., & Lubin, B. (1985). *Manual for the Multiple Affect Adjective Checklist-Revised.* San Diego, CA.: Educational and Industrial Testing Service.

INDEX

About the Author

George S. Howard is professor and chairman of the Department of Psychology and director of the Laboratory for Social Research at the University of Notre Dame. He received his Ph.D. in Counseling psychology in 1975 from Southern Illinois University. Professor Howard is currently the President of both the Division of Theoretical and Philosophical Psychology and the Division of Humanistic Psychology of the American Psychological Association (APA). A Fellow of six divisions of APA, he also serves as a member of the organization's Council of Representatives. Author of six books and more than 130 professional articles and chapters, Dr. Howard's research focuses upon philosophical and methodological issues in counseling, clinical, personality, educational, sports and ecological psychology.

He and his wife, Nancy Gulanick, are the parents of two sons, John Gulanick and Gregory Howard.